Ouida

Madame la Marquise

And Other Novelettes

Ouida

Madame la Marquise
And Other Novelettes

ISBN/EAN: 9783742821867

Manufactured in Europe, USA, Canada, Australia, Japa

Cover: Foto ©Andreas Hilbeck / pixelio.de

Manufactured and distributed by brebook publishing software (www.brebook.com)

Ouida

Madame la Marquise

COLLECTION
OF
BRITISH AUTHORS

TAUCHNITZ EDITION.

VOL. 1258.

MADAME LA MARQUISE BY OUIDA.

IN ONE VOLUME.

TAUCHNITZ EDITION.
By the same Author,

IDALIA	2 vols.
TRICOTRIN	2 vols.
PUCK	2 vols.
CHANDOS	2 vols.
STRATHMORE	2 vols.
UNDER TWO FLAGS	2 vols.
FOLLE-FARINE	2 vols.
A LEAF IN THE STORM . .	1 vol.
CECIL CASTLEMAINE'S GAGE .	1 vol.

MADAME LA MARQUISE

AND OTHER NOVELETTES.

BY

OUIDA,

AUTHOR OF "IDALIA," "A LEAF IN THE STORM,"
ETC. ETC.

COPYRIGHT EDITION.

LEIPZIG
BERNHARD TAUCHNITZ
1872.

CONTENTS.

	Page
Madame la Marquise	7
The General's Match-making; or, Coaches and Cousinship	31
The Story of a Crayon-Head; or, a Doubled-down Leaf in a Man's Life	74
The Beauty of Vicq d'Azyr; or, "Not at all a Proper Person"	109
A Line in the "Daily:" Who did it, and Who was done by It	139
Fitz's Election; or, Blue and Yellow	182
"Redeemed." An Episode with the Confederate Horse	234
The Marquis's Tactics; or, Lord Glen's Wager	260
Sir Galahad's Raid: an Adventure on the Sweet Waters	290

MADAME LA MARQUISE.

SHE was surpassingly fair, Madame la Marquise. Mignard's portraits of her may fully rival his far-famed Portrait aux Amours. One of them has her painted as Venus Victrix, in the fashion of the day; one of them, as herself, as Léontine Opportune de Vivonne de Rennecourt, Marquise de la Rivière, with her crève-cœurs, and her diamonds, and her gay smile, showing her teeth, white and gleaming as the pearls mingled with her curls à la mode Montespan. Not Louise de la Beaume-le-Blanc, when the elm-boughs of St. Germain first flung their shadow on her golden head, before it bent for the Carmelite veil before the altar in the Rue St. Jacques; not Henriette d'Angleterre, when she listened to the trouvères' romances sung under her balcony at St. Cloud, before her young life was quenched by the hand of Morel and the order of Monsieur; not Athénaïs de Mortemart, when the liveries of lapis lazuli blue dashed through the streets of Paris, and the outriders cleared her path with their whips, before the game was lost, and the iron spikes were fastened inside the Montespan bracelets;—none of them, her contemporaries and acquaintances, eclipsed in loveliness Madame la Marquise. Had she but been fair instead of dark, the brown Bourbon eyes would have fallen on her of a surety; she would have outshone the lapis lazuli liveries with a royal guard of scarlet and gold, and her friend Athénaïs would have hated her as that fair lady hated "la sotte Fontanges" and "Saint Maintenon;" for their sex, in all ages, have remembered the sage's precept, "Love as though you will one day hate," and invariably carry about with them, ready for need, a little essence of the acid of Malice, to sour in an instant the sugared cream of their loves and their friendships, if occasion rise up and the storm-cloud of rivalry loom in the horizon.

She was a beauty, Madame la Marquise, and she knew it, as she leaned out over the balcony of her château of Petite Forêt, that lay close to Clagny, under the shadow of the wood of Ville d'Avrée, outside the gates of Versailles, looking down on her bosquets, gardens, and terraces designed by Le Nôtre; for though she was alone, and there was nothing but her little dog Osmin to admire her white skin, and her dark eyes, and her beautiful hands and arms, and her diamond pendants that glittered in the moonlight, she smiled, her flashing triumphant smile, as she whispered to herself, "He is mine—mine! Bah! how can he help himself?" and pressed the ruby agraffe on her bosom with the look of a woman who knew no resistance, and brooked no reluctance to worship at her shrine.

Nothing ever opposed Madame la Marquise, and life went smoothly on with her. If Bossuet ever reproved her, it was in those *anathèmes cachés sous des fleurs d'oranger* in which that politic priest knew how to deal when expedient, however haughty and relentless to the world in general. M. le Marquis was not a savage eccentricity like M. de Pardaillon de Gondran, would never have dreamt of imitating the eccentricity of going into mourning, but if the Bourbon eye *had* fallen on his wife, would have said, like a loyal peer of France, that all his household treasures were the King's. Disagreeables fled before the scintillations of her smiles, as the crowd fled before her gilded carriage and her Flanders horses; and if ever a little fit of piety once in a while came over her, and Conscience whispered a mal à propos word in her delicate ear, she would give an enamelled lamp to Sainte Marie Reparatrice, by the advice of the Comtesse de Soubise and the Princesse de Monaco (who did such expiatory things themselves, and knew the comfort they afforded), and emerge from her repentance one of the most radiant of all the brilliant butterflies that fluttered their gorgeous wings in the Jardin de Flore under the sunny skies of Versailles.

The moonlight glittered on the fountains, falling with measured splash into their marble basins; the lime-leaves, faintly stirred by the sultry breezes, perfumed the night with their voluptuous fragrance, and the roses, twining round the carved and gilded balustrade, shook off their bowed heads drops of dew, that gleamed brightly as the diamonds among the curls of the woman who leaned above, resting her delicately rouged cheek on her jewelled hand, alone—a very rare circumstance with the Marquise de la Rivière. Osmin did not admire the rare solitude, for he rattled his silver bells and barked—an Italian greyhound's shrill, fretful bark—as his quick ears caught the distant sound of steps coming swiftly over the turf below, and his mistress smiled as she patted his head:

"Ah, Osmin!—here he is?"

A man came out from under the heavy shadow of limes and chesnuts, whose darkness the moon's rays had no power to pierce, crossed the lawn just under the balcony, and, coming up the terrace steps, stood near her—a man young, fair, handsome, whose age and form the uniform of a Captain of the Guards would have suited far better than the dark robes of a priest, which he wore;

his lips were pressed closely together, and his face was pale with a pallor that consorted painfully with the warm passionate gleam of his eyes.

"So! You are late in obeying my commands, monsieur!"

Surely no other man in France would have stood silent beside her, under the spell of her dazzling glances, with such a picture before him as Madame la Marquise, in her azure silk and her point d'Angleterre, with her diamond pendants shaking among her hair, and her arched eyebrows lifted imperiously? But he did; his lips pressed closer, his eyes gleaming brighter. She changed her tone; it was soft, seductive, reproachful, and the smile on her lips was tender—as tender as it ever could be with the mockery that always lay under it; and it broke at last the spell that bound him, as she whispered, "Ah! Gaston, you love me no longer!"

"Not love you? O God!"

They were but five words, but they told Madame la Marquise of a passion such as she had never roused, despite all her fascinations and intrigues, in the lovers that crowded round her in the salons within, or at Versailles, over the trees yonder, where love was gallantry, and all was light comedy, with nothing so foolish as tragedy known.

He clasped her hands so closely that the sharp points of the diamond rings cut his own, though he felt them not.

"Not love you? Great Heaven! Not love you? Near you, I forget my oath, my vows, my God!—I forget all, save you, whom I adore, as, till I met you, I adored my Church. Torture endured with you were dearer than Paradise won alone! Once with you, I have no strength, you bow me to your will as the wind bows the lime-leaf. Oh! woman, woman! could you have no mercy, that with crowds round you, daily worshipping your slightest smile, you must needs bow *me* down before your glance, as you bow those who have no oaths to bind them, no need to scourge themselves in midnight solitude for the mere crime of Thought? Had you no mercy, that with all hearts yours, you must have mine to sear it and destroy it? Have you not lives enough vowed to you, that you seek to blast mine for ever? I was content, untroubled, till I met you; no woman's glance stirred my heart, no woman's eyes haunted my vigils, no woman's voice came in memory between my soul and prayer! What devil tempted you to throw your spells over me—could you not leave *one* man in peace?"

"Ah bah! the tempted love the game of temptation generally full as well as the tempters!" thought Madame la Marquise, with an inward laugh.

Why did she allow such language to go unrebuked? Why did she, to whom none daréd to breathe any but words the most polished, and love vows the most honeyed, permit herself to be addressed in such a strain? Possibly it was very new to her, such energy as this, and such an outbreak of passion amused her. At any rate she only drew her hands away, and her brilliant brown eyes filled with tears;—tears *were* to be had at Versailles when needed, even her friend Montespan knew how to use them as the worst weapons against the artillery of the Evêque de Condom—and her heart heaved under the filmy lace.

"Ah, Gaston! what words! 'What devil tempted me?' I know scarcely whether love be angel or devil; he seems either or both! But you love me little, unless in that name you recognise a plea for every madness and every thought!"

The scarlet blood flushed over his face, and his eyes shone and gleamed like fire, while he clenched his hands in a mortal anguish.

"Angel or devil? Ay! which, indeed! The one when it comes to us, the other when it leaves us! You have roused love in me I shall bear to my grave; but what gage have I that you give it me back? How do I know but that even now you are trifling with me, mocking at me, smiling at the beardless priest who is unlearned in all the gay gallantries of libertine churchmen and soldierly courtiers! My Heaven! how know, as I stand beside you, whether you pity or disdain me, love or scorn me?"

The passionate words broke in a torrent from his lips, stirred the stillness of the summer eve with a fiery anguish little akin to it.

"Do I not love you?"

Her answer was simple; but as Léontine de Rennecourt spoke it, leaning her cheek against his breast, with her eyes dazzling as the diamonds in her hair, looking up into his by the light of the stars, they had an eloquence far more dangerous than speech, and delirious to the senses as magician's perfumes. His lips lingered on hers, and she felt the loud fast throbs of the heart she had won as he bent over her, pressing her closer and closer to him—vanquished and conquered, as men in all ages and of all creeds have been vanquished and conquered by women, all other thoughts fleeing away into oblivion, all fears dying out, all vows forgotten in the warm, living life of passion and of joy, that, for the first time in a brief life, flooded his heart with its golden voluptuous light.

"You love me? So be it," he murmured; "but beware

what you do; my life lies in your hands, and you must be mine till death parts us!"

"Till my fancy change rather!" thought Madame la Marquise, as she put her jewelled hand on his lips, her hair softly brushing his cheek, with a touch as soft, and an odour as sweet, as the leaves of one of the roses twining below.

Two men strolling below under the limes of Petite Forêt—discussing the last scandals of Versailles, talking of the ascendancy of La Fontanges, of the Spanish dress his Majesty had reassumed to please her, of the Brinvilliers' Poudre de Succession, of the new château given to Père de La Chaise, of D'Aubigny's last extravagance and Lauzun's last mot, and the last gossip about Bossuet and Mademoiselle de Mauléon, and all the chit-chat of that varied day, glittering with wit and prolific of poison—glanced up to the balcony by the light of the stars.

"That cursed priest!" muttered the younger, le Vicomte de Saint-Elix, as he struck the head off a lily with his delicate cane.

"In a fool's paradise! Ah-ha! Madame la Marquise!" laughed the other—the old Duc de Clos-Vougeot—taking a chocolate sweetmeat out of his emerald-studded bonbonnière as they walked on, while the lime-blossoms shook off in the summer night wind and dropped dead on the grass beneath, laughing at the story of the box D'Artagnan had found in Lauzun's rooms when he seized his papers, containing the portraits of sixty women of high degree who had worshipped the resistless Captain of the Guard, with critical and historical notices penned under each; notices D'Artagnan and his aide could not help indiscreetly retailing, in despite of the Bourbon command of secrecy—secrecy so necessary where sixty beauties and saints were involved!

"A fool's paradise!" said the Duc de Clos-Vougeot, tapping his bonbonnière, enamelled by Petitot: the Duc was old, and knew women well, and knew the value and length of a paradise dependent on that most fickle of butterflies—female fidelity; he had heard Ninon de Lenclos try to persuade Scarron's wife to become a coquette, and Scarron's wife in turn beseech Ninon to discontinue her coquetries; had seen that, however different their theories and practice, the result was the same; and already guessed right, that if Paris had been universally won by the one, its monarch would eventually be won by the other.

"A fool's paradise!"

The courtier was right, but the priest, had he heard him, would never have believed; *his* heaven shone in those dazzling eyes: till the eyes closed in death, his heaven was safe! He had never loved, he had seen nothing of women; he had come straight from the monastic gloom of a Dominican abbey, in the very heart of the South, down in Languedoc, where costly missals were his only idol, and rigid pietists, profoundly ignorant of the ways and thoughts of their brethren of Paris, had reared him up in anchorite rigidity, and scourged his mind with iron philosophies and stoic-like doctrines of self-mortification that would have repudiated the sophistries and ingenuities of Sanchez, Escobar, and Mascarenhas, as suggestions of the very Master of Evil himself. From the ascetic gloom of that Languedoc convent he had been brought straight, by superior will, into the glare of the life at Versailles, that brilliant, gorgeous, sparkling, bizarre life, scintillating with wit, brimful of intrigue, crowded with the men and women who formed the Court of that age and the History of the next; where he found every churchman an *abbé galant*, and heard those who performed the mass jest at it with those who attended it; where he found no lines marked of right and wrong, but saw them all fused in a gay, tangled web of two court colours—Expediency and Pleasure. A life that dazzled and tired his eyes, as the glitter of light in a room dazzles and tires the eyes of a man who comes suddenly in from the dark night air, till he grew giddy and sick, and in the midst of the gilded salons, or soft confessions of titled sinners, would ask himself if indeed he could be the same man who had sat calm and grave with the mellow sun streaming in on his missal-page in the monastic gloom of the Languedoc abbey but so few brief months before, when all this world of Versailles was unknown? The same man? Truly not—never again the same, since Madame la Marquise had bent her brown eyes upon him, been amused with his singular difference from all those around her, had loved him as women loved at Versailles, and bowed him down to her feet, before he guessed the name of the forbidden language that stirred in his heart and rushed to his lips, untaught and unbidden.

"A fool's paradise!" said the Duc, sagaciously tapping his gold bonbonnière. But many a paradise like it has dawned and faded, before and since the Versailles of Louis Quatorze.

He loved, and Madame la Marquise loved him. Through one brief tumult of struggle he passed: struggle between the creed of the Dominican abbey, where no sin would have been held so thrice accursed, so unpardonable, so deserving of the scourge and the stake as this—and the creed of the Bourbon Court, where churchmen's gallantries were every-day gossip; where the Abbé de Rancé, ere he founded the saintly gloom of La Trappe, scandalised town and court as much as Lauzun; where the Père de la Chaise smiled complacently on La Fontanges' ascendancy; where three nobles rushed to pick up the handkerchief of that royal confessor, who washed out with holy water the royal indiscretions, as you wash off grains of dust with perfumed water; where the great and saintly Bishop of Condom could be checked in a rebuking harangue, and have the tables turned on him by a mischievous reference to Mademoiselle de Mauléon; where life was intrigue for churchmen and laymen alike, and where the abbé's rochet and the cardinal's scarlet covered the same vices as were openly blazoned on the gold aiglettes of the Garde du Corps and the costly lace of the Chambellan du Roi. A storm, brief and violent as the summer storms that raged over Versailles, was roused between the conflicting thoughts at war within him, between the principles deeply rooted from long habit and stern belief, and the passions sprung up unbidden with the sudden growth and gorgeous glow of a tropical flower —a storm, brief and violent, a struggle, ended that night, when he stood on the balcony with the woman he loved, felt her lips upon his, and bowed down to her feet delirious and strengthless.

"I have won my wager with Adeline; I have vanquished *mon beau* De Launay," thought Madame la Marquise, smiling, two days after, as she sat, en negligé, in her broidered chair, pulling Osmin's ears, and stirring the frothy chocolate handed to her by her negro, Azor, brought over in the suite of the African embassy from Adra, full of monkeyish espièglerie, and covered with gems—a priceless dwarf, black as ink, and but two feet high, who could match any day with the Queen's little Moor. "He amuses me with his vows of eternal love. Eternal love?—how *de trop* we should find it, here in Versailles! But it is amusing enough to play at for a season. No, that is not half enough—he adores! This poor Gaston!"

So in the salons of Versailles, and in the world, where Ninon reigned, by the Court ladies, while they loitered in the new-made gardens of Marly, among other similar things jested of, was this new amour of Madame de la Rivière for the young Père de Launay. "She was always eccentric, and he *was* very handsome, and would have charming manners if he were not so grave and so silent," the women averred; while the young nobles swore that these meddling churchmen had always the best luck, whether in amatory conquest, or on fat lands and rich revenues. What the Priest of Languedoc thought a love that would outlast life, and repay him for peace of conscience and heaven both lost, was only one of the passing bubbles of gossip and scandal floating for an hour, amidst myriads like it, on the glittering, fast-rushing, diamond-bright waters of life at Versailles!

A new existence had dawned for him; far away in the dim dusky vista of forgotten things, though in reality barely distant a few short months, lay the old life in Languedoc, vague and unremembered as a passed dream; with its calm routine, its monastic silence, its unvarying alternations of study and prayer, its iron-bound thoughts, its rigid creed. It had sunk away as the peaceful grey twilight of a summer's night sinks away before the fiery burst of an artificial illumination, and a new life had dawned for him, radiant, tumultuous, conflicting, delicious —that dazzled his eyes with the magnificence of boundless riches and unrestricted extravagance; that charmed his intellect with the witty coruscations, the polished esprit, of an age unsurpassed for genius, grace, and wit; and that swayed alike his heart, his imagination, and his passions with the subtle intoxication of this syren of

Love, whose forbidden song had never before, in faintest echo, fallen on his ear.

Far away in the dim, lifeless, pulseless past, sank the memory of the old Dominican abbey, of all it had taught him, of all it had exacted, in its iron, stoical, merciless creed. A new life had arisen for him, and Gaston de Launay, waking from the semi-slumber of the living death he had endured in Languedoc, and liked because he knew no other, was happy—happy as a prisoner is in the wild delight with which he welcomes the sunlight after lengthened imprisonment, happy as an opium-eater is in the delicious delirium that succeeds the lulling softness of the opiate.

"He loves me, poor Gaston! Bah! But how strangely he talks! If love were this fiery, changeless, earnest thing with us that it is with him, what in the world should we do with it? We should have to get a lettre de cachet for it, and forbid it the Court; send it in exile to Pignerol, as they have just done Lauzun. Love in earnest? We should lose the best spice for our wine, the best toy for our games, and, mon Dieu! what embroilments there would be! Love in earnest? Bagatelle! Louise de la Vallière shows us the folly of that; but for its Quixotisms she would now be at Vaujours, instead of buried alive in that Rue St. Jacques, with nothing to do but to weep for 'Louison,' count her beads, and listen to M. de Condom's merciless eloquence! Like the king,

J'aime qu'on m'aime, mais avec de l'esprit.

People have no right to reproach each other with inconstancy; one's caprices are not in one's own keeping; and one can no more help where one's fancy blows, than that lime-leaf can help where the breeze chooses to waft it. But poor Gaston! how make *him* comprehend that?" thought Madame la Marquise, as she turned, and smiled, and held out her warm jewelled hands, and listened once again to the words of the man who was in her power as utterly as the bird in the power of the snake when it has once looked up into the fatal eyes that lure it to its doom.

"You will love me ever?" he would ask, resting his lips on her white low brow.

"Ever!" would softly answer Madame la Marquise.

And her lover believed her: should his deity lie? He believed her! What did he, fresh from the solitude of his monastery, gloomy and severe as that of the Trappist abbey, with its perpetual silence, its lowered glances, its shrouded faces, its ever-present "memento mori," know of women's faith, of women's love, of the sense in which *they* meant that vow "for ever"? He believed her, and never asked what would be at the end of a path strewn with such odorous flowers. Alone, it is true, in moments when he paused to think, he stood aghast at the abyss into which he had fallen, at the sin into which, a few months before, haughty and stern in virtue against the temptation that had never entered his path, he would have defied devils in legion to have lured him, yet into which he had now plunged at the mere smile of a woman! Out of her presence, out of her spells, standing by himself under the same skies that had brooded over his days of peace in Languedoc, back on his heart, with a sickening anguish, would come the weight of his sin; the burden of his broken oaths, the scorch of that curse eternal which, by his creed, he held drawn down on him here and hereafter; and Gaston de Launay would struggle again against this idolatrous passion, which had come with its fell delusion betwixt him and his God; struggle —vainly, idly—struggle, only to hug closer the sin he loved while he loathed; only to drink deeper of the draught whose voluptuous perfume was poison; only to forget all, forsake all, dare all, at one whisper of her voice, one glance of her eyes, one touch of the lips whose caress he held would be bought by a curse through eternity.

Few women love aught "for ever," save, perchance, diamonds, lace, and their own beauty, and Madame la Marquise was not one of those few; certainly not—she had no desire to make herself singular in her generation, and could set fashions much more likely to find disciples, without reverting to anything so eccentric, plebeian, and out of date. Love *one* for ever! She would have thought it as terrible waste of her fascinations, as for a jewel to shine in the solitude of its case, looked on by only one pair of eyes, or for a priceless enamel, by Petitot, to be only worn next the heart, shrouded away from the light of day, hidden under the folds of linen and lace.

"Love one for ever?"—Madame la Marquise laughed at the thought, as she stood dressed for a ball, after assisting at the representation of a certain tragedy, called "Bérénice" (in which Mesdames Deshoulières and De Sévigné, despite their esprit, alone of all Paris and the Court could see no beauty), and glanced in the mirror at her radiant face, her delicate skin, her raven curls, with their pendants shaking, her snow-white arms, and her costly dress of the newest mode, its stomacher gleaming one mass of gems. "Love one for ever? The droll idea! Is it not enough that I have loved him once?"

It was more than enough for his rivals, who bitterly envied him; courtly abbés, with polished smiles, and young chanoines, with scented curls and velvet toques, courtiers, who piqued themselves on reputations only second to Lauzun's, and men of the world, who laughed at this new caprice of Madame la Marquise, alike bore no good-will to this Languedoc priest, and gave him a significant sneer, or a compliment that roused his blood to fire, and stung him far worse than more open insult, when they met in the salons, or crossed in the corridors, at Versailles or Petite Forêt.

"Those men! those men! Should he ever lose her to any one of them?" he would think over and over again, clenching his hand, in impotent agony of passion that he had not the sword and the license of a soldier to strike them on the lips with his glove for the smile with which they dared to speak her name; to make them wash out in blood under the trees, before the sun was up, the laugh, the sneer, the delicate satire, which were worse to bear than a blow to the man who could not avenge them.

"Pardieu! Madame must be very unusually faithful to her handsome priest; she has smiled on no other for two months! What unparalleled fidelity!" said the Vicomte de Saint-Elix, with petulant irritation.

"Jealous, Léonce?" laughed the old Duc, whom he spoke to, tapping the medallion portrait on his bonbonnière. "Take comfort: when the weather has been so long fixed, it is always near a change. Ah, M. de Launay overhears! He looks as if he would slay us. Very unchristian in a priest!"

Gaston de Launay overheard, as he stood by a croisée at Petite Forêt, playing with Osmin—he liked even the dog, since the hand he loved so often lay on its slender neck, and toyed with its silver chain—and, sworn as he was to the service of his Church, sole mistress as his Church had been, till Léontine de Rennecourt's eyes had lured him to his desertion of her, apostate in his own eyes as such a thought confessed him to have grown, he tongue; there was Madame de Sévigné and Madame de Grignan, the Duchesse de Richelieu and the Duchesse de Lesdiguières; there was Bussy Rabutin and Hamilton. Who was there not that was brilliant, that was distinguished, that was high in rank and famed in wit at the fête of Madame la Marquise?—Madame la Marquise, who floated through the crowd that glittered in her salon and gardens, who laughed and smiled, showing her dazzling white teeth, who had a little Cupid gleaming with jewels (emblematic enough of Cupid as he was known at Versailles) to present the Princesse de Conti with a bridal bouquet whose flowers were of pearls and whose leaves were of emeralds; who piqued herself that the magnificence of her fête was scarcely eclipsed by His Majesty himself; who yielded the palm neither to La Vallière's lovely daughter, nor to her friend Athénaïs, nor to any one of the beauties who shone with them, and whose likeness by Mignard laughed down from the wall where it hung, matchless double of her own matchless self.

The priest of Languedoc watched her, the relentless fangs of passion gnawing his heart, as the wolf the Spartan. For the first time he was forgotten! His idol passed him carelessly, gave him no glance, no smile, but lavished a thousand coquetries on Saint-Elix, on De Rohan-Soubise, on the boy Vermandois—on any who sought them. Once he addressed her. Madame la Marquise shrugged her snow-white shoulders, and arched her eyebrows with petulant irritation, and turned to laugh gaily at Saint-Elix, who was amusing her, and La Montespan, and Madame de Thianges, with some gay mischievous scandal concerning Madame de Lesdiguières and the Archbishop of Paris; for scandals, if not wholly new, are ever diverting when concerning an enemy, specially when dressed and served up with the piquant sauce of wit.

"I no longer then, madame, lead a dog's life in jealousy of this priest," whispered Saint-Elix, after other whispers, in the ear of Madame la Marquise. The Vicomte adored her, not truly in Languedoc fashion, but very warmly—à la mode de Versailles.

The Marquise laughed:

"Perhaps not! You know I bet Mme. de Montevreau that I would conquer him. I have won now. Hush! He is close. There will be a tragedy, *mon ami!*"

"M. le Vicomte, if you have the honour of a noble, the heart of a man, you fight me to-night. *I* seek no shelter under my cloth!"

Saint-Elix turned as he heard the words, laughed scornfully, and signed the speaker away with an insolent sneer:

"Bah! *Révérend Père!* we do not fight with women and churchmen!"

The fête was ended at last, the lights that had gleamed among the limes and chesnuts had died out, the gardens and salons were emptied and silent, the little Cupid had laid aside his weighty jewelled wings, the carriages with their gorgeous liveries, their outriders, and their guards of honour, had rolled from the gates of Petite Forêt to the Palace of Versailles. Madame la Marquise stood alone once more in the balcony of her salons, leaning her white arms on its guilded balustrade, looking down on to the gardens beneath, silvered with the breaking light of the dawn, smiling, her white teeth gleaming between her parted rose-hued lips, and thinking of what? Who shall say?

Still, still as death lay the gardens below, that an hour ago had been peopled with a glittering crowd, re-echoing with music, laughter, witty response, words of intrigue. Where the lights had shone on diamonds and pearl-broidered trains, on softly rouged cheeks, and gold-laced coats, on jewelled swords and broideries of gold, the grey hue of the breaking day now only fell on the silvered leaves of the limes, the turf wet with dew, the drooped heads of the Provence roses; and Madame la Marquise, standing alone, started as a step through the salon within broke the silence.

"Madame, will you permit me a word *now?*"

Gaston de Launay took her hands off the balustrade, and held them tight in his, while his voice sounded, even in his own ears, strangely calm, yet strangely harsh:

"Madame, you love me no longer?"

"Monsieur, I do not answer questions put to me in such a manner."

She would have drawn her hands away, but he held them in a fierce grasp till her rings cut his skin as they had done once before.

"No trifling! Answer—yes or no!"

"Well! 'no,' then, monsieur. Since you *will* have the truth, do not blame me if you find it uncomplimentary and unacceptable."

He let go her hands and reeled back, staggered, as if struck by a shot.

"Mon Dieu! it is true—you love me no longer! And you tell it me *thus!*"

Madame la Marquise, for an instant, was silenced and touched; for the words were uttered with the faint cry of a man in agony, and she saw, even by the dim twilight of dawn, how livid his lips turned, how ashy grey grew the hue of his face. But she smiled, playing with Osmin's new collar of pearls and coral.

"Tell it you 'thus'? I would not have told it you 'thus,' monsieur, if you had been content with a hint, and had not evinced so strong a desire for candour undisguised; but if people will not comprehend a delicate suggestion, they must be wounded by plainer truths—it is their own fault. Did you think I was like a little shepherdess in a pastoral, to play the childish game of constancy without variations? Had you presumption enough to fancy you could amuse me for ever——"

He stopped her, his voice broken and hoarse, as he gasped for breath.

"Silence! Woman, have you no mercy? For you—for such as you—I have flung away heaven, steeped myself in sin, lost my church, my peace, my all—forfeited all right to the reverence of my fellows, all hope for the smile of my God! For you—for such as you—I have become a traitor, a hypocrite, an apostate, whose prayers are insults, whose professions are lies, whose oaths are perjury! At your smile, I have flung away eternity; for your kiss, I have risked my life here, my life hereafter; for your love I held no price too vast to pay; weighed with it, honour, faith, heaven, all seemed valueless—all were forgotten! You lured me from tranquil calm, you broke in on the days of peace which but for you were unbroken still, you haunted my prayers, you placed yourself between Heaven and me, you planned to conquer my anchorite's pride, you wagered you would lure me from my priestly vows, and yet you have so little mercy, that when your bet is won, when your amusement grows stale, when the victory grows valueless, you can turn on me with words like these without one self-reproach?"

"Ma foi, monsieur! it is you who may reproach yourself, not I," cried his hearer insolently. "Are you so very provincial still, that you are ignorant that when a lover has ceased to please he has to blame his own lack of power to retain any love he may have won, and is far too well bred to utter a complaint? Your language is very new to me. Most men, monsieur, would be grateful for my slightest preference; I permit none to rebuke me for either giving or withdrawing it."

The eyes of Madame la Marquise sparkled angrily, and the smile on her lips was a deadly one, full of irony, full of malice. As he beheld it, the scales fell at last from the eyes of Gaston de Launay, and he saw what this woman was whom he had worshipped with such mad, blind, idolatrous passion.

He bowed his head with a low, broken moan, as a man stunned by a mortal blow; while Madame la Marquise stood playing with the pearl-and-coral chain, and smiling the malicious and mischievous smile that showed her white teeth, as they are shown in the portrait by Mignard.

"*Comme les hommes sont fous!*" laughed Madame la Marquise.

He lifted his eyes, and looked at her as she stood in the faint light of the dawn, with her rich dress, her gleaming diamonds, her wicked smile, her matchless beauty; and the passion in him broke out in a bitter cry:

"God help me! my sin has brought home its curse!"

He bent over her, his burning lips scorching her own like fire, holding her in one last embrace, that clasped her in a vice of iron she had no power to break.

"Angel! devil! temptress! *This* for what I have deemed thee—*that* for what thou art!"

He flung her from him with unconscious violence, maddened with pain, as a man by the blow that has blinded him, and left her—lying where she fell.

The grey silvery dawn rose, and broke into the warmth and sunlight of a summer day; the deer nestled in their couches under the chequered shadows of the woodlands round, and the morning chimes were rung in musical cadence from the campanile of the château; the Provence roses tossed their delicate heads, joyously shaking the dew off their scented petals; the blossoms of the limes fell in a fragrant shower on to the turf below, and the boughs, swayed softly by the wind, brushed their leaves against the sparkling waters of the fountains; the woods and gardens of Petite Forêt lay, bright and laughing, in the mellow sunlight of the new day to which the world was waking. And with his face turned up to the sky, clasped in his hand a medallion enamel, on which was painted the head of a woman, the grass and ferns where he had fallen stained crimson with his life-blood, lay a dead man, while in his bosom nestled a little dog, moaning piteous, plaintive cries, and vainly seeking its best to wake him to the day that for him would never dawn.

When her household, trembling, spread the news that the dead priest had been found lying under the limes, slain by his own hand, and it reached Madame la Marquise in her private chambers, she was startled, shocked, wept, hiding her radiant eyes in her broidered handkerchief, and called Azor, and bade him bring her her flask of scented waters, and bathed her eyes, and turned them dazzling bright on Saint-Elix, and stirred her chocolate, and asked the news. "*On peut être émue aux larmes et aimer le chocolat,*" thought Madame la Marquise, with her friend Montespan;—while, without, under the waving shadow of the linden boughs, with the sunlight streaming round him, the little dog nestling in his breast, refusing to be comforted, lay the man whom she had murdered.

The portrait by Mignard still hangs on the walls of the château, and in its radiant colours Madame la Marquise still lives, fair type of her age, smiling her victorious smile, with the diamonds shining among her hair, and her brilliant eyes flashing defiance, irony, and coquetry as of yore, when she reigned amidst the beauties of Versailles;—and in the gardens beyond, in the summer nights, the lime boughs softly shake their fragrant flowers on the turf, and the moonlight falls in hushed and mournful calm, streaming through the network of the boughs on to the tangled mass of violets and ferns that has grown up in rank luxuriance over the spot where Gaston de Launay died.

THE GENERAL'S MATCH-MAKING;

OR,

COACHES AND COUSINSHIP.

"WHERE the devil shall I go this Long? Paris is too hot; the inside of my adorable Château des Fleurs would give one a lively idea of the feelings of eels in a frying-pan. Rome's only fit to melt down puffy cardinals, as jocks set themselves before the kitchen fire preparatory to the Spring Meetings. In Switzerland there's nothing fit to eat. Spain might be the ticket—the Andalusians are a good-looking lot, but they haven't a notion of beer. Scotland I daren't enter, because I know I should get married under their rascally laws. I'd go to the Bads, but the V. P.'s fillies say they mean to do 'em this summer, and I won't risk meeting them if I know it; the baits they set to catch the unsuspecting are quite frightful. Where the devil *shall* I go?"

So spoke Sydenham Morton, whilom Captain of Eton, now in due course having passed up to King's, discussing ham-pie and audit, devils and coffee, while the June sun streamed through the large oriel windows.

"*To* the devil, I fear, if you only find your proper fraternity," said a man, coming in. Oak was never sported by Sydie, except when he was rattling certain little squares of ivory in boxes lined with green felt.

"Ah, Mr. Keane, is that you? Come in."

The permission was needless, insomuch as Keane was already in and down on a rocking-chair.

"One o'clock, and only just begun your breakfast! I have finished more than half my day's work."

"I dare say," answered Sydie; "but one shining light like you, monseigneur, is enough for a college. Why should I exert myself? I swore I hadn't four marks a year, and I've my fellowship for telling the furbelow. We all go in for the dolce here, except you, and you're such a patent machine for turning out Q.E.D.s by the dozen, that you can no more help working than the bedmaker can help taking my tea and saying the cat did it, and 'May she never be forgiven if she ever so much as looked at that there blessed lock.' I say, find a Q.E.D. for me, to the most vexatious problem, where I'm to go this Long?"

"Go a quiet reading tour; mark out a regular plan, and travel somewhere rugged and lonely, with not a crinoline, or a trout-stream, or a pack of hounds within a hundred miles; the middle of Stonehenge, for example, or with the lighthouse men out at the Smalls or Eddystone. You'd do wonders when you came back, Sydie."

Sydie shook his head and puffed gravely at his pipe.

"Thank you, sir. Cramming's not my line. As for history, I don't see anything particularly interesting in the blackguardisms of men all dust and ashes and gelatine now; if I were the Prince of Wales, I might think it my duty to inquire into the characters of my grandfathers; but not being that individual, I find the Derby list much more suited to my genius. As for the classics, they won't help me to ask for my dinner at Tortoni's, nor to ingratiate myself with the women at the Maison Dorée; and I prefer following Ovid's counsels, and enjoying the Falernian of life represented in these days by milk-punch, to plodding through the De Officiis. As for mathematics, it *may* be something very grand to draw triangles and circles till A meets B because C is as long as D; but I know, when I did the same operation in chalk when I was a small on the nursery floor, my nurse (who might have gone along with the barbarian who stuck Archimedes) called me an idle brat. Well, I say, about the Long? Where are *you* going, most grave and reverent seignior?"

"Where there are no impertinent boys, if there be such a paradise on earth," rejoined Keane, lighting his pipe. "I go to my moor, of course, for the 12th, but until then I haven't made up my mind. I think I shall scamper over South America; I want freshening up, and I've a great fancy to see those buried cities, not to mention a chance of buffalo hunting."

"Travelling's such a bore," interrupted Sydie, stretching himself out like an india-rubber tube. "Talk of the cherub that's always sitting up aloft to watch over poor Jack, there are always ten thousand demons watching over the life of any luckless Æothen; there are the custom-house men, whose natural prey he becomes, and the hotel-keepers, who fasten on him to suck his life-blood, and there are the mosquitoes, and other things less minute but not less agonising; and there are guides and muleteers, and waiters and ciceroni—oh, hang it! travelling's a dreadful bore, if it were only for the inevitable widow with four daughters whom you've danced with once at a charity ball, who rushes up to you on the Boulevards or a Rhine steamer, and tacks herself on to you, and whom it's well for you if you can shake off when you scatter the dust of the city from the sole of your foot."

"You can't chatter, can you?"

"Yes; my frænum was happily cut when I was a baby. Fancy what a loss the world would have endured if it hadn't been!" said Sydie, lazily shutting his half-closed blue eyes. "I say, the governor has been bothering my life out to go down to St. Crucis; he's an old brick, you know, and has the primest dry in the kingdom. I wish you'd come, will you? There's capital fishing and cricketing, and you'd keep me company. Do. You shall have the best mount in the kingdom, and the General will do you no end of good on Hippocrates' rule—contrarieties cure contrarieties!"

"I'll think about it; but you know I prefer solitude generally; misanthropical, I admit, but decidedly lucky for me, as my companions through life will always be my inkstand, my terrier, and my papers. I have never wished for any other yet, and I hope I never shall. Are you going to smoke and drink audit on that sofa all day?"

"No," answered Sydie, "I'm going to take a turn at beer and Brown's for a change. Well, I shall take you down with me on Tuesday, sir, so that's settled."

Keane laughed, and after some few words on the business that had brought him thither, went across the quad to his own rooms to plunge into the intricacies of Fourrier and Laplace, or give the vigour of his brain to stuffing some young goose's empty head, or cramming some idle young dog with ballast enough to carry him through the shoals and quicksands of his Greats.

Gerald Keane was a mathematical Coach, and had taken high honours—a rare thing for a Kingsman to do, for are they not, by their own confession, the laziest disciples of the Dolce in the whole of Granta, invariably bumped and caught out, and from sheer idleness letting other men beat at Lord's and shame the Oxford Eleven, and graduate with Double Firsts, while they lie perdus in the shades of Holy Henry? Keane, however, was the one exception to the rule. He was dreadfully wild, as ladies say, for his first term or two, though equally eloquent at the Union; then his family exulting in the accuracies of their prophecies regarding his worthlessness, and somebody else daring him to go in for honours, his pluck was put up, and he set himself to work to show them all what he could do if he chose. Once roused to put out his powers, he liked using them; the bother of the training over, it is no trouble to keep place as stroke-oar; and now men pointed him out in the Senate House, and at the Senior Fellows' table, and he bid fair to rank with the writer on Jasher and the author of the Inductive Sciences.

People called him very cold. It was popularly averred that he had no more feeling than Roubilliac's or Thorwaldsen's statues; but as he was a great favourite with the under-grads, and always good-natured to them, there were a few men who doubted the theory, though *he* never tried to refute or dispute it.

Of all the young fellows, the one Keane liked the best, and to whom he was kindest, was Sydenham Morton —Sydie to everybody in Granta, from the little fleuriste opposite in King's Parade, to the V. P.'s wife, who petted him because his uncle was a millionnaire—the dearest fellow in the world, according to all the Cambridge young ladies—the darling of all the milliner and confectioner girls in Trumpington-street and Petty Cury—the best chap going among the kindred spirits, who got gated, and lectured, and rusticated for skying over to Newmarket, or pommelling bargees, or taking a lark over at Cherryhinton—the best-dressed, fastest, and most charming of Cantabs, as he himself would gravely assure you.

They were totally dissimilar, and far asunder in position; but an affair on the slope of the Matterhorn, when the boy had saved the elder man's life, had riveted attachment between them, and bridged over the difference of their academical rank.

The Commencement came and went, with its speeches, and its H.R.H. Chancellor, and its pretty women gliding among the elms of Neville's Court (poor Leslie Ellis's daily haunt), filling the grim benches of the Senate House, and flitting past the carved benches of King's Chapel. Granta was henceforth a desert to all Cambridge belles; they could walk down Trumpington-street without meeting a score of little straw hats, and Trumpington-street became as odious as Sahara; the "darling Backs" were free to them, and, of course, they who, by all relations, from those of Genesis to those of Vanity Fair, have never cared, save for *fruit défendu*, saw nothing to admire in the trees, and grass, and river, minus outriggers and collegians. There was a general exodus: Masters' red hoods, Fellows Commoners' gold-lace, Fellows' gown and mortar boards, morning chapel surplices, and under-grads' straw-hats and cut-away coats, all vanished from court and library, street and cloister. Cambridge was empty; the married Dons and their families went off to country-houses or Rhine steamers; Fellows went touring with views to mediæval architecture, Roman remains, Greek inscriptions, Paris laisser aller, or Norwegian fishing, according to their tastes and habits; under-grads scattered themselves over the face of the globe, and were to be found in knots of two or three calling for stout in Véfour's, kicking up a row with Austrian gendarmerie, chalking up effigies of Bomba on Italian walls, striding up every mountain from Skiddaw to the Pic du Midi, burrowing like rabbits in a warren for reading purposes on Dartmoor, kissing sunny-haired Gretchens in German hostelries, swinging through the Vaterland with knapsacks and sticks, doing a walking tour—in fact, swarming everywhere with their impossible

French, and hearty voices, and lithe English muscle, Granta marked on them as distinctly as an M.B. waistcoat marks an Anglican, or utter ignorance of modern politics a "great classic."

Cambridge had emptied itself of the scores of naughty boys that lie in the arms of Mater, and on Tuesday Keane and Sydie were shaking and rattling over those dreadful nervous Eastern Counties tenders, through that picturesque and beautiful country that does permutations with such laudable perseverance on pollards, fens, and flats—flats, fens, and pollards—at the snail's pace that, according to the G.E.R., we must believe to be "express."

"I wrote and told the governor you were coming down with me, sir," said Sydie, hanging up his hat. "I didn't tell him what a trouble I had to make you throw over South America for a fortnight, and come and taste his curry at the Beeches. You'll like the old boy; he's as hot and choleric, and as genial and good-hearted, as any old brick that ever walked. He was born as sweet-tempered and soft-mouthed as mamma when an eldest son waltzes twice with Adeliza, and the pepper's been put into him by the curry-powder, the gentlemanlike transportation, and the unlimited command over black devils, enjoyed by gentlemen of the H.E.I.C.S."

"A nabob uncle," thought Keane. "Oh, I see, yellow, dyspeptic, always boring one with 'How to govern India,' and recollections of 'When I served with Napier.' What a fool I was to let Sydie persuade me to go. A month in Lima and the Pampas would be much pleasanter."

"He came over last year," continued Sydie, in blissful ignorance, "and bought the Beeches, a very jolly place, only he's crammed it with everything anybody suggested, and tried anything that any farmer recommended, so that the house and the estate present a peculiar compendium of all theories of architecture, and a general exhibition of all sorts of tastes. He's his hobbies; pouncing on and apprehending small boys is one of 'em, for which practice he is endeared to the youth of St. Crucis as the 'old cove,' the 'Injian devil,' and like affectionate cognomens. But the General's weak point is me—me and little Fay."

"His mare, I suppose?"

"His mare!—bless my heart, no!—his mare!" And Sydie lay back, and laughed silently. "His mare! By George! what would she say? She's a good deal too lively a young lady to run in harness for anybody, though she's soft-mouthed enough when she's led. Mare! No, Fay's his niece—my cousin. Her father and my father went to glory when we were both smalls, and left us in legacy to the General, and a pretty pot of money the legacy has cost him."

"Your cousin, indeed! The name's more like a mare's than a girl's," answered Keane, thinking to himself. "A cousin! I just wish I'd known that. One of those Indian girls, I bet, tanned brown as a berry, flirts à outrance, has run the gauntlet of all the Calcutta balls, been engaged to men in all the Arms, talks horridly broad Anglo-Indian-English. I know the style."

The engine screamed, and pulled up at the St. Crucis station, some seventy miles farther on, lying in the midst of Creswickian landscapes, with woodlands, and cottages, and sweet fresh stretches of meadow-land, such as do one's heart good after hard days and late nights in dust and gaslight.

"Deuced fine points," said Sydie, taking the ribbons of a high-stepping bay that had brought one of the neatest possible traps to take him and Keane to the Beeches, and springing, in all his glory, to the box, than which no imperial throne could have offered to him one-half so delightful a seat. "Governor never keeps screws. What a crying shame we're not allowed to keep the sorriest hack at King's. That comes of gentlemen slipping into shoes that were meant for beggars. Hallo! there are the old beech-trees; I vow I can almost taste the curry and dry from looking at them."

In dashed the bay through the park-gates, sending the shingle flying up in small simooms, and the rooks cawing in supreme surprise from their nests in the branches of the beech-trees.

"Hallo, my ancient, how are you?" began Sydie to the butler, while that stately person expanded into a smile of welcome. "Down, dog, down! 'Pon my life, the old place looks very jolly. What have you hung all that armour up for;—to make believe our ancestors dwelt in these marble halls? How devilish dusty I am. Where's the General? Didn't know we were coming till next train. Fay! Fay! where are you? Ashton, where's Miss Morton?"

"Here, Sydie dear," cried the young lady in question, rushing across the hall with the most ecstatic delight, and throwing herself into the Cantab's arms, who received her with no less cordiality, and kissed her straightway, regardless of the presence of Keane, the butler, and Harris.

"Oh, Sydie," began the young lady, breathlessly, "I'm so delighted you're come. There's the archery fête, and a pic-nic at Shallowton, and an election ball over at Coverdale, and I want you to dance with me, and to try the new billiard-table, and to come and see my aviary, and to teach me pistol-shooting (because Julia Dupuis can shoot splendidly, and talks of joining the Rifles), and to show me how to do Euclid, and to amuse me, and to play with me, and to tell me which is the prettiest of Snowdrop's pups to be saved, and to——" She stopped suddenly, and dropped from enthusiastic tirade to subdued surprise, as she caught sight of Keane for the first time. "Oh, Sydie, why did you not introduce me to your friend? How rude I have been!"

"Mr. Keane, my cousin, the torment of my existence, Miss Morton in public, Little Fay in private life. There, you know one another now. I can't say any more. Do tell me where the governor is."

"Mr. Keane, what can you think of me?" cried Fay. "Any friend of Sydenham's is most welcome to the Beeches, and my uncle will scold me frightfully for giving you such a reception. Please do forgive me, I was so delighted to see my cousin."

"Which I can fully enter into, having a weakness for Sydie myself," smiled Keane. "I am sure he is very fortunate in being the cause of such an excuse."

Keane said it *par complaisance*, but rather carelessly; young ladies, as a class, being one of his aversions. He looked at Fay Morton, however, and saw she was not an Indianised girl after all. She was not yellow, but, *au contraire*, had waving fair hair, long dark eyes, and a mischievous, sunny face—

> A rosebud set with little wilful thorns,
> And sweet as English air could make her.

"Where's the governor, Fay?" reiterated Sydie.

"Here, my dear boy. Thought of your old uncle the first thing, Sydie? God bless my soul, how well you look! Confound you, why didn't you tell me what train you were coming by? Devil take you, Ashton, why's there no fire in the hall? Thought it was warm, did you? Hum! more fool you then."

"Uncle dear," said Miss Fay, "here is Sydie's friend, Mr. Keane; you are being as rude as I have been."

The General, at this conjuration, swung sharp round, a stout, hale, handsome old fellow, with grey moustaches and a high colour, holding a spade in his hand and clad in a linen coat.

"Bless my soul, sir," cried the General, shaking Keane's hand with the greatest possible energy, "charmed to see you—delighted, 'pon my honour; only hope you're come to stay till Christmas; there are plenty of bachelors' dens. Devil take me! of what was I thinking? I was pleased to see that boy, I suppose. More fool I, you'll say, a lazy, good-for-nothing young dog like him. Don't let me keep you standing in the hall. Cursed cold, isn't it? and there's Little Fay in muslin! Ashton, send some hot water into the west room for Mr.—Mr.——Confound you, Sydie, why didn't you tell—I mean, introduce me?—Mr. Keane. Luncheon will be on the table in ten minutes. Like curry, Mr. Keane? There, get along, Sydie, you foolish boy; you can talk to Fay after luncheon."

"Sydie," whispered Fay, an hour before dinner, when she had teased the Cantab's life out of him till he had consented to pronounce judgment on the puppies, "what a splendid head that man has you brought with you; he'd do for Plato, with that grand calm brow and lofty unapproachable look. Who is he?"

"The greatest philosopher of modern times," responded her cousin, solemnly. "A condensation of Solon, Thales, Plutarch, Seneca, Cicero, Lucullus, Bion, Theophrastes, and Co.; such a giant of mathematical knowledge, and all other knowledge, too, that every day, when he passes under Bacon's Gate, we are afraid the old legend will come to pass, and it will tumble down as flat as a pancake; a homage to him, but a loss to Cambridge."

"Nonsense," said Miss Fay, impatiently. "(I like that sweet little thing with the black nose best, dear.) *Who is he? What is he?* How old is he? What's his name? Where does he live?"

"Gently, young woman," cried Sydie. "He is Tutor and Fellow of King's, and a great gun besides; he's some twenty-five years older than you. His name on the rolls is Gerald, I believe, and he dwells in the shadow of Mater, beyond the reach of my cornet; for which fact, not being musically inclined, he is barbarian enough to return thanks daily in chapel."

"I am sorry he is come. It was stupid of you to bring him."

"Wherefore, *ma cousine?* Are you afraid of him? You needn't be. Young ladies are too insignificant atoms of creation for him to criticise. He'll no more expect sense from you than from Snowdrop and her pups."

"Afraid!" repeated Fay, with extreme indignation. "I should like to see any man of whom I should feel afraid! If he doesn't like fun and nonsense, I pity him; but if he despise me ever so much for it, I shall enjoy myself before him, and in spite of him. I was sorry you brought him, because he will take you away when I want you all to myself; and he looks so haughty, that——"

"You *are* afraid of him, Fay, and won't own it?"

"I am *not*," reiterated Fay, impetuously; "and I will smoke a cigar with him after dinner, to show you I am not one bit."

"I bet you six pair of gloves you do no such thing, young lady."

"Done. Do keep the one with a black nose, Sydie; and yet that little liver-coloured darling is too pretty to be killed. Suppose we save them all? Snowdrop will be so pleased."

Whereon Fay kissed all the little snub noses with the deepest affection, and was caught in the act by Keane and the General.

"There's that child with her arms full of dogs," said the General, beaming with satisfaction at sight of his niece. "She's a little, spoilt, wilful thing. She's an old bachelor's pet, and you must make allowances. I call her the fairy of the Beeches, God bless her! She nursed me last winter, when I was at death's door from these cursed cold winds, sir, better than Miss Nightingale could have done. What a devilish climate it *is;* never two days alike. I don't wonder Englishwomen are such icicles, poor things; they're frost-bitten from their cradle upwards."

"India warms them up, General, doesn't it?"

The General shook with laughter.

"To be sure, to be sure; if prudery's the fashion, they'll wear it, sir, as they would patches of hair powder; but they're always uncommonly glad to leave it off and lock it out of sight when they can. What do you think of the kennels? I say, Sydie, confound you, why did you bring any traps down with you? Haven't room for 'em; not for one. Couldn't cram a tilbury into the coach-house."

"A trap, governor?" said Sydie, straightening his back after examination of the pups; "can't keep even a wall-eyed cab-horse; wish I could."

"Where's your drag, then?" demanded the General.

"My drag? Don't I just wish I had one, to offer my bosom friend the V.P. a seat on the box. Calvert, of Trinity, tooled us over in his to the Spring Meetings, and his greys are the sweetest pair of goers—the leaders especially—that ever you saw in harness. We came back 'cross country, to get in time for hall, and a pretty mess we made of it, for we broke the axle, and lamed the off-wheeler, and——"

"But, God bless my soul!" stormed the General, excited beyond measure, "you wrote me word you were going to bring a drag down with you, and of course I supposed you meant what you said, and I had Harris in about it, and he swore the coach-house was as full of traps as ever it could hold, so I had my tax-cart and Fay's phaeton turned into one of the stalls, and then, after all, it comes out you've never brought it! Devil take you, Sydie, why can't you be more thoughtful——"

"But my dear governor——"

"Nonsense; don't talk to me!" cried the General, trying to work himself into a passion, and diving into the recesses of six separate pockets one after another. "Look here, sir; I suppose you'll believe your own words? Here it is in black and white.—'P.S. I shall bring *my Coach* down with me.' There, what do you say now? Confound you, what are you laughing at? *I* don't see anything to laugh at. In my day, young fellows didn't make fools of old men in this way. Bless my soul! why the devil don't you leave off laughing, and talk a little common sense? The thing's plain enough. —'P.S. *I shall bring my Coach down with me.*'"

"So I have," said Sydie, screaming with laughter. "Look at him—he's a first-rate Coach, too! Wheels always oiled, and ready for any road; always going up hill, and never caught coming down; started at a devil of a pace, and now keeps ahead of all other vehicles on all highways. A first-class Coach, that will tool me through the tortuous lanes and treacherous pitfalls of the Greats with flying colours. My Coach! Bravo, General! that's the best bit of fun I've had since I dressed up like Sophonisba Briggs, and led the V.P. a dance all round the quad, every hair on his head standing erect in his virtuous indignation at the awful morals of his college."

"Eh, what?" grunted the General, light beginning to dawn upon him. "Do you mean Mr. Keane? Hum! how's one to be up to all your confounded slang? How could I know? Devil take you, Sydie, why can't you write common English? You young fellows talk as bad jargon as Sepoys. You're sure I'm delighted to see you, Mr. Keane, though I did make the mistake."

"Thank you, General," said Keane; "but it's rather cool of you, Master Sydie, to have forced me on to your uncle's hands without his wish or his leave."

"Not at all, not at all," swore the General, with vehement cordiality. "I gave him carte blanche to ask whom he would, and unexpected guests are always most welcome; *not* that you were unexpected though, for I'd told that boy to be sure and bring somebody down here——"

"And have had the tax-cart and my phaeton turned out to make comfortable quarters for him," said Miss Fay, with a glance at The Coach to see how he took chaff, "and I only hope Mr. Keane may like his accommodation."

"Perhaps, Miss Morton," said Keane, smiling, "I shall like it so well that you will have to say to me as poor Voltaire to his troublesome abbé, 'Don Quichotte prenait les auberges pour les châteaux, mais vous avez pris les châteaux pour les auberges.'"

"Tiresome man," thought Fay. "I wish Sydie hadn't brought him here; but I shall do as I always do, however grand and supercilious he may look. He has lived among all those men and books till he has grown as cold as granite. What a pity it is people don't enjoy existence as I do!"

"You are thinking, Miss Morton," said Keane, as he walked on beside her, with an amused glance at her face, which was expressive enough of her thoughts, "that if your uncle is glad to see me, you are not, and that Sydie was very stupid not to bring down one of his kindred spirits instead of——Don't disclaim it now; you should veil your face if you wish your thoughts not to be read."

"I was not going to disclaim it," said Fay, quickly looking up at him with a rapid glance, half penitence, half irritation. "I always tell the truth; but I was *not* thinking exactly that; I don't want any of Sydie's friends —I detest boys—but I certainly *was* thinking that as you look down on everything that we all delight in, I fancied you and the Beeches will hardly agree. If I am rude, you must not be angry; you wanted me to tell you the truth."

Keane smiled again.

"Do I look down on the things you delight in? I hardly know enough of you, as we have only addressed about six syllables to each other, to be able to judge what you like and what you don't like; but certainly I must admit, that caressing the little round heads of those puppies yonder, which seemed to afford you such extreme rapture, would not be any source of remarkable gratification to me."

Fay looked up at him and laughed.

"Well, I am fond of animals as you are fond of books. Is it not an open question whether the live dog or sheepskin is not as good as the dead Morocco or Russian leather?"

"Is it an open question, whether Macaulay's or Arago's brain weighs no more than a cat's or a puppy's?"

"Brain!" said impudent little Fay; "are your great

men always as honest and as faithful as my poor little Snowdrop? I have an idea that Sheridan's brains were often obscured by brandy; that Richelieu had the weakness to be prouder of his bad poems than his magnificent policies; and that Pope and Byron had the folly to be more tenacious of a glance at their physical defect than an onslaught on their noblest works. I could mention a good many other instances where brain was not always a voucher for corresponding strength of character."

Keane was surprised to hear a sensible speech from this volatile little puss, and honoured her by answering her seriously.

"Say, rather, Miss Morton, that those to whom many temptations fall should have many excuses made. Where the brain preponderates, excelling the creative faculty and rapid thought, there will the sensibilities be proportionately acute. The vivacity and vigorous life which produced the rapid flow of Sheridan's eloquence led him into the dissipation which made him end his days in a spunging-house. Men of cooler minds and natures must not presume to judge him. They had not his temptation; they cannot judge of his fault. Richelieu, in all probability, amused himself with his verses as he amused himself with his white kitten and its cork, as a *délassement;* had he piqued himself upon his poetry as they say, he would have turned poetaster instead of politician. As for the other two, you must remember that Pope's deformity made him a subject of ridicule to the woman he was fool enough to worship, and Byron, poor fellow, was over-susceptible on all points, or he would scarcely have allowed the venomed arrows from the Scotch Reviewers to wound him, nor would he have cared for the desertion of a wife who was to him like ice to fire. When you are older, you will learn that it is very dangerous and unjust to say this thing is right, that wrong, that feeling wise, or this foolish; for all temperaments are different, and the same circumstances may produce very different effects. Your puppies will grow up with dissimilar characters; how much more so, then, must men?"

Miss Fay was quiet for a minute, then she flashed her mischievous eyes on him.

"Certainly; but then, by your own admission, you have no right to decide that your love for mathematics is wise, and my love for Snowdrop foolish; it may be quite *au contraire*. Perhaps, after all, I may have 'chosen the better part.'"

"Fay, go in and dress for dinner," interrupted the General, trotting up; "your tongue would run on for ever if nobody stopped it; you're no exception to your sex on that point. Is she?"

Keane laughed.

"Perhaps Miss Morton's frænum, like Sydie's, was cut too far in her infancy, and therefore she has been 'unbridled' ever since."

"In all things!" cried Little Fay. "Nobody has put the curb on me yet, and nobody ever shall."

"Don't be too sure, Fay," cried Sydie. "Rarey does wonders with the wildest fillies. Somebody may bring you down on your knees yet."

"You'll have to see to that, Sydie," laughed the General. "Come, get along, child, to your toilette. I never have my soup cold and my curry overdone. To wait for his dinner is a stretch of good-nature and patience that ought not to be expected of any man."

The soup was not cold nor the curry overdone, and the dinner was pleasant enough, in the long dining-room, with the June sun streaming in through its bay-windows from out the brilliant-coloured garden, and the walls echoing with the laughter of Sydie and his cousin, the young lady keeping true to her avowal of "not caring for Plato's presence." "Plato," however, listened quietly, peeling his peaches with tranquil amusement; for if the girl talked nonsense, it was clever nonsense, as rare, by the way, and quite as refreshing as true wit.

"My gloves are safe; you're too afraid of him, Fay," whispered Sydie, bending forwards to give her some hautboys.

"Am I?" cried Miss Fay, with a *moue* of supreme contempt. Neither the whisper nor the *moue* escaped Keane, as he talked with the governor on model drainage.

"Where's my hookah, Fay?" asked the General, after dessert. "Get it, will you, my pet?"

"Voilà!" cried Miss Fay, lifting the narghilé from the sideboard. Then taking some cigars off the mantelpiece, she put one in her own mouth, struck a fusee, and, handing the case to Keane, said, with a saucy smile in her soft bright eyes, though, to tell the truth, she was a little bit afraid of taking liberties with him:

"If you are not above such a sublunary indulgence, will you have a cigar with me?"

"With the greatest pleasure," said Keane, with a grave bow; "and if you would like to further rival George Sand, I shall be very happy to give you the address of my tailor."

"Thank you exceedingly; but as long as crinoline is the type of the sex that are a little lower than the angels, and ribbon-ties the seal of those but a trifle better than Mephistopheles, I don't think I will change it," responded Little Fay, contemptuously, as she threw herself down on a couch with an indignant defiant glance, and puffed at her Manilla.

Madame la Marquise, etc. 4

"I *hate* him, Sydie," said the little lady, vehemently, that night.

"Do you, dear," answered the Cantab; "you see, you've never had anybody to be afraid of, or had any man neglect you before."

"He may neglect me if he please, I am sure I do not care," rejoined Fay, disdainfully; "only I do wish, Sydie, that you had never brought him here to make us all uncomfortable."

"He don't make me uncomfortable, quite otherwise; nor yet the governor; you're the only victim, Fay."

Fay saw little enough of Keane for the next week or two. He was out all day with Sydie trout-fishing, or walking over his farms with the General, or sitting in the study reading, and writing his articles for the *Cambridge Journal*, *Leonville's Mathematical Journal*, or the *Westminster Review*. But when she was with him, there was no mischief within her reach that Miss Fay did not perpetrate. Keane, to tease her, would condemn—so seriously that she believed him—all that she loved the best; he would tell her that he admired quiet, domestic women; that he thought girls should be very subdued and retiring; that they should work well, and not care much for society; at all of which, being her extreme antipodes, Little Fay would be vehemently wrathful. She would get on her pony without any saddle in her evening dress, and ride him at the five-bar gate in the stable-yard; she would put on Sydie's smoking-cap, and look very pretty in it, and take a Queen's on the divan of the smoking-room, reading *Bell's Life*, and asking Keane how much he would bet on the October; she would spend all the morning making wreaths of roses, dressing herself and the puppies up in them, inquiring if it was not a laudable and industrious occupation. There was no nonsense or mischief Fay would not imagine and forthwith commit, and anything they wanted her not to do she would do straightway, even to the imperilling of her own life and limb. She tried hard to irritate or rouse "Plato," as she called him, but "Plato" was not to be moved, and treated her as a spoilt child, whom he alone had sense enough to resist.

"It will be great folly for you to attempt it, Miss Morton. Those horses are not fit to be driven by any one, much less by a woman," said Keane, quietly, one morning.

They were in the stable-yard, and chanced to be alone when a new purchase of the governor's—two scarcely broken-in thorough-bred colts—were brought with a new mail-phaeton into the yard, and Miss Fay forthwith announced her resolution of driving them round the avenue. The groom that came with them told her they were almost more than he could manage, their own coachman begged and implored, Keane reasoned quietly, all to no purpose. The rosebud had put out its little wilful thorns; Keane's words added fuel to fire. Up she sprang, looking the daintiest morsel imaginable perched up on that very exalted box-seat, told the horrified groom to mount behind, and started them off, lifting her hat with a graceful bow to "Plato," who stood watching the phaeton with his arms folded and his cigar in his mouth.

Soon after, he started in the contrary direction, for the avenue circled the Beeches in an oval of four miles, and he knew he should meet her coming back. He strolled along under the pleasant shadow of the great trees, enjoying the sunset and the fresh air, and capable of enjoying them still more but for an inward misgiving. His presentiment was not without its grounds. He had walked about a mile and a half round the avenue, when a cloud of dust told him what was up, and in the distance came the thorough-breds, broken away as he had prophesied, tearing along with the bits between their teeth, Little Fay keeping gallantly hold of the ribbons, but as powerless over the colts now they had got their heads as the groom leaning from the back seat.

On came the phaeton, bumping, rattling, oscillating, threatening every second to be turned over. Keane caught one glance of Fay's face, resolute and pale, and of her little hands grasping the ribbons, till they were cut and bleeding with the strain. There was nothing for it but to stand straight in the animals' path, catch their heads, and throw them back on their haunches. Luckily, his muscles were like iron—luckily, too, the colts had come a long way, and were not fresh. He stood like a rock, and checked them; running a very close risk of dislocating his arms with the shock, but saving Little Fay from destruction. The colts stood trembling, the groom jumped out and caught the reins, Keane amused himself silently with the mingled penitence, vexation, shame, and rebellion visible in the little lady's face.

"Well," said he, quietly, "as you were so desirous of breaking your neck, will you ever forgive me for defeating your purpose?"

"Pray don't!" cried Fay, passionately. "I do thank you so much for saving my life; I think it so generous and brave of you to have rescued me at such risk to yourself. I feel that I can never be grateful enough to you, but don't talk in that way. I know it was silly and self-willed of me."

"It was; that fact is obvious."

"Then I shall make it more so," cried Miss Fay, with her old wilfulness. "I do feel very grateful, and I would tell you so, if you would let me; but if you think it has made me afraid, you are quite wrong, and so you shall see."

And before he could interfere, or do more than mechanically spring up after her, she had caught the reins from the groom, and started the trembling colts off again. But Keane put his hand on the ribbons.

"Foolish child; are you mad?" he said, so gravely yet so gently that Fay let them go, and let him drive her back to the stable-yard, where she sprang out, and rushed away to her own room, terrified the governor with a few vehement sentences, which gave him a vague idea that Keane was murdered and both Fay's legs broken, and then had a private cry all to herself, with her arms round Snowdrop's neck, curled up in one of the drawing-room windows, where she had not been long when the General and Keane passed through, not noticing her, hidden as she was in curtains, cushions, and flowers.

"She's a little wilful thing, Keane," the General was saying, "but you mustn't think the worse of her for that."

"I don't. I am sick of those conventional young ladies who agree with everything one says to them—who keep all the frowns for mothers and servants, and are as serene as a cloudless sky abroad, smile blandly on all alike, and haven't an opinion of their own."

"Fay's plenty of opinions of her own," chuckled the General; "and she tells 'em pretty freely, too. Bless the child, she's not ashamed of any of her thoughts, and never will be."

"I hope not. Your little niece can do things that no other young lady could, and they are so pretty in her, that it would be a thousand pities for her to grow one atom less natural and wilful. Grapes growing wild are charming—grapes trained to a stake are ruined. I assure you, if I were you, I would not scold her for driving those colts to-day. High spirits and love of fun led her on, and the courage and presence of mind she displayed are too rare among her sex for us to do right in checking them."

"To be sure, to be sure," assented the governor, gleefully. "God bless the child! she's one among a thousand, sir. Cognac, not milk-and-water. There's the dinner-bell; confound it."

Whereat the General made his exit, and Keane also; and Fay kissed the spaniel with even more passionate attachment than ordinary.

"Ah, Snowdrop, I don't hate him any more; he is a darling!"

One glowing August morning Keane was in the study pondering whether he would go to his moor or not. The General had besought him to stay. His gamekeeper wrote him that it was a horridly bad rainy season in Invernessshire; the trout and the rabbits were very good sport in a mild way here. Altogether, Keane felt half disposed to keep where he was, when a shadow fell across his paper, and, as he looked up, he saw in the open window the English rosebud.

"Is it not one of the open questions, Mr. Keane," asked Fay, "whether it is very wise to spend all this glorious morning shut out of the sight of the sun-rays and the scent of the flowers?"

"How have *you* been spending it, then?"

"Putting bouquets in all the rooms, cleaning my aviary, talking to the puppies, and reading Jocelyn under the limes in the shrubberies—all very puerile, but all very pleasant. Perhaps if you descended to a lazy day like that now and then, you might be none the worse!"

"Is that a challenge? Will you take me under the limes?"

"No, indeed! I do not admit men who despise them to my gardens of Armida, any more than you would admit me into your Schools. I have as great a scorn for a sceptic as you have for a tyro."

"Pardon me. I have no scorn for a tyro. But you would not come to the Academe; you dislike 'Plato' too much."

Fay looked up at him half shyly, half mischievously.

"Yes, I do dislike you, when you look down on me as Richelieu might have looked down on his kitten."

"Liking to see its play?" said Keane, half sadly. "Contrasting its gay insouciance with his own toil and turmoil, regretting, perhaps, the time when trifles made his joy as they did his kitten's? If I were to look on you so, there would not be much to offend you."

"You do not think so of me, or you would speak to me as if I were an intelligent being, not a silly little thing."

"How do you know I think you silly?"

"Because you think all women so."

"Perhaps; but then you should rather try to redeem me from my error in doctrine. Come, let us sign a treaty of peace. Take me under the limes. I want some fresh air after writing all day; and in payment I will teach you Euclid, as you vainly beseeched your cousin to do yesterday."

"Will you?" cried Fay, eagerly. Then she threw back her head. "I never am won by bribes."

"Nor yet by threats? What a difficult young lady you are. Come, show me your shrubbery sanctum now you have invaded mine."

The English rosebud laid aside its wilful thorns, and

Fay, a little less afraid of her Plato, and therefore a little less defiant to him, led him over the grounds, filled his hands with flowers, showed him her aviary, read some of Jocelyn to him, to show him, she said, that Lamartine was better than the Œdipus in Coloneus, and thought, as she dressed for dinner, "I wonder if he does despise me—he has such a beautiful face, if he were not so haughty and cold!"

The next day Keane gave her an hour of Euclid in the study. Certainly The Coach had never had such a pretty pupil; and he wished every dull head he had to cram was as intelligent as this fair-haired one. Fay was quick and clever; she was stimulated, moreover, by his decree concerning the stupidity of all women; she really worked as hard as any young man studying for degrees when they supposed her fast asleep in bed, and she got over the Pons Asinorum in a style that fairly astonished her tutor.

The Coach did not dislike his occupation either; it did him good, after his life of solitude and study, something as the kitten and cork did Richelieu good after his cabinets and councils; and Little Fay, with her flowers and fun, mischief and impudence, and that winning wilfulness which it amused him gradually to tame down, unbent the chillness which had grown upon him. He was the better for it, as a man after hard study or practice is the better for some fresh sea-breezes, and some days of careless dolce.

"Well, Fay, have you had another poor devil flinging himself at your feet by means of a postage-stamp?" said Sydie one morning at breakfast. "You can't disguise anything from me, your most interested, anxious, and near and dear relative. Whenever the governor looks particularly stormy I see the signs of the times, that if I do not forthwith remove your dangerously attractive person, all the bricks, spooneys, swells, and do-nothings in the county will speedily fill the Hanwell wards to overflowing."

"Don't talk such nonsense, Sydie," said Fay, impatiently, with a glance at Keane, as she handed him his chocolate.

"Ah! deuce take the fellows," chuckled the General. "Love, devotion, admiration! What a lot of stuff they do write. I wonder if Fay were a little beggar, how much of it all would stand the test? But we know a trick worth two of that. Try those sardines, Keane. House is let, Fay—eh? House is let; nobody need apply. Ha, ha!"

And the General took some more curry, laughing till he was purple, while Fay blushed scarlet, a trick of which she was rarely guilty; Sydie smiled, and Keane picked out his sardines with calm deliberation.

"Hallo! God bless my soul!" burst forth the General again. "Devil take me! I'll be hanged if I stand it! Confound 'em all! I do call it hard for a man not to be able to sit at his breakfast in peace. Good Heavens! what will come to the country, if all those little devils grow up to be food for Calcraft? He's actually pulling the bark off the trees, as I live! Excuse me, I *can't* sit still and see it."

Wherewith the General bolted from his chair, darted through the window, upsetting three dogs, two kittens, and a stand of flowers in his exit, and bolted breathlessly across the park with the poker in his hand.

"Bless his old heart! Ain't he a brick?" shouted Sydie. "Do excuse me, Fay, I must go and hear him blow up that boy sky-high, and give him a shilling for tuck afterwards; it will be so rich."

The Cantab made his exit, and Fay busied herself

calming the kittens' minds, and restoring the dethroned geraniums. Keane read his *Times* for ten minutes, then looked up.

"Miss Morton, where is your tongue? I have not heard it for a quarter of an hour, a miracle that has never happened in the two months I have been at the Beeches."

"You do not want to hear it."

"What! am I in *mauvais odeur* again?" smiled Keane. "I thought we were good friends. Have you found the Q.E.D. to the problem I gave you?"

"To be sure!" cried Fay, exultantly. And kneeling down by him, she went through the whole thing in exceeding triumph.

"You are a good child," said her tutor, smiling, in himself amazed at this volatile little thing's capacity for mathematics. "I think you will be able to take your degree, if you like. Come, do you hate me now, Fay?"

"No," said Fay, a little shyly. "I never hated you, I always admired you; but I was afraid of you, though I would never confess it to Sydie."

"Never be afraid of me," said Keane, putting his hand on hers as it lay on the arm of his chair. "You have no cause. You can do things few girls can; but they are pretty in you, where they might be—not so pretty in others. *I* like them at the least. You are very fond of your cousin, are you not?"

"Of Sydie? Oh, I love him dearly!"

Keane took his hand away, and rose, as the General trotted in:

"God bless my soul, Keane, how warm it is! Confoundedly hot without one's hat, I can tell you. Had my walk all for nothing, too. That cursed little idiot wasn't trespassing after all. Stephen had set him to spud out the daisies, and I'd thrashed the boy before I'd listen to him. Devil take him!"

August went out and September came in, and Keane stayed on at the Beeches. They were pleasant days to them all, knocking over the partridges right and left, enjoying a cold luncheon under the luxuriant hedges, and going home for a dinner, full of laughter, and talk, and good cookery; and Fay's songs afterwards, as wild and sweet in their way as a goldfinch's on a hawthorn spray.

"You like Little Fay, don't you, Keane?" said the General, as they went home one evening.

Keane looked startled for a second.

"Of course," he said, rather haughtily. "That Miss Morton is very charming every one must admit."

"Bless her little heart! She's a wild little filly, Keane; but she'll go better and truer than your quiet broken-in ones, who wear the harness so respectably, and are so wicked and vicious in their own minds. And what do you think of my boy?" asked the General, pointing to Sydie, who was in front. "How does he stand at Cambridge?"

"Sydie? Oh, he's a nice young fellow. He is a great favourite there, and he is—the best things he can be—generous, sweet-tempered, and honourable——"

"To be sure," echoed the General, rubbing his hands. "He's a dear boy—a very dear boy. They're both exactly all I wished them to be, dear children; and I must say I am delighted to see 'em carrying out the plan I had always made for 'em from their childhood."

"Being what, General, may I ask?"

"Why, any one can see, as plain as a pikestaff, that they're in love with each other," said the General, glowing with satisfaction; "and I mean them to be married and happy. They dote on each other, Keane, and I shan't put any obstacles in their way. Youth's short enough, Heaven knows; let 'em enjoy it, say I, it don't come back again. Don't say anything to him about it; I want to have some fun with him. They've settled it all, of course, long ago; but he hasn't confided in me, the sly dog. Trust an old campaigner, though, for twigging an *affaire de cœur*. Bless them both, they make me feel a boy again. We'll have a gay wedding, Keane; mind you come down for it. I dare say it'll be at Christmas."

Keane walked along, drawing his cap over his eyes. The sun was setting full in his face.

"Well, what sport?" cried Fay, running up to them.

"Pretty fair," said Keane, coldly, as he passed her.

It was an hour before the dinner-bell rang. Then he came down cold and calm, particularly brilliant in conversation, more courteous, perhaps, to her than ever, but the frost had gathered round him that the sunny atmosphere of the Beeches had melted; and Fay, though she tried to teaze, and to coax, and to win him, could not dissipate it. She felt him an immeasurable distance from her again. He was a learned, haughty, grave philosopher, and she a little naughty child.

As Keane went up-stairs that night, he heard Sydie talking in the hall.

"Yes, my worshipped Fay, I shall be intensely and utterly miserable away from the light of your eyes; but, nevertheless, I must go and see Kingslake from John's next Tuesday, because I've promised; and let one idolise your divine self ever so much, one can't give up one's larks, you know."

Keane ground his teeth with a bitter sigh and a fierce oath.

"Little Fay, I would have loved you more tenderly than that!"

He went in and threw himself on his bed, not to sleep. For the first time for many years he could not summon sleep at his will. He had gone on petting her and amusing himself, thinking of her only as a winning, wayward child. Now he woke with a shock to discover, too late, that she had stolen from him unawares the heart he had so long refused to any woman. With his high intellect and calm philosophy, after his years spent in severe science and cold solitude, the hot well-springs of passion had broken loose again. He longed to take her bright life into his own grave and cheerless one; he longed to feel her warm young heart beat with his own, icebound for so many years; but Little Fay was never to be his.

In the bedroom next to him the General sat, with his feet in his slippers and his dressing-gown round him, smoking his last cheroot before a roaring fire, chuckling complacently over his own thoughts.

"To be sure, we'll have a very gay wedding, such as the county hasn't seen in all its blessed days," he muttered, with supreme satisfaction. "Sydie shall have this place. What do I want with a great town of a house like this, big enough for a barrack? I'll take that shooting-box that's to let four miles off; that'll be plenty large enough for me and my old chums to smoke in and chat over bygone times, and it will do our hearts good— freshen us up a bit to see those young things enjoying themselves. My Little Fay will be the prettiest bride that ever was seen. Silly young things to suppose I don't see through them. Trust an old soldier! However, love is blind, they say. How could they have helped falling in love with one another? and who'd have the heart to part 'em, I should like to know?"

Keane stayed that day: the next, receiving a letter which afforded a true though a slight excuse to return to Cambridge, he went, the General, Fay, and Sydie believing him gone only for a few days, he knowing that he would never set foot in the Beeches again. He went back to his rooms, whose dark monastic gloom in the dull October day seemed to close round him like an iron shroud. Here, with his books, his papers, his treasures of intellect, science and art, his "mind a kingdom" to him, he had spent many a happy day, with his brain growing only clearer and clearer as he followed out a close reasoning or clenched a subtle analysis. Now, for the sake of a mischievous child but half his age, he shuddered as he entered.

"Well, my dear boy," began the General one day after dinner, "I've seen your game, though you thought I didn't. How do you know, you young dog, that I shall give my consent?"

"Oh, bother, governor, I know you will," cried Sydie, aghast; "because, you see, if you let me have a few cool hundreds I can give the men such slap-up wines—and it's my last year, General."

"You sly dog!" chuckled the governor, "I'm not talking of your wine-merchant, and you know I'm not, Master Sydie. It's no good playing hide-and-seek with me; I can always see through a millstone when Cupid is behind it; and there's no need to beat round the bush with me, my boy. I never gave my assent to anything with greater delight in my life; I've always meant you to marry Fay, and——"

"Marry Fay!" shouted Sydie. "Good Heavens! governor, what next?" And the Cantab threw himself back and laughed till he cried, and Snowdrop and her pups barked furiously in a concert of excited sympathy.

"Why, sir, why?—why, because—devil take you, Sydie—I don't know what you are laughing at, do you?" cried the General, starting out of his chair.

"Yes, I do, governor; you're labouring under a most delicious delusion."

"Delusion!—eh?—what? Why, bless my soul, I don't think you know what you are saying, Sydie?" stormed the General.

"Yes, I do; you've an idea—how you got it into your head Heaven knows, but there it is—you've an idea that Fay and I are in love with one another; and I assure you you were never more mistaken in your life."

Seeing the General standing bolt upright staring at him, and looking decidedly apoplectic, Sydie made the matter a little clearer.

"Fay and I would do a good deal to oblige you, my beloved governor, if we could get up the steam a little, but I'm afraid we really can *not*. Love ain't in one's own hands, you see, but a skittish mare, that gets her head, and takes the bit between her teeth, and bolts off with you wherever she likes. Is it possible that two people who broke each other's toys, and teased each other's lives out, and caught the measles of each other, from their cradle upwards, should fall in love with each other when they grow up? Besides, I don't intend to marry for the next twenty years, if I can help it. I couldn't afford a milliner's bill to my tailor's, and I should be ruined for life if I merged my bright particular star of a self into a respectable, lark-shunning, bill-paying, shabby-hatted, family man. Good Heavens, what a train of horrors comes with the bare idea!"

"Do you mean to say, sir, you won't marry your cousin?" shouted the General.

"Bless your dear old heart, *no*, governor—ten times over, *no!* I wouldn't marry anybody, not for half the universe."

"Then I've done with you, sir—I wash my hands of you!" shouted the General, tearing up and down the room in a quick march, more beneficial to his feelings than his carpet. "You are an ungrateful, unprincipled, shameless young man, and are no more worthy of the affection and the interest I've been fool enough to waste on you than a tom-cat. You're an abominably selfish, ungrateful, unnatural boy; and though you *are* poor Phil's son, I will tell you my mind, sir; and I must say I think your conduct with your cousin, making love to her— desperate love to her—winning her affections, poor unhappy child, and then making a jest of her and treating it with a laugh, is disgraceful, sir—*disgraceful*, do you hear?"

"Yes, I hear, General," cried Sydie, convulsed with laughter; "but Fay cares no more for me than for those geraniums. We are fond of one another, in a cool, cousinly sort of way, but—"

"Hold your tongue!" stormed the General. "Don't dare to say another word to me about it. You know well enough that it has been the one delight of my life, and if you'd had any respect or right feeling in you, you'd marry her to-morrow."

"She wouldn't be a party to that. Few women *are* blind to my manifold attractions; but Fay's one of 'em. Look here, governor," said Sydie, laying his hand affectionately on the General's shoulder, "did it never occur to you that though the pretty castle's knocked down, there may be much nicer bricks left to build a new one? Can't you see that Fay doesn't care two buttons about me, but cares a good many diamond studs about somebody else?"

"Nothing has occurred to me but that you and she are two heartless, selfish, ungrateful chits. Hold your tongue, sir!"

"But, General——"

"Hold your tongue, sir; don't talk to me, I tell you. In love with somebody else? I should like to see him show his face here. Somebody she's talked to for five minutes at a race-ball, and proposed to her in a corner, thinking to get some of my money. Some swindler, or Italian refugee, or blackleg, I'd be bound—taken her in, made her think him angel, and will persuade her to run away with him. I'll set the police round the house— I'll send her to school in Paris. What fools men are to have anything to do with women at all! You seem in their confidence; who's the fellow?"

"A man very like a swindler or a blackleg—Keane!"

"Keane!" shouted the General, pausing in the middle of his frantic march.

"Keane," responded Sydie.

"Keane!" shouted the General again. "God bless my soul, she might as well have fallen in love with the man in the moon. Why couldn't she like the person I'd chosen for her?"

"If one can't guide the mare oneself, 'tisn't likely the governors can for one," muttered Sydie.

"Poor dear child! fallen in love with a man who don't care a button for her, ch? Humph!—that's always the way with women—lose the good chances, and fling themselves at a man's feet who cares no more for their tomfoolery of worship than he cares for the blacking on his boots. Devil take young people, what a torment they are! The ungrateful little jade, how dare she go and smash all my plans like that? and if I ever set my heart on anything, I set it on that match. Keane! he'll no more love anybody than the stone cherubs on the terrace. He's a splendid head, but his heart's every atom as cold as granite. Love her? Not a bit of it. When I told him you were going to marry her (I thought you would, and so you will, too, if you've the slightest particle of gratitude or common sense in either of you), he listened as quietly and as calmly as if he had been one of the men in armour in the hall. Love, indeed! To the devil with love, say I! It's the head and root of everything that's mischievous and bad."

"Wait a bit, uncle," cried Sydie; "you told him all about your previous match-making, eh? And didn't he go off like a shot two days after, when we meant him to stay on a month longer? Can't you put two and two together, my once wide-awake governor? 'Tisn't such a difficult operation.".

"No, I can't!" shouted the General; "I don't know anything, I don't see anything, I don't believe in anything, I hate everybody and everything, I tell you; and I'm a great fool for having ever set my heart on any plan that wanted a woman's concurrence—

> For if she will she will, you may depend on't,
> And if she won't she won't, and there's an end on't."

Wherewith the General stuck his wide-awake on fiercely, and darted out of the bay-window to cool himself. Half way across the lawn, he turned sharp round, and came back again.

"Sydie, do you fancy Keane cares a straw for that child?"

"I can't say. It's possible."

"Humph! Well, can't you go and see? That's come of those mathematical lessons. What a fool I was to allow her to be so much with him!" growled the General, with many grunts and half-audible oaths, swinging round again, and trotting through the window as hot and peppery as his own idolised curry.

Keane was sitting writing in his rooms at King's some few days after. The backs looked dismal with their leafless, sepia-coloured trees; the streets were full of sloppy mud and dripping under-grads' umbrellas; his own room looked sombre and dark, without any sunshine on its heavy oak bookcases, and massive library-table, and dark bronzes. His pen moved quickly, his head was bent over the paper, his mouth sternly set, and his forehead paler and more severe than ever. The gloom in his chambers had gathered round him himself, when his door was burst open, and Sydie dashed in and threw himself down in a green leather arm-chair.

"Well, sir, here am I back again. Just met the V.P. in the quad, and he was so enchanted at seeing me, that he kissed me on both cheeks, flung off his gown, tossed up his cap, and performed a *pas d'extase* on the spot. Isn't it delightful to be so beloved? Granta looks very delicious to-day, I must say—about as refreshing and lively as an acidulated spinster going district-visiting in a snow-storm. And how are you, most noble lord?"

"Pretty well."

"Only that? Thought you were all muscle and iron, I say. What *do* you think the governor has been saying to me?"

"How can I tell?"

"Tell! No, I should not have guessed it if I'd tried for a hundred years! By George! nothing less than that I should marry Fay. What do you think of that, sir?"

Keane traced Greek unconsciously on the margin of

his *Times*. For the life of him, with all his self-command, he could not have answered.

"Marry Fay! *I!*" shouted Sydie. "Ye gods, what an idea! I never was so astonished in all my days. Marry Little Fay!—the governor must be mad, you know."

"You will not marry your cousin?" asked Keane, tranquilly, though the rapid glance and involuntary start did not escape Sydie's quick eyes.

"Marry! I! By George, no! She wouldn't have me, and I'm sure I wouldn't have her. She is a dear little monkey, and I'm very fond of her, but I wouldn't put the halter round my neck for any woman going. I don't like vexing the General, but it would be really too great a sacrifice merely to oblige him."

"She cares nothing for you, then?"

"Nothing? Well, I don't know. Yes, in a measure, she does. If I should be taken home on a hurdle one fine morning, she'd shed some cousinly tears over my inanimate body; but as for *the other thing*, not one bit of it. 'Tisn't likely. We're a great deal too like one another, too full of devilry and carelessness, to assimilate. Isn't it the delicious contrast and fiz of the sparkling acid of divine lemons with the contrariety of the fiery spirit of beloved rum that makes the delectable union known and worshipped in our symposia under the blissful name of PUNCH? Marry Little Fay! By Jove, if all the governor's match-making was founded on no better reasons for success, it is a small marvel that he's a bachelor now! By George, it's time for hall!"

And the Cantab took himself off, congratulating himself on the adroit manner in which he had cut the Gordian knot that the General had muddled up so inexplicably in his unpropitious match-making.

Keane lay back in his chair some minutes, very still; then he rose to dine in hall, pushing away his books and papers, as if throwing aside with them a dull and heavy weight. The robins sang in the leafless backs, the sun shone out on the sloppy streets; the youth he thought gone for ever was come back to him. Oh, strange stale story of Hercules and Omphale, old as the hills, and as eternal! Hercules goes on in his strength slaying his Hydra and his Laomedon for many years, but he comes at last, whether he like it or not, to his Omphale, at whose feet he is content to sit and spin long golden threads of pleasure and of passion, while his lion's skin is motheaten and his club rots away.

Little Fay sat curled up on the study hearth-rug, reading a book her late guest had left behind him—a very light and entertaining volume, being Delolme "On the Constitution," but which she preferred, I suppose, to "What Will He Do With It?" or the "Feuilles d'Automne," for the sake of that clear autograph, "Gerald Keane, King's Coll.," on its fly-leaf. A pretty picture she made, with her handsome spaniels; and she was so intent on what she was reading—the fly-leaf, by the way—that she never heard the opening of the door, till a hand drew away her book. Then Fay started up, oversetting the puppies one after another, radiant and breathless.

Keane took her hands and drew her near him.

"You do not hate me now, then?"

Fay put her head on one side with her old wilfulness.

"Yes I do—when you go away without any notice, and hardly bid me good-bye. You would not have left one of your men pupils so unceremoniously."

Keane smiled involuntarily, and drew her closer.

"If you do not hate me, will you go a step farther—and love me? Little Fay, my own darling, will you come and brighten my life? It has been a saddened and a stern one, but it shall never throw a shade on yours."

The wild little filly was conquered—at least, she came to hand docile and subdued, and acknowledged her master. She loved him, and told him so with that frankness and fondness which would have covered faults far more glaring and weighty than Little Fay's.

"But you must never be afraid of me," whispered Keane, some time after.

"Oh no."

"And you do not wish Sydie had never brought me here to make you all uncomfortable."

"Oh, please don't!" cried Fay, plaintively. "I was a child then, and I did not know what I said."

"'Then,' being three months ago, may I ask what you are now?"

"A child still in knowledge, but *your* child," whispered Fay, lifting her face to his, "to be petted and spoiled, and never found fault with, remember?"

"My little darling, who would have the heart to find fault with you, whatever your sins?"

"God bless my soul, what's this?" cried a voice in the doorway.

There stood the General in wide-awake and shooting-coat, with a spade in one hand and a watering-pot in the other, too astonished to keep his amazement to himself. Fay would fain have turned and fled, but Keane smiled, kept one arm round her, and stretched out his hand to the governor.

"General, I came once uninvited, and I am come again. Will you forgive me? I have a great deal to say to you, but I must ask you one question first of all. Will you give me your treasure?"

"Eh! humph! What? Well—I suppose—yes," ejaculated the General, breathless from the combined effects of amazement and excessive and vehement gardening. "But bless my soul, Keane, I should as soon have thought of one of the stone cherubs, or that bronze Milton. Never mind, one lives and learns. Mind? Devil take me, what am I talking about? I don't mind at all; I'm very happy, only I'd set my heart on—you know what. More fool I. Fay, you little imp, come here. Are you fairly broken in by Keane, then?"

"Yes," said Miss Fay, with her old mischief, but a new blush, "as he has promised never to use the curb."

"God bless you, then, my little pet," cried the General, kissing her some fifty times. Then he laughed till he cried, and dried his eyes and laughed again, and grunted, and growled, and shook both Keane's hands vehemently. "I was a great fool, sir, and I dare say you've managed much better. I *did* set my heart on the boy, you know, but it can't be helped now, and I don't wish it should. Be kind to her, that's all; for though she mayn't bear the curb, the whip from anybody she cares about would break her heart. She's a dear child, Keane—a very dear child. Be kind to her, that's all."

On the evening of January 13th, beginning the Lent Term, Mr. Sydenham Morton sat in his own rooms with half a dozen spirits like himself, a delicious aroma surrounding them of Maryland and rum-punch, and a rapid flow of talk making its way through the dense atmosphere.

"To think of Granite Keane being caught!" shouted one young fellow, "I should as soon have thought of the Pyramids walking over to the Sphinx, and marrying her."

"Poor devil! I pity him," sneered Henley of Trinity, aged nineteen.

"He don't require much pity, my dear fellow; I think he's pretty comfortable," rejoined Sydie. "He did, to be sure, when he was trying to beat sense into your brain-box, but that's over for the present."

"Come, tell us about the wedding," said Somerset of King's. "I was so sorry I couldn't go down."

"Well," began Sydie, stretching his legs and putting down his pipe, "she—*the* she was dressed in white tulle and——"

"Bother the dress. Go ahead!"

"The dress was no bother, it was the one subject in life to the women. You must listen to the dress, because I asked the prettiest girl there for the description of it to enlighten your minds, and it was harder to learn than six books of Horace. The bridesmaids wore tarlatane à la Princesse Stéphanie, trois jupes bouillonnées, jupe dessous de soie glacée, guirlandes couleur des yeux impériaux d'Eugénie, corsets décolletés, garnis de ruches de ruban du——"

"For Heaven's sake, hold your tongue!" cried Somerset, "That jargon's worse than the Yahoos'. The dead languages are bad enough to learn, but women's living language of fashion is ten hundred times worse. The twelve girls were dressed in blue and white, and thought themselves angels—we understand. Cut along."

"Gunter was prime," continued Sydie, "and the governor was prime, too—splendid old buck; only when he gave her away he was very near saying, 'Devil take it!' which might have had a novel, but hardly a solemn, effect. Little Fay was delightful—for all the world like a bit of incarnated sunshine. Keane was granite all over, except his eyes, and they were lava; if we hadn't, for our

THE GENERAL'S MATCH-MAKING. 73

own preservation, let him put her in a carriage and started 'em off, he might have become dangerous, after the manner of Etna, ice outside and red-hot coals within. The bridesmaids' tears must have washed the church for a week, and made it rather a damp affair. One would scarcely think women were so anxious to marry, to judge from the amount of grief they get up at a friend's sacrifice. It looks uncommonly like envy; but it *isn't*, we're sure! The ball was like most other balls: alternate waltzing and flirtation, a vast lot of nonsense talked, and a vast lot of champagne drunk—Cupid running about in every direction, and a tremendous run on all the amatory poets—Browning and Tennyson being worked as hard as cab-horses, and used-up pretty much as those quadrupeds—dandies suffering self-inflicted torture from tight boots, and saying, like Cranmer, when he held his hand in the fire, that it was rather agreeable than otherwise, considering it drew admiration—spurs getting entangled in ladies' dresses, and ladies making use thereof for a display of amiability, which the dragoons are very much mistaken if they fancied continued into private life—girls believing all the pretty things said to them—men going home and laughing at them all—wallflowers very black, women engaged ten deep very sunshiny—the governor very glorious, and my noble self very fascinating. And now," said Sydie, taking up his pipe, "pass the punch, old boy, and never say I can't talk!"

THE STORY OF A CRAYON-HEAD;

OR,

A DOUBLED-DOWN LEAF IN A MAN'S LIFE.

I WAS dining with a friend, in his house on the Lung' Arno (he fills, never mind what, post in the British Legation), where I was passing an autumn month. The night was oppressively hot; a still, sultry sky brooded over the city, and the stars shining out from a purple mist on to the Campanile near, and the slopes of Bellosguardo in the distance. It was intensely hot; not all the iced wines on his table could remove the oppressive warmth of the evening air, which made both him and me think of evenings we had spent together in the voluptuous lassitude of the East, in days gone by, when we had travelled there, fresh to life, to new impressions, to all that gives "greenness to the grass, and glory to the flower."

The Arno ran on under its bridge, and we leaned out of the balcony where we were sitting and smoking, while I tossed over, without thinking much of what I was doing, a portfolio of his sketches. Position has lost for art many good artists since Sir George Beaumont: my friend is one of them; his sketches are masterly; and had he been a vagrant Bohemian instead of an English peer, there might have been pictures on the walls of the R.A. to console one for the meretricious daubs and pet vul-

THE STORY OF A CRAYON-HEAD. 75

garities of nursery episodes, hideous babies, and third-class carriage interiors, which make one's accustomed annual visit to the rooms that once saw the beauties of Reynolds, and Wilson, and Lawrence, a positive martyrdom to anybody of decent refinement and educated taste. The portfolio stood near me, and I took out a sketch or two now and then between the pauses of our conversation, looking lazily up the river, while the moonlight shone on Dante's city, that so long forgot, and has, so late, remembered him.

"Ah! what a pretty face this is? Who's the original?" I asked him, drawing out a female head, done with great finish in pastel, under which was written, in his own hand, "Florelle." It was a face of great beauty, with a low Greek brow and bronze-dark hair, and those large, soft, liquid eyes that you only see in a Southern, and that looked at you from the sketch with an earnest, wistful regard, half childlike, half impassioned. He looked up, glanced at the sketch, and stretched out his hand hastily, but I held it away from him. "I want to look at it; it is a beautiful head; I wish we had the original here now. Who is she?"

As I spoke—holding the sketch up where the light from the room within fell on what I had no doubt was a likeness of some fair face that had beguiled his time in days gone by, a souvenir of one of his loves more lasting than souvenirs of such episodes often are, if merely trusted to that inconstant capricieuse, Memory—I might have hit him with a bullet rather than asked him about a mere *étude à deux crayons*, for he shuddered, and drank off some white Hermitage quickly.

"I had forgotten that was in the portfolio," he said, hurriedly, as he took it from me and put it behind him, with its face against the wall, as though it had been the sketch of a Medusa.

"What do you take it away for? I had not half done looking at it. Who is the original?"

"One I don't care to mention."

"Because?"

"Because the sight of that picture gives me a twinge of what I ought to be hardened against—regret."

"Regret! Is any woman worth that?"

"She was."

"I don't believe it; and I fancied you and I thought alike on such points. Of all the women for whom we feel twinges of conscience or self-reproach in melancholy moments, how many *loved us?* Moralists and poets sentimentalise over it, and make it a stalking-horse whereby to magnify our sins and consign us more utterly to perdition, while they do for themselves a little bit of poetic morality cheaply; but in reality there are uncommonly few women who can love, to begin with, and in the second, vanity, avarice, jealousy, desires for pretty toilettes, one or other, or all combined, have quite as much to do with their 'sacrifice' for us as anything."

"Quite true; but—there are women and women, perhaps, and it was not of that sort of regret that I spoke."

"Of what sort, then?"

He made me no reply; he broke the ash off his Manilla, and smoked silently some moments, leaning over the balcony and watching the monotonous flow of the Arno, with deeper gloom on his face than I remembered to have seen there any time before. I was sorry I had chanced to light upon a sketch that had brought him back such painful recollections of whatever kind they might be, and I smoked too, sending the perfumed tobacco out into the still sultry night that was brooding over Florence.

"Of what sort?" said he, abruptly, after some minutes' pause. "Shall I tell you? Then you can tell *me* whether I was a fool who made one grand mistake, or a sensible man of the world who kept himself from a grand folly. I have been often in doubt myself."

He leaned back, his face in shadow, so that I could not see it, while the Arno's ebb and flow was making mournful river-music under our windows;—the purple glories of the summer night deepened round Giotto's Tower, where, in centuries past, the Immortal of Florence had sat dreaming of the Paradiso, the mortals passing by whispering him as "the man who had seen hell;" and the light within the room shone on the olives and grapes, the cut glass and silver claret-jugs, the crimson Monte-pulciano and the white Hermitage, on the table, as he told me the story of the head in crayons.

"Two years ago I went into the south of France. I was Chargé d'Affaires at —— then, you remember, and the climate had told upon me. I was not over well, and somebody recommended me the waters of Eaux Bonnes. The waters I put little faith in, but in the air of the Pyrenees, in the change from diplomacy to a life *en rase campagne*, I put much, and I went to Eaux Bonnes accordingly, for July and August, with a vow to forswear any society I might find at the baths—I had had only too much of society as it was—and to spend my days in the mountains with my sketching-block and my gun. But I did not like Eaux Bonnes; it was intensely warm. There were several people who knew me really; no end of others who got hold of my name, and wanted me to join their riding parties, and balls, and pic-nics. That was not what *I* wanted, so I left the place and went to

Luz, hoping to find solitude there. That valley of Luz—you know it?—is it not as lovely as any artist's dream of Arcadia, in the evening, when the sunset light has passed off the meadows and corn-lands of the lower valley, and just lingers golden and rosy on the crests of the mountains, while the glow-worms are coming out among the grasses, and the lights are being lit in the little homesteads nestling among their orchards one above another on the hill-sides, and its hundred streams are rushing down the mountains and under the trees, foaming, and tumbling, and rejoicing on their way! When I have had my fill of ambition and of pleasure, I shall go and live at Luz, I think.

"*When!* Well! you are quite right to repeat it ironically; that time will never come, I dare say, and why should it? I am not the stuff to cogitate away my years in country solitudes. If prizes are worth winning, they are worth working for till one's death; a man should never give up the field while he has life left in him. Well! I went to Luz, and spent a pleasant week or so there, knocking over a few chamois or izards, or sketching on the sides of the Pic du Midi, or Tourmalet, but chiefly lying about under the great beech-trees in the shade, listening to the tinkle of the sheep-bells, like an idle fellow, as I meant to be for the time I had allotted myself. One day——"

He stopped and blew some whiffs from his Manilla into the air. He seemed to linger over the prelude to his story, and shrink from going on with the story itself, I thought; and he smothered a sigh as he raised himself.

"How warm the night is; we shall have a tempest. Reach me that wine, there's a good fellow. No, not the Amontillado, the Château Margaux, please; one can't drink hot dry wines such a night as this. But to satisfy your curiosity about this crayon study.—One day I thought I would go to Gavarnie. I had heard a good deal, of course, about the great marble wall, and the mighty waterfalls, the rocks of Marboré, and the Brêche de Roland, but, as it chanced, I had never been up to the Cercle, nor, indeed, in that part of the Midi at all, so I went. The gods favoured me, I remember: there were no mists, the sun was brilliant, and the great amphitheatre was for once unobscured; the white marble flashing brown and purple, rose and golden, in the light; the cascades tumbling and leaping down into the gigantic basin; the vast plains of snow glittering in the sunshine; the twin rocks standing in the clear air, straight and fluted as any two Corinthian columns hewn and chiselled by man. Good Heaven! before a scene like Gavarnie, what true artist must not fling away his colours and his brushes in despair and disgust with his own puerility and impotence? What can be transferred to canvas of such a scene as that? What does the best beauty of Claude, the grandest sublimity of Salvator, the greatest power of Poussin, look beside Nature when she reigns as she reigns at Gavarnie? I am an art worshipper, as you know: but there are times in my life, places on earth, that make me ready to renounce art for ever!

"The day was beautiful, and thinking I knew the country pretty well, I took no guides. I hate them when I can possibly dispense with them. But the mist soon swooped down over the Cercle, and I began to wish I had had one when I turned my horse's head back again. You know the route, of course? Through the Chaos—Heaven knows it is deserving of its name;—down the break-neck little bridle-path, along the Gave, and over the Scia bridge to St. Sauveur. You know it? Then you know that it is much easier to break your neck down it than to find your way by it, though by some hazard I did not break my neck, nor the animal's knees either, but managed to get over the bridge without falling into the torrent, and to pick my way safely down into more level ground; once there, I thought I should easily enough find my way to St. Sauveur, but I was mistaken: the mists had spread over the valley, a heavy storm had come up, and somehow or other I lost the way, and could not tell where I was, whether St. Sauveur was to the left or the right, behind me or in front of me. The horse, a miserable little Pyrennean beast, was too frightened by the lightning to take the matter into his hands as he had done on the road through the Chaos, and I saw nothing for it but to surrender and come to grief in any way the elements best pleased; swearing at myself for not having stayed at the inn at Gavarnie or Gedre; wishing myself at the vilest mountain auberge that ever sheltered men and mules pêle-mêle; and calling myself hard names for not having listened to my landlady's dissuasions of that morning as I left her door, from my project of going to Gavarnie without a guide, which seemed to her the acme of all she had ever known or heard of English strangers' fooleries. The storm only increased, the great black rocks echoing the roll of the thunder, and the Gave lashing itself into fury in its narrow bed; happily I was on decently level ground, and the horse being, I suppose, tolerably used to storms like it, I pushed him on at last, by dint of blows and conjurations combined, to where, in the flashes of the lightning, I saw what looked to me like the outline of a homestead: it stood in a cleft between two shelving sides of rock, and a narrow bridle-path led up to it, through high yews and a tangled wilderness of rhododendrons, boxwood, and birch—one of those green slopes, so common in the Pyrenees, that look in full sunlight doubly bright and Arcadian-like, from the contrast of the dark, bare, perpendicular rocks that shut them in. I could see but little of its beauty then in the fog that shrouded both it and me, but I saw the shape and semblance of a house, and urging the horse up the ascent, thundered on its gate-panels with my whip-handle till the rocks round echoed.

"There was no answer, and I knocked a little louder, if possible, than before. I was wet to the skin with that wretched storm, and swore not mildly at the inhospitable roof that would not admit me under it. I knocked again, inclined to pick up a bit of granite and beat the panel in; and at last a face—an old woman's weather-beaten face, but with black Southern eyes that had lost little of their fire with age—looked through a grating at me and asked me what I wanted.

"'I want shelter if you can give it me,' I answered her. 'I have lost my way coming from Gavarnie, and am drenched through. I will pay you liberally if you will give me an asylum till the weather clears.'

"Her eyes blazed like coals through the little grille.

"'M'sieu, we take no money here—have you mistaken it for an inn? Come in if you want shelter, in Heaven's name! The Holy Virgin forbid we should refuse refuge to any!'

"And she crossed herself and uttered some conjurations to Mary to protect them from all wolves in sheep's clothing, and guard their dwelling from all harm, by which I suppose she thought I spoke fairly and looked harmless, but might possibly be a thief or an assassin, or both in one. She unlocked the gate, and calling to a boy to take my horse into a shed, admitted me under a covered passage-way into the house, which looked like part, and a very ruined part, too, of what had probably been, in the times of Henri Quatre and his grandfather, a feudal château fenced by natural ramparts from the rocks that surrounded it, shutting in the green slope on which it stood, with only one egress, the path through which I had ascended, into the level plain below. She marshalled me through this covered way into an interior passage, dark and vaulted, cheerless enough, and opened a low oak door, ushering me into a chamber, bare, gloomy, yet with something of lost grandeur and past state lingering about its great hearth, its massive walls, its stained windows, and its ragged tapestry hangings. The woman went up to one of the windows and spoke with a gentleness to which I should have never thought her voice could have been attuned with its harsh patois.

"'Mon enfant, v'là un m'sieu étranger qui vient chercher un abri pour un petit peu. Veux-tu lui parler?'

"The young girl she spoke to turned, rose, and, coming forward, bade me welcome with the grace, simplicity, and the naïve freedom from embarrassment of a child, looking up in my face with her soft clear eyes. She was like——No matter! you have seen that crayon-head, it is but a bad portrayal of a face whose expression Raphael and Sassoferrato themselves would have failed to render in its earnest, innocent, elevated regard. She was very young—

> Standing with reluctant feet
> Where the brook and river meet—
> Womanhood and childhood fleet.

Good Heavens, I am quoting poetry! what will you think of me, to have gone back to the Wertherian and Tennysonian days so far as to repeat a triplet of Longfellow's? No man quotes *those* poets after his salad days, except in a moment of weakness. Caramba! why *has* one any weaknesses at all? we ought not to have any; we live in an atmosphere that would kill them all if they were not as obstinate and indestructible as all other weeds whose seeds will linger and peer up and spoil the ground, let one root them out ever so! I owed you an apology for that lapse into Longfellow, and I have made it. Am I to go on with this story?"

He laughed as he spoke, and his laugh was by no means heartfelt. I told him to go on, and he lighted another Manilla and obeyed me, while the Arno murmured on its way, and the dusky, sultry clouds brooded nearer the earth, and the lights were lit in the distant windows of the palace of the Marchese Acqua d'Oro, that fairest of Florentines, who rouges so indiscriminately and flirts her fan so inimitably, to one of whose balls we were going that night.

He settled himself back in his chair, with his face darkened again by the shadow cast on it from the pillar of the balcony; and took his cigar out of his mouth.

"She looked incongruous in that bare and gloomy room, out of place with it, and out of keeping with the old woman—a French peasant woman, weather-beaten and bronzed, such as you see any day by the score riding to market or sitting knitting at their cottage doors. It was impossible that the girl could be either daughter or grand-daughter, or any relation at all to her. In that room she looked more as one of these myrtles might do, set down in the stifling gloomy horrors of a London street than anything else, save that in certain traces about the chamber, as I told you, there were relics of a faded grandeur which harmonised better with her. I can see her now, as she stood there with a strange foreign grace, an indescribable patrician delicacy mingled with extreme youthfulness and naïveté, like an old picture in costume, like one of Raphael's child-angels in face—poor little Florelle!

"'You would stay till the storm is over, monsieur? you are welcome to shelter if you will,' she said, coming forward to me timidly yet frankly. 'Cazot tells me you are a stranger, and our mountain storms are dangerous if you have no guide.'

"I did not know who Cazot was, but I presumed her to be the old woman, who seemed to be portress, mistress, domestic, cameriste, and all else in her single person, but I thanked her for her permitted shelter, and accepted her invitation to remain till the weather had cleared, as you can imagine. When you have lost your way any asylum is grateful, however desolate and tumble-down. They made me welcome, she and the old peasant woman, with that simple, unstrained, and unostentatious hospitality which is, after all, the true essence of good breeding, and of which your parvenu knows nothing, when he keeps you waiting, and shows you that you are come at an inapropos moment, in his fussy fear lest everything should not be *comme il faut* to do due credit to *him*. Old Cazot set before me some simple refreshment, a *grillade de châtaignes*, some maize and milk, and a dish of trout just caught in the Gave below, while I looked at my châtelaine, marvelling how that young delicate creature could come to be shut up with an old peasant on a remote hill-side. I did my best to draw her out and learn her history; she was shy at first of a complete stranger, as was but natural, but I spoke of Gavarnie, of the beauty of the Pyrenees, or Tourmalet, and the Lac Bleu, and, warming with enthusiasm for her birthplace, the girl forgot that I was a foreign tourist, unknown to her, and indebted to her for an hour's shelter, and before my impromptu supper was over I had drawn from her, by a few questions which she was too much of a child and had too little to conceal not to answer with a child's ingenuousness, the whole of her short history, and the explanation of her anomalous position. Her name was Florelle de l'Heris, a name once powerful enough among the nobles of the Midi, and the old woman, Madame Cazot, was her father's foster-sister. Of her family, beggared in common with the best aristocracy of France, none were now left; they had dwindled and fallen away, till of the once great house of L'Heris this child remained alone its representative: her mother had died in her infancy, and her father, either too idle or too brokenhearted to care to retrieve his fortunes, lived the life of a hermit among these ruins where I now found his daughter, educating her himself till his death, which occurred when she was only twelve years old, leaving her to poverty and obscurity, and such protection and companionship as her old nurse Cazot could afford her. Such was the story Florelle de l'Heris told me as I sat there that evening waiting till the clouds should clear and the mists roll off enough to let me go to St. Sauveur—a story told simply and pathetically, and which Cazot, sitting knitting in a corner, added to by a hundred gesticulations, expletives, appeals to the Virgin, and prolix addenda, glad, I dare say, of any new confidant, and disposed to regard me with gratitude for my sincere praises of her fried trout. It was a story which seemed to me to suit the delicate beauty of the flower I had found in the wilderness, and read more like a chapter of some versified novelette, like 'Lucille,' than a *bona fide* page out of the book of one's actual life, especially in a life like mine, of essentially material pleasures and emphatically substantial and palpable ambitions. But there *are* odd stories in real life!—strange pathetic ones, too

—stranger, often, than those that found the plot and underplot of a novel or the basis of a poem; but when such men as I come across them they startle us, they look bizarre and unlike all the other leaves of the book that glitter with worldly aphorisms, philosophical maxims, and pungent egotisms, and we would fain cut them out; they have the ring of that Arcadia whose golden gates shut on us when we outgrew boyhood, and in which, *en revanche*, we have sworn ever since to disbelieve—keeping our word sometimes, perhaps to our own hindrance—Heaven knows!

"I stayed as long as I could that evening, till the weather had cleared up so long, and the sun was shining again so indisputably, that I had no longer any excuse to linger in the dark tapestried room, with the chesnuts sputtering among the wood-ashes, and Madame Cazot's needles clicking one continual refrain, and the soft gazelle eyes of my young châtelaine glancing from my sketches to me with that mixture of shyness and fearlessness, innocence and candour, which gave so great a charm to her manner. She was a new study to me, both for my palette and my mind—a pretty fresh toy to amuse me while I should stay in the Midi. I was not going to leave without making sure of a permission to return. I wanted to have that face among my pastels, and when I had thanked her for her shelter and her welcome, I told her my name, and asked her leave to come again where I had been so kindly received.

"'Come again, monsieur? Certainly, if you care to come. But you will find it a long way from Luz, I fear,' she said, naïvely, looking up at me with her large clear fawn-like eyes—eyes so cloudless and untroubled *then*—as she let me take her hand, and bade me adieu et bonsoir.

"I reassured her on that score, you can fancy, and left her standing in the deep embrasured window, a great stag-hound at her feet, and the setting sun, all the brighter for its past eclipse, bathing her in light. I can always see her in memory as I saw her then, poor child!—— Faugh! How hot the night is! Can't we get more air anyhow?

"'If you come again up here, m'sieu, you will be the first visitor the Nid de l'Aigle has seen for four years,' said old Cazot, as she showed me out through the dusky vaulted passage. She was a cheerful, garrulous old woman, strong in her devotion to the De l'Heris of the bygone past; stronger even yet in her love for their single orphan representative of the beggared present. 'Visitors! Is it likely we should have any, m'sieu? Those that would suit me would be bad company for Ma'amselle Florelle, and those that should seek her never do. I recollect the time, m'sieu, when the highest in all the departments were glad to come to the bidding of a De l'Heris; but generations have gone since then, and lands and gold gone too, and, if you cannot feast them, what care people for you? That is true in the Pyrenees, m'sieu, as well as in the rest of the world. I have not lived eighty years without finding out that. If my child yonder were the heiress of the De l'Heris, there would be plenty to court and seek her; but she lives in these poor broken-down ruins with me, an old peasant woman, to care for her as best I can, and not a soul takes heed of her save the holy women at the convent, where, maybe, she will seek refuge at last!'

"She let me out at the gate where I had thundered for admittance two hours before, and, giving her my thanks for her hospitality—money she would not take—I wished her good day, and rode down the bridle-path to

St. Sauveur, and onwards to Luz, thinking at intervals of that fair young life that had but just sprung up, and was already destined to wither away its bloom in a convent. Any destiny would be better to proffer to her than that. She interested me already by her childlike loveliness and her strange solitude of position, and I thought she would while away some of the long summer hours during my stay in the Midi when I was tired of chamois and palette, and my lazy dolce under the beech-wood shades. At any rate, she was newer and more charming than the belles of Eaux Bonnes.

"The next morning I remembered her permission and my promise, and I rode out through the town again, up the mountain-road, to the Nid de l'Aigle; glad of anything that gave me an amusement and a pursuit. I never wholly appreciate the far niente, I think; perhaps I have lived too entirely in the world—and a world ultra-cold and courtly, too—to retain much patience for the meditative life, the life of trees and woods, sermons in stones, and monologues in mountains. I am a restless, ambitious man; I must have a *pursuit*, be it of a great aim or a small, or I grow weary, and my time hangs heavily on hand. Already having found Florelle de l'Heris among these hills reconciled me more to my *pro tempo* banishment from society, excitement, and pleasure, and I thanked my good fortune for having lighted upon her. She was very lovely, and I always care more for the physical than the intellectual charms of any woman. I do not share some men's visionary requirements on their mental score; I ask but material beauty, and am content with it.

"I rode up to the Nid de l'Aigle: by a clearer light it stood on a spot of great picturesqueness, and before the fury of the revolutionary peasantry had destroyed what was the then habitable and stately château, must have been a place of considerable extent and beauty, and in the feudal times, fenced in by the natural ramparts of its shelving rocks, no doubt all but impregnable. There were but a few ruins now that held together and had a roof over them—the part where Madame Cazot and the last of the De l'Heris lived; it was perfectly solitary; there was nothing to be heard round it but the foaming of the river, the music of the sheep-bells from the flocks that fed in the clefts and on the slopes of grass-land, and the shout of some shepherd-boy from the path below: but it was as beautiful a spot as any in the Pyrenees, with its overhanging beech-woods, its wilderness of wild flowers, its rocks covered with that soft grey moss whose tint defies one to repeat it in oil or water colours, and its larches and beeches drooping over into the waters of the Gave. In such a home, with no companions save her father, old Cazot, and her great stag-hound, and, occasionally, the quiet recluses of St. Marie Purificatrice, with everything to feed her native poetry and susceptibility, and nothing to teach her anything of the actual and ordinary world, it were inevitable that the character of Florelle should take its colouring from the scenes around her, and that she should grow up singularly childlike, imaginative, and innocent of all that in any other life she would unavoidably have known. Well educated she was, through her father and the nuns, but it was a semi-religious and peculiar education, of which the chief literature had been the legendary and sacred poetry of France and Spain, the chief amusement copying the illuminated missals lent her by the nuns, or joining in the choral services of the convent; an education that taught her nothing of the world from which she was shut out, and encouraged all that was self-devoted, visionary, and fervid in her nature, leaving her at seventeen as unconscious of evil as the youngest child. I despair of making you imagine what Florelle then was. Had I never met her, I should have believed in her as little as yourself, and would have discredited the existence of so poetic a creation out of the world of fiction; her ethereal delicacy, her sunny gaiety when anything amused her, her intense sensitiveness, pained in a moment by a harsh word, pleased as soon by a kind one, her innocence of all the blots and cruelties, artifices and evils, of that world beyond her Nid de l'Aigle, made a character strangely new to me, and strangely winning, but which, to you, I despair of portraying: I could not have *imagined* it. Had I never seen her, and had I met with it in the pages of a novel, I should have put it aside as a graceful but impossible conception of romance.

"I went up that day to the Nid de l'Aigle, and Florelle received me with pleasure; perhaps Madame Cazot had instilled into her some scepticism that 'a grand seigneur,' as the woman was pleased to term me, would trouble himself to ride up the mountains from Luz merely to repeat his thanks for an hour's shelter and a supper of roasted chesnuts. She was a simple-minded, goodhearted old woman, who had lived all her life among the rocks and rivers of the Hautes-Pyrénées, her longest excursion a market-day to Luz or Bagnères. She looked on her young mistress and charge as a child—in truth, Florelle was but little more—and thought my visit paid simply from gratitude and courtesy, never dreaming of attributing it to 'cette beauté héréditaire des L'Heris,' which she was proud of boasting was an inalienable heirloom to the family.

"I often repeated my visits; so often, that in a week or so the old ruined château grew a natural resort in the long summer days, and Florelle watched for my coming from the deep arched window where I had seen her first, or from under the boughs of the great copper-beech that grew before the gate, and looked for me as regularly as though I were to spend my lifetime in the valley of Luz. Poor child! I never told her my title, but I taught her to call me by my Christian name. It used to sound very pretty when she said it, with her long Southern pronunciation—prettier than it ever sounds now from the lips of Beatrice Acqua d'Oro yonder, in her softest moments, when she plays at sentiment. She had a great natural talent for art, hitherto uncultivated, of course, save by such instructions as one of the women at the convent, skilful in illuminating, had occasionally given her. I amused myself with teaching her to transfer to paper and canvas the scenery she loved so passionately. I spent many hours training this talent of hers, that was of very unusual calibre, and, with due culture, might have ranked her with Elisabetta Sirani or Rosa Bonheur. Sitting with her in the old room, or under the beech-trees, or by the side of the torrents that tore down the rocks into the Gave, it pleased me to draw out her unsullied thoughts, to spread her mind out before me like a book —a pure book enough, God knows, with not even a stain of the world upon it—to make her eyes glisten and glow and dilate, to fill them with tears or laughter at my will, to wake up her young life from its unconscious, untroubled, childish repose to a new happiness, a new pain, which she felt but could not translate, which dawned in her face for me, but never spoke in its true language to her, ignorant then of its very name—it amused me. Bah! our amusements are cruel sometimes, and costly too!

"It was at that time I took the head in pastels which you have seen, and she asked me, in innocent admiration of its loveliness, if she was *indeed* like that?—This night is awfully oppressive. Is that water in that caraffe? Is it iced? Push it to me. Thank you.

"I was always welcome at the Nid de l'Aigle. Old Cazot, with the instinct of servants who have lived with people of birth till they are as proud of their master's heraldry as though it were their own, discerned that I was of the same rank as her adored House of De l'Heris —if indeed she admitted any equal to them—and with all the cheery familiarity of a Frenchwoman treated me with punctilious deference, being as thoroughly imbued with respect and adoration for the aristocracy as any of those who died for the white lilies in the Place de la Révolution. And Florelle—Florelle watched for me, and counted her hours by those I spent with her. You are sure I had not read and played with women's hearts so long—women, too, with a thousand veils and evasions and artifices, of which she was in pure ignorance even of the existence—without having this heart, young, unworn, and unoccupied, under my power at once, plastic to mould as wax, ready to receive any impressions at my hands, and moulded easily to my will. Florelle had read no love-stories to help her to translate this new life to which I awoke her, or to put her on her guard against it. I went there often, every day at last, teaching my pupil the art which she was only too glad and too eager to learn, stirring her vivid imagination with descriptions of that brilliant outside world, of whose pleasures, gaieties, and pursuits she was as ignorant as any little gentian flower on the rocks; keeping her spell-bound with glimpses of its life, which looked to her like fairy-land, bizarre bal masqué though it be to us; and pleasing myself with awakening new thoughts, new impressions, new emotions, which swept over her tell-tale face like the lights and shades over meadow-land as the sun fades on and off it. She was a new study, a new amusement to me, after the women of our world, and I beguiled my time with her, not thoughtlessly, as I might have done, not too hastily, as I *should* have done ten years before, but pleased with my new amusement, and more charmed with Florelle than I at first knew, though I confess I soon wished to make her love me, and soon tried my best to make her do so—an easy task when one has had some practice in the rose-hued atmosphere of the boudoir, among the most difficile and the most brilliant coquettes of Europe! Florelle, with a nature singularly loving, and a mind singularly imaginative, with no rival for me even in her fancy, soon lavished on me all the love of which her impassioned and poetic character was capable. She did not know it, but I did. She loved me, poor child!—love more pure, unselfish, and fond than I ever won before, than I shall ever win again.

"Basta! why need you have lighted on that crayon-head, and make me rake up this story? I loathe looking at the past. What good ever comes of it? A wise man lives only in his present. 'La vita è appunto una memoria, una speranza, un punto,' writes the fool of a poet, as though the bygone memories and the unrealised hopes were worth a straw! It is that very present 'instant' that he despises which is available, and, in which, when we are in our senses, we absorb ourselves, knowing that that alone will yield a fruit worth having. What are the fruits of the others? only Dead Sea apples that crumble into ash.

"I knew that Florelle loved me; that I, and I alone, filled both her imagination and her heart. I would not precipitately startle her into any avowal of it. I liked to see it dawn in her face and gleam in her eyes, guilelessly and unconsciously. It was a new pleasure to me, a new charm in that book of Woman of which I had thought I knew every phase, and had exhausted every reading. I taught Florelle to love me, but I would not give her a name to my teaching till she found it herself. I returned it? Oh yes, I loved her, selfishly, as most people, men or women, do love, let them say what they will; *very* selfishly, perhaps—a love that was beneath her —a love for which, had she seen into my heart, she might have disdained, and hated me, if her soft nature could have been moved to so fierce a thing as hate—a love that sought its own gratification, and thought nothing of her welfare—a love *not* worthy of her, as I sometimes felt then, as I believe now.

"I had been about six weeks in the Pyrenees since the day I lost myself en route from Gavarnie; most of the days I had spent three or four hours, often more, at the Nid de l'Aigle, giving my painting lessons to Florelle, or being guided by her among the beech-wooded and mountain passes near her home. The dreariest fens and flats might have gathered interest from such a guide, and the glorious beauties of the Midi, well suited to her, gained additional poetry from her impassioned love for them, and her fond knowledge of all their legends, superstitions, histories, and associated memories, gathered from the oral lore of the peasantry, the cradle songs of Madame Cazot, and the stories of the old chronicles of the South. Heavens! what a wealth of imagination, talent, genius, lay in her if *I* had not destroyed it!

"At length the time drew near when my so-called sojourn at the Baths must end. One day Florelle and I were out sketching, as usual; she sat under one of the great beeches, within a few feet of one of the cascades that fell into the Gave du Pau, and I lay on the grass by her, looking into those clear gazelle eyes that met mine so brightly and trustfully, watching the progress of her brush, and throwing twigs and stones into the spray of the torrent. I can remember the place as though it were yesterday, the splash of the foam over the rocks, the tinkle of the sheep-bells from the hills, the scent of the wild flowers growing round, the glowing golden light that spread over the woodlands, touching even the distant crest of Mont Aigu and the Pic du Midi. Strange how some scenes will stamp themselves on the camera of the brain never to be effaced, let one try all that one may.

"There, that morning, I for the first time since we had met, spoke of leaving Luz, and of going back to that life which I had so often amused her by describing. Happy in her present, ignorant of how soon the scenes so familiar and dear to her would tire and pall on me, and infinitely too much of a child to have looked beyond, or speculated upon anything which I had not spoken of to her, it had not presented itself to her that this sort of life could not go on for ever; that even she would not reconcile me long to the banishment from my own world, and that in the nature of things we must either become more to each other than we were now, or part as strangers, whom chance had thrown together for a little time. She loved me, but, as I say, so innocently and uncalculatingly, that she never knew it till I spoke of leaving her; then she grew very pale, her eyes filled with tears, and shunned mine for the first time, and, as an anatomist watches the quiver of pain in his victim, so I watched the suffering of mine. It was her first taste of the bitterness of life, and while I inflicted the pain I smiled at it, pleased in my egotism to see the power I had over her. It was cruel, I grant it, but in confessing it I only confess to what nine out of ten men have felt, though they conceal or deny it.

"'You will miss me, Florelle?' I asked her. She looked at me reproachfully, wistfully, piteously, the sort of look I have seen in the eyes of a dying deer; too bewildered by this sudden mention of my departure to answer in words. No answer was needed with eyes so eloquent as hers, but I repeated it again. I knew I gave pain, but I knew, too, I should soon console her. Her lips quivered, and the tears gathered in her eyes; she had not known enough of sorrow to have learnt to dissemble it. I asked her if she loved me so much that she was unwilling to bid me farewell. For the first time her eyes sank beneath mine, and a hot painful colour flushed over her face. Poor child! if ever I have been loved by any woman, I was loved by her. Then I woke her heart from its innocent peaceful rest, with words that spoke a language utterly new to her. I sketched to her a life with me that made her cheeks glow, and her lips quiver, and her eyes grow dark. She was lovelier in those moments than any art could ever attempt to picture! She loved me, and I made her tell me so over and over again. She put her fate unhesitatingly into my hands, and rejoiced in the passion I vowed her, little understanding how selfishly I sought her, little thinking, in her ignorance of the evil of the world, that while she rejoiced in the fondness I lavished on her, and worshipped me as though I were some superior unerring god-like being, she was to me only a new toy, only a pursuit of the hour, a plaything, too, of which I foresaw I should tire! Isn't it Benjamin Constant who says, 'Malheureux l'homme qui, dans le commencement d'un amour, prévoit avec une précision cruelle l'heure où il en sera lassé'?

"As it happened, I had made that morning an appointment in Luz with some men I knew, who happened to be passing through it, and had stopped there that day to go up the Pic du Midi the next, so that I could spend only an hour or two with Florelle. I took her to her home, parted with her for a few hours, and went down the path. I remember how she stood looking after me under the heavy grey stone-work of the gateway, the tendrils of the ivy hanging down and touching her hair that glistened in the sunshine as she smiled me her adieux. My words had translated, for the first time, all the newly-dawned emotions that had lately stirred in her heart, while she knew not their name.

"I soon lost sight of her through a sharp turn of the bridle-path round the rocks, and went on my way thinking of my new love, of how completely I held the threads of her fate in my hands, and how entirely it lay in my power to touch the chords of her young heart into acute pain or into as acute pleasure with one word of mine—of how utterly I could mould her character, her life, her fate, whether for happiness or misery, at my will. I loved her well enough, if only for her unusual beauty, to feel triumph at my entire power, and to feel a tinge of her own poetry and tenderness of feeling stirring in me as I went on under the green, drooping, fanlight boughs of the pines, thinking of Florelle de l'Heris.

"'M'sieu! permettez-moi vous parle un p'tit mot?'

"Madame Cazot's patois made me look up, almost startled for the moment, though there was nothing astonishing in her appearance there, in her accustomed spot under the shade of a mountain-ash and a great boulder of rock, occupied at her usual task, washing linen in the Gave, as it foamed and rushed over its stones. She raised herself from her work and looked up at me, shading her eyes from the light—a sunburnt, wrinkled, hardy old woman, with her scarlet capulet, her blue cloth jacket, and her brown woollen petticoat, so strange a contrast to the figure I had lately left under the gateway of the Nid de l'Aigle, that it was difficult to believe them even of the same sex or country.

"She spoke with extreme deference, as she always did, but so earnestly, that I looked at her in surprise, and stopped to hear what it might be she had to say. She was but a peasant woman, but she had a certain dignity of manner for all that, caught, no doubt, from her long service with, and her pride in, the De l'Heris.

"'M'sieu, I have no right, perhaps, to address you; you are a grand seigneur, and I but a poor peasant woman. Nevertheless, I must speak. I have a charge to which I shall have to answer in the other world to God and to my master. M'sieu, pardon me what I say, but you love Ma'amselle Florelle?'

"I stared at the woman, astonished at her interference and annoyed at her presumption, and motioned her aside with my stick. But she placed herself in the path—a narrow path—on which two people could not have stood without one or other going into the Gave, and stopped me resolutely and respectfully, shading her eyes from the sun, and looking steadily at my face.

"'M'sieu, a little while ago, in the gateway yonder, when you parted with Ma'amselle Florelle, I was coming out behind you to bring my linen to the river, and I saw you take her in your arms and kiss her many times, and whisper to her that you would come again "ce soir!" Then, m'sieu, I knew that you must love my little lady, or, at least, must have made her love you. I have thought her—living always with her—but a beautiful child still; but you have found her a beautiful woman, and loved her, or taught her love, m'sieu. Pardon me if I wrong your honour, but my master left her in my charge, and I am an ignorant old peasant, ill-fitted for such a trust; but is this love of yours such as the Sieur de l'Heris, were he now on earth, would put his hand in your own and thank you for, or is it such that he would wash out its insult in your blood or his?'

"Her words amazed me for a moment, first at the presumption of an interference of which I had never dreamt, next at the iron firmness with which this old woman, nothing daunted, spoke, as though the blood of a race of kings ran in her veins. I laughed a little at the absurdity of this cross-questioning from her to me, and not choosing to bandy words with her, bade her move aside; but her eyes blazed like fire; she stood firm as the earth itself.

"'M'sieu, answer me! You love Ma'amselle Florelle —you have asked her in marriage?'

"I smiled involuntarily:

"'My good woman, men of my class don't marry every pretty face they meet; we are not so fond of the institution. You mean well, I know; at the same time, you are deucedly impertinent, and I am not accustomed to interference. Have the goodness to let me pass, if you please.'

"But she would not move. She folded her arms across her chest, quivering from head to foot with passion, her deep-set eyes flashed like coals under her bushy eyebrows.

"'M'sieu, I understand you well enough. The house of the L'Heris is fallen, ruined, and beggared, and you deem dishonour may approach it unrebuked and unrevenged. Listen to me, m'sieu; I am but a woman, it is true, and old, but I swore by Heaven and Our Lady to the Sieur de l'Heris, when he lay dying yonder, years ago, that I would serve the child he left, as my forefathers had served his in peace and war for centuries, and keep and guard her as best I might dearer than my own heart's blood. Listen to me. Before this love of yours shall breathe another word into her ear to scorch and sully it; before your lips shall ever meet hers again; before you say again to a De l'Heris poor and powerless, what you would never have dared to say to a De l'Heris rich and powerful, I will defend her as the eagles by the Nid de l'Aigle defend their young. You shall only reach her across my dead body!'

"She spoke with the vehemence and passionate gesticulation of a Southern; in her patois, it is true, and with rude eloquence, but there was an odd *timbre* of pathos in her voice, harsh though it was, and a certain wild dignity about her through the very earnestness and passion that inspired her. I told her she was mad, and would have put her out of my path, but, planting herself before me, she laid hold of my arm so firmly that I could not have pushed forwards without violence, which I would not have used to a woman, and a woman, moreover, as old as she was.

"'Listen to one word more, m'sieu. I know not what title you may bear in your own country, but I saw a coronet upon your handkerchief the other day, and I can tell you are a grand seigneur—you have the air of it, the manner. M'sieu, you can have many women to love you; cannot you spare this one? you must have many pleasures, pursuits, enjoyments in your world, can you not leave me this single treasure? Think, m'sieu! If Ma'amselle Florelle loves you now, she will love you only the dearer as years go on; and *you*, you will tire of her, weary of her, want change, fresh beauty, new excitement

—you must know that you will, or why should you shrink from the bondage of marriage?—you will weary of her; you will neglect her first and desert her afterwards; what will be the child's life *then?* Think! You have done her cruel harm enough now with your wooing words, why will you do her more? What is your love beside hers? If you have heart or conscience you cannot dare to contrast them together; *she* would give up everything for you and *you* would give up nothing! M'sieu, Florelle is not like the women of your world; she is innocent of evil as the holy saints; those who meet her should guard her from the knowledge, and not lead her to it. Were the Sieur de l'Heris living now, were her House powerful as I have known them, would you have dared or dreamt of seeking her as you do now? M'sieu, he who wrongs trust, betrays hospitality, and takes advantage of that very purity, guilelessness, and want of due protection which should be the best and strongest appeal to every man of chivalry and honour— he, whoever he be, the De l'Heris would have held, as what he is, a coward! Will you not now have pity upon the child, and let her go?'

"I have seldom been moved in, never been swayed from, any pursuit or any purpose, whether of love, or pleasure, or ambition; but something in old Cazot's words stirred me strangely, more strangely still from the daring and singularity of the speaker. Her intense love for her young charge gave her pathos, eloquence, and even a certain rude majesty, as she spoke; her bronzed wrinkled features worked with emotions she could not repress, and hot tears fell over her hard cheeks. I felt that what she said was true; that as surely as the night follows the day would weariness of it succeed to my love for Florelle, that to the hospitality I had so readily received I had, in truth, given but an ill return, and that I had deliberately taken advantage of the very ignorance of the world and faith in me which should have most appealed to my honour. I knew what she said was true, and this epithet of 'coward' hit me harder from the lips of a woman, on whom her sex would not let me avenge it, with whom my conscience would not let me dispute it, than it would have done from any man. *I* called a coward by an old peasant woman! absurd idea enough, wasn't it? It is a more absurd one still that I could not listen to her unmoved, that her words touched me—how or why I could not have told—stirred up in me something of weakness, unselfishness, or chivalrousness—I know not what exactly —that prompted me for once to give up my own egotistical evanescent passions and act to Florelle as though all the males of her house were on earth to make me render account of my acts. At old Cazot's words I shrank for once from my own motives and my own desires, shrank from classing Florelle with the *cocottes* of my world, from bringing her down to their level and their life.

"'You will have pity on her, m'sieu, and go?' asked old Cazot, more softly, as she looked in my face.

"I did not answer her, but put her aside out of my way, went down the mountain-path to where my horse was left cropping the grass on the level ground beneath a plane-tree, and rode at a gallop into Luz without looking back at the grey-turreted ruins of the Nid de l'Aigle.

"And I left Luz that night without seeing Florelle de l'Heris again—a tardy kindness—one, perhaps, as cruel as the cruelty from which old Cazot had protected her. Don't you think I was a fool, indeed, for once in my life, to listen to an old woman's prating! Call me so if you like, I shall not dispute it; we hardly know when we are fools, and when wise men! Well! I have not been much given to such weaknesses.

"I left Luz, sending a letter to Florelle, in which I bade her farewell, and entreated her to forget me—an entreaty which, while I made it, I felt would not be obeyed—one which, in the selfishness of my heart, I dare say, I hoped might not be. I went back to my old diplomatic and social life, to my customary pursuits, amusements, and ambitions, turning over the leaf of my life that contained my sojourn in the Pyrenees, as you turn over the page of a romance to which you will never recur. I led the same life, occupied myself with my old ambitions, and enjoyed my old pleasures; but I could not forget Florelle as wholly as I wished and tried to do. I had not usually been troubled with such memories; if unwelcome, I could generally thrust them aside; but Florelle I did not forget; the more I saw of other women the sweeter and brighter seemed by contrast her sensitive, delicate nature, unsullied by the world, and unstained by artifice and falsehood. The longer time went on, the more I regretted having given her up—perhaps on no better principle than that on which a child cares most for the toy he cannot have; perhaps because, away from her, I realised that I had lost the purest and the strongest love I had ever won. In the whirl of my customary life I sometimes wondered how she had received my letter, and how far the iron had burnt into her young heart—wondered if she had joined the Sisters of Sainte Marie Purificatrice, or still led her solitary life among the rocks and beech-woods of Nid de l'Aigle. I often thought of her, little as the life I led was conducive to regretful or romantic thoughts. At length, my desire to see her again grew ungovernable. I had never been in the habit of refusing myself what I wished; a man is a fool who does, if his wishes are in any degree attainable. And at the end of the season I went over to Paris, and down again once more into the Midi. I reached Luz, lying in the warm golden Pyrennean light as I had left it, and took once more the old familiar road up the hills to the Nid de l'Aigle. There had been no outward change from the year that had flown by; there drooped the fanlike branches of the pines; there rushed the Gave over its rocky bed; there came the silvery sheep-bell chimes down the mountain-sides; there, over hill and wood, streamed the mellow glories of the Southern sunlight. There is something unutterably painful in the sight of any place after one's lengthened absence, wearing the same smile, lying in the same sunlight. I rode on, picturing the flush of gladness that would dawn in Florelle's face at the sight of me, thinking that Mme. Cazot should not part me from her again, even, I thought, as I saw the old grey turrets above the beech-woods, if I paid old Cazot's exacted penalty of marriage! I loved Florelle more deeply than I had done twelve months before. 'L'absence allument les grandes passions et éteignent les petites,' they say. It had been the reverse with me.

"I rode up the bridle-path and passed through the old gateway. There was an unusual stillness about the place; nothing but the roar of the torrent near, and the songs of the birds in the branches speaking in the summer air. My impatience to see Florelle, or to hear her, grew ungovernable. The door stood open. I groped my way through the passage and pushed open the door of the old room. Under the oriel window, where I had seen her first, she lay on a little couch. I saw her again—but *how!* My God! to the day of my death I shall never

THE STORY OF A CRAYON-HEAD.

forget her face as I saw it then; it was turned from me, and her hair streamed over her pillows, but as the sunlight fell upon it, I knew well enough what was written there. Old Cazot, sitting by the bed with her head on her arms, looked up, and came towards me, forcing me back.

"'You are come at last to see her die. Look on your work—look well at it—and then go; with my curse upon you!'

"I shook off her grasp, and forcing my way towards the window, threw myself down by Florelle's bed; till then I never knew how well I loved her. My voice awoke her from her sleep, and, with a wild cry of joy, she started up, weak as she was, and threw her arms round my neck, clinging to me with her little hands, and crying to me deliriously not to leave her while she lived—to stay with her till death should take her; where had I been so long? why had I come so late? *So late!*—those piteous words! As I held her in my arms, unconscious from the shock, and saw the pitiless marks that disease, the most hopeless and the most cruel, had made on the face that I had left fair, bright, and full of life as any child's, I felt the full bitterness of that piteous reproach, 'Why had I come so late?'

"What need to tell you more. Florelle de l'Heris was dying, and I had killed her. The child that I had loved so selfishly had loved me with all the concentrated tenderness of her isolated and impassioned nature; the letter I wrote bidding her farewell had given her her death-blow. They told me that from the day she received that letter everything lost its interest for her. She would sit for hours looking down the road to Luz, as though watching wearily for one who never came, or kneeling before the pictures I had left as before some altar, praying to Heaven to take care of me, and bless me, and let her see me once again before she died. Consumption had killed her mother in her youth; during the chill winter at the Nid de l'Aigle the hereditary disease settled upon her. When I found her she was dying fast. All the medical aid, all the alleviations, luxuries, resources, that money could procure, to ward off the death I would have given twenty years of my life to avert, I lavished on her, but they were useless; for my consolation they told me that, used a few months earlier, they would have saved her! She lingered three weeks, fading away like a flower gathered before its fullest bloom. Each day was torture to me. I knew enough of the disease to know from the first there was no hope for her or me. Those long terrible night-hours, when she lay with her head upon my shoulder, and her little hot thin hands in mine, while I listened, uncertain whether every breath was not the last, or whether life was not already fled! By God! I cannot think of them!

"One of those long summer nights Florelle died: happy with me, loving and forgiving me to the last; speaking to the last of that reunion in which *she*, in her innocent faith, believed and hoped, according to the promise of her creed!—died with her hands clasped round my neck, and her eyes looking up to mine, till the last ray of light was quenched in them—died while the morning dawn rose in the east and cast a golden radiance on her face, the herald of a day to which she never woke!"

There was a dead silence between us; the Arno splashed against the wall below, murmuring its eternal song beneath its bridge, while the dark heavy clouds drifted over the sky with a sullen roll of thunder. He lay back in his chair, the deep shadow from the balcony pillar hiding his face from me, and his voice quivered painfully as he spoke the last words of his story. He was silent for many minutes, and so was I, regretting that my careless question had unfolded a page out of his life's history written in characters so painful to him. Such skeletons dwell in the hearts of most; hands need be tender that disentomb them and drag out to daylight ashes so mournful and so grievous, guarded so tenaciously, hidden so jealously. Each of us is tender over his own, but who does not think his brother's fit subject for jest, for gibe, for mocking dance of death?

He raised himself with a laugh, but his lips looked white as death as he drank down a draught of the Hermitage.

"Welll what say you: is the maxim right, *y-a-i-il femmes et femmes?* Caramba! why need you have pitched upon that portfolio?—There are the lights in the Acqua d'Oro's palace; we must go, or we shall get into disgrace."

We went, and Beatrice Acqua d'Oro talked very ardent Italian to him, and the Comtesse Bois de Sandal remarked to me what a brilliant and successful man Lord —— was, but how unimpressionable!—as cold and as glittering as ice. Nothing had ever made him *feel*, she was quite certain, pretty complimentary nonsense though he often talked. What would the Marchesa and the Comtesse have said, I wonder, had I told them of that little grave under the Pyrennean beech-woods? So much does the world know of any of us! In the lives of all men are doubled-down pages written on in secret, folded out of sight, forgotten as they make other entries in the diary, never read by their fellows, only glanced at by themselves in some midnight hour of solitude.

Basta! they are painful reading, my friends. Don't

you find them so? Let us leave the skeletons in the closet, the pictures in the portfolio, the doubled-down pages in the locked diary, and go to Beatrice Acqua d'Oro's, where the lights are burning gaily. What is Madame Bois de Sandal, *née* Dashwood, singing in the music room?

> The tender grace of a day that is dead
> Will never come back to me!

That is the burden of many songs sung in this world, for some dead flowers strew most paths, and grass grows over myriad graves, and many leaves are folded down in many lives, I fear. And—retrospection is very idle, my good fellow, and regret is as bad as the tic, and flirting is deucedly pleasant; the white Hermitage we drank tonight is gone, we know, but are there no other bottles left of wine every whit as good? Shall we waste our time sighing after spilt lees? Surely not. And yet—ah me!—the dead fragrance of those vines that yielded us the golden nectar of our youth!"

THE BEAUTY OF VICQ D'AZYR;

OR,

"NOT AT ALL A PROPER PERSON."

———

BON AMI, do you consider the possession of sisters an agreeable addition to anybody's existence? *I* hold it very intensely the reverse. Who puts a man down so spitefully as his sisters? Who refuses so obstinately to see any good in the Nazarene they have known from their nurseries? Who snubs him so contumaciously, when he's a little chap in jackets and they young ladies already out? Who worries him so pertinaciously to marry their pet friend, "who has ten thousand a year, dear! Red hair? I'm sure she has not! It's the most lovely auburn! But you never see any beauty in *refined* women!" Who, if you incline towards a pretty little ineligible, rakes up so laboriously every scrap of gossip detrimental to her, and pours into your ear the delightful intelligence that she has been engaged to Powell of the Greys, is a shocking flirt, wears false teeth, is full five years older than she says she is, and has most objectionable connexions? Who, I should like to know, does any and all of these things, my good fellow, so amiably and unremittingly as your sisters? till—some day of grace, perhaps—you make a telling speech at St. Stephen's, and fling a second-hand aroma of distinction upon them; or marry a co-heiress and lady-in-her-own-right, and they *raffolent* of that charming creature, speculating on the desirability of being invited to your house when the men are down for September. Then, what a dear fellow you become! they always *were* so fond of you! a little wild! oh yes! but they are *so* glad you are changed, and think more seriously now! it was only from a *real* interest in your welfare that they used to grieve, &c. &c.

My sisters were my natural enemies, I remember, when I was in the daisy age and exposed to their thraldom; they were so blandly superior, so ineffably condescending, and wielded, with such smiling dexterity, that feminine power of torture known familiarly as "nagging!" Now, of course, they leave me in peace; but from my earliest to my emancipated years they were my natural enemies. I might occasionally excite the enmity, it is possible. I remember, when I was aged eight, covering Constance, a stately brunette, with a mortifying amount of confusion, by asking her, as she welcomed a visitor with effusion, why she said she was delighted to see her, when she had cried, "There's that odious woman again!" as we saw the carriage drive up. I have a criminal recollection of taking Gwendolina's fan, fresh from Howell and James's, and stripping it of its gold-powdered down before her face ere she could rush to its rescue, as an invaluable medium in the manufacture of May-flies. I also have a dim and guilty recollection of saying to the Hon. George Cursitt, standing then in the interesting position of my prospective brother-in-law, "Mr. Cursitt, Agnéta doesn't care one straw for you. I heard her saying so last night to Con; and that if you weren't so near the title, she would never have accepted you;" which revelation inopportunely brought that desirable alliance to an end, and Olympian thunders on my culprit's head.

I had my sins, doubtless, but they were more than

avenged on me; my sisters were my natural enemies, and I never knew of any man's who weren't so, more or less. Ah! my good sirs, those domesticities are all of them horrid bores, and how any man, happily and thrice blessedly free from them, can take the very worst of them voluntarily on his head by the Gate of Marriage (which differs thus remarkably from a certain Gate at Jerusalem, that at the one the camels kneel down to be lightened of all *their* burdens ere they can pass through it; at the other, the poor human animal kneels down to be loaded with all *his* ere he is permitted to enter), does pass my comprehension, I confess. I might amply avenge the injuries of my boyhood received from *mesdemoiselles mes sœurs*. Could I not tell Gwendolina of the pot of money dropped by her caro sposo over the Cesarewitch Stakes? Could I not intimate to Agneta where her Right Honourable lord and master spent the small hours last night, when popularly supposed to be nodding on the Treasury benches in the service of the state? Could I not rend the pride of Constance, by casually asking monsieur her husband, as I sip her coffee in her drawing-room this evening, who was that very pretty blonde with him at the Crystal Palace yesterday? the blonde being as well known about town as any other star of the demi-monde. Of course I could: but I am magnanimous; I can too thoroughly sympathise with those poor fellows. My vengeance would recoil on innocent heads, so I am magnanimous and silent.

My sisters have long ceased to be mesdemoiselles, they have become mesdames, in that transforming crucible of marriage in which, assuredly, all that glitters is not gold, but in which much is swamped, and crushed, and fused with uncongenial metal, and from which the elixir of happiness but rarely exhales, whatever feminine alchemists, who patronise the hymeneal furnace, may choose to assure us to the contrary. My sisters are indisputably very fine women, and develop in full bloom all those essential qualities which their moral and mental trainers sedulously instilled into them when they were limited to the schoolroom and thorough-bass, Garcia and an "expurgated" Shakspeare, the society of Mademoiselle Colletmonté and Fräulein von Engel, and the occasional refection of a mild, religious, respectably-twaddling fiction of the milk-and-water, pious-tendency, nursery-chronicling, and grammar-disregarding class, now-a-days indited for the mental improvement of a common-place generation in general, and growing young ladies in particular. My sisters are women of the world to perfection; indeed, for talent in refrigerating with a glance; in expressing disdain of a toilette or a ton by an upraised eyebrow; in assuming a various impenetrable plaît-il? expression at a moment's notice; in sweeping past intimate friends with a charming unconsciousness of their existence, when such unconsciousness is expedient or desirable; in reducing an unwished-for intruder into an instantaneous and agonising sense of his own de trop-ism and insignificance—in all such accomplishments and acquirements necessary to existence in all proper worlds, I think they may be matched with the best-bred lady to be found any day, from April to August, between Berkeley-square and Wilton-crescent. Constance, now Lady Maréchale, is of a saintly turn, and touched with fashionable fanaticism, pets evangelical bishops and ragged-school boys, drives to special services, and is called our noble and Christian patroness by physicians and hon. secs., holds doctrinal points and strong tracts, mixed together in equal proportion, an infallible chloride of lime for the disinfectance of our polluted globe, and appears to receive celestial telegrams of indisputable veracity and charming acrimony concerning the destiny of the vengeful contents of the Seven Vials. Agneta, now Mrs. Albany Protocol, is a Cabinet Ministress, and a second Duchesse de Longueville (in her own estimation at the least); "is strengthening her party" when she issues her dinner invitations, whispers awfully of a "crisis" when even penny-paper leaders can't get up a breeze, and spends her existence in "pushing" poor Protocol, who, thorough Englishman that he is, considers it a point of honour to stand still in all paths with praiseworthy Britannic obstinacy and opticism. Gwendolina, now Lady Frederic Farniente, is a butterfly of fashion, has delicate health, affects dilettanteism, is interested by nothing, has many other charming minauderies, and lives in an exclusive circle—so tremendously exclusive, indeed, that it is possible she may at last draw the *cordon sanitaire* so *very* tight, that she will be left alone with the pretty woman her mirrors reflect.

They have each of them attained to what the world calls a "good position"—an eminence the world dearly reveres; if you can climb to it, *do;* never mind what dirt may cling to your feet, or what you may chance to pull down in your ascent, no questions will be asked you at the top, when you wave your flag victoriously from a plateau at a good elevation. They haven't all their ambitions—who has? If a fresh Alexander conquered the world he would fret out his life for a standing-place to be able to try Archimedes' little experiment on his newly-won globe. Lady Maréchale dies for entrance to certain salons which are closed to her; she is but a Baronet's wife, and, though so heavenly-minded, has *some* weaknesses of earth. Mrs. Protocol grieves because she thinks a grateful country ought to wreathe her lord's brow with laurels—*Anglicè*, strawberry-leaves—and the country remains ungrateful, and the brows bare. Lady Frederic frets because her foe and rival, Lady Maria Fitz-Sachet, has footmen an inch taller than her own. They haven't all their ambitions satisfied. We are too occupied with kicking our dear friends and neighbours down off the rounds of the social ladder to advance ourselves always perhaps as entirely as we otherwise might do. But still they occupy "unexceptionable positions," and from those fortified and impregnable citadels are very severe upon those who are not, and very jealous of those who are, similarly favoured by fortune. When St. Peter lets ladies through the celestial portals, he'll never please them unless he locks out all their acquaintance, and indulges them with a gratifying peep at the rejected candidates.

The triad regard each other after the manner of ladies; that is to say, Lady Maréchale holds Mrs. Protocol and Lady Frederic "frivolous and worldly;" Lady Frederic gives them both one little supercilious expressive epithet, "*précieuses;*" Mrs. Protocol considers Lady Maréchale a "pharisee," and Lady Frederic a "butterfly;"—in a word, there is that charming family love to one another which ladies so delight to evince, that I suppose we must excuse them for it on the plea that

'Tis their nature to!

which Dr. Watts puts forward so amiably and grammatically in excuse for the bellicose propensities of the canine race, but which is never remembered by priest or layman in extenuation of the human.

They dislike one another—relatives always do—still, the three Arms will combine their Horse, Line, and Field Batteries in a common cause and against a common enemy; the Saint, the Politician, and the Butterfly have several rallying-points in common, and when it comes to the question of extinguishing an ineligible, of combining a sneer with a smile, of blending the unexceptionably-courteous with the indescribably-contemptuous, of calmly shutting their doors to those who won't aggrandise them, and blandly throwing them open to those who will, it would be an invidious task to give the golden apple, and decide which of the three ladies most distinguishes herself in such social prowess.

Need I say that I *don't* see very much of them?—severe strictures on society in general, with moral platitudes, over the luncheon wines at Lady Maréchale's; discourse redolent of blue-books, with vindictive hits at Protocol and myself for our disinclination to accept a "mission," and our levity of life and opinions at "a period so full of social revolutions and wide-spread agitation as the present," through the soup and fish at Agneta's; softly hissed acerbities and languidly yawned satires on the prettiest women of my acquaintance, over the coffee at Lady Frederic's; are none of them particularly inviting or alluring. And as they or similar conversational confections are invariably included in each of the three ladies' entertainments *en petite comité*, it isn't wonderful if I forswear their drawing-rooms. Chères dames, you complain, and your chosen defenders for you, that men don't affect your society now-a-days save and except when making love to you. It isn't *our* fault, indeed: you bore us, and —what can we do?—we shrink as naturally and pardonably from voluntary boredom as from any other voluntary suffering, and shirk an air redolent of ennui from the same principle as we do an air redolent of diphtheria. Self-preservation is a law of nature, and female society consists too exclusively of milk-and-water, dashed here and there with citric acid of malice, to be either a recherché or refreshing beverage to palates that have tasted warmer spices or more wholesome tonics.

So I don't see much of my triad of sisters unless accidentally, but last August I encountered them by chance at Vicq d'Azyr. Do you know Vicq d'Azyr? No? All right! when it is known universally it will be spoilt; it will soon be fashionable, dyspeptic, artificial, like the crowds that will flock to it; its warm, bubbling springs will be gathered into long upright glasses, and quaffed by yellow-visaged groups; brass bands will bray where now the thrushes, orioles, and nightingales have the woodlands to themselves; cavalcades of hired hacks will cut up its thyme-covered turf, and young ladies will sketch in tortured outline and miserable washes the glorious sweep of its mountains, the crimson tints of its forests, the rush of its tumbling torrents, the golden gleam of its southern sun. Vicq d'Azyr will be a Spa, and will be spoilt; dyspepsia and bronchia, vanities and flirtations, cares and conquests, physicians and intrigantes, real marchionesses puffing under asthma, fictitious marquises strewing chaff for pigeons, monde and demi-monde, grandes dames and dames d'industrie will float into it, a mighty army of butterflies with a locust power of destruction: Vicq d'Azyr will be no more, and in its stead we shall have—a Fashionable Bath. Vicq d'Azyr, however, is free *yet* from the hand of the spoiler, and is charming—its vine-clad hills stretching up in sunny slopes; its little homesteads nestling on the mountains' sides among the pines that load the air with their rich heavy perfume; its torrents foaming down the ravines, flinging their snowy spray far over the boughs of arbutus and mountain-ash that bend across the brinks of their rushing courses; its dark-eyed peasant girls that dance at sunset under the linden-trees like living incarnations of Florian's pastorals; its sultry brilliant summer nights, when all is still, when the birds are sleeping among the ilex-leaves, and the wind barely stirs the tangled boughs of the woodland; when night is down on the mountains, wrapping hill and valley, crag and forest in one soft purple mist, and the silence around is only broken by the mystic music of the rushing waters, the soft whir of the night-birds' wings, or the distant chime of a village clock faintly tolling through the air:——Caramba, messieurs! I beg your pardon! I don't know why I poetise on Vicq d'Azyr. *I* went there to slay, not to sketch, with a rifle, not with a stylus, to kill izzards and chamois, not to indite a poem à la mode, with double-barrelled adjectives, no metre, and a "purpose;" nor to add my quota to the luckless loaded walls of the Academy by a pre-Raphaelite landscape of arsenical green, with the effete trammels of perspective gallantly disregarded, and trees like Dr. Syntax's wife, "roundabout and rather squat," with just two-dozen-and-seven leaves apiece for liberal allowance. I went to Vicq d'Azyr, amongst other places, last August, for chamois-hunting with Dunbar, of the Queen's Bays, taking up our abode at the Toison d'Or, whither all artists, tourists, men who come for the sport, women who come for its scenery, or invalids who come for its waters (whose properties, *miserabile dictu!* are just being discovered as a panacea for every human ill—from a migraine to an "incurable pulmonary affliction"), seek accommodation if they can have it, since it is the only hotel in the place, though a very good one; is adorned with a balcony running round the house, twined and buried in honeysuckle and wild clematis, which enchants young ladies into instant promotion of it into their sketch-books; and gives you, what is of rather more importance, and what makes you ready to admire the clematis when, under gastronomic exasperation, you might swear at it as a harbour for tarantule—an omelette, I assure you, well-nigh as well cooked as you have it at Mivart's or Meurice's.

At the Toison d'Or we took up our abode, and at the Toison d'Or we encountered my two elder sisters, Constance and Agneta, travelling for once on the same road, as they had left Paris together, and were together going on to the fashionable capital of a fashionable little toy duchy on the other side of the Rhine, when they should have finished with the wilder beauties and more unknown charms of Vicq d'Azyr and its environs. Each lady had her little train of husband, courier, valet, lady's-maid, small dog, and giant jewel-box. I have put the list in the inverse ratio of their importance, I believe. Your husband *versus* your jewel-box? Of course, my dear madam; absurd! What's the value of a little simple gold ring against a dozen glittering circlets of diamonds, emeralds, rubies, and garnets?

Each lady was bent on recruiting herself at Vicq d'Azyr after the toils of the season, and of shining *après* with all the brilliance that a fair share of beauty, good positions, and money, fairly entitled them to expect, at the little Court of—we will call it, Lemongenseidlitz—dominated by its charming Duchess, Princess Hélène of Lemongenseidlitz-Phizzstrclitz, the loveliest and most volage of all minor royalties. Each lady was strongly opposed to whatever the other wished; each thought the weather "sultry" when the other thought it "chilly," and *vice versâ*. Each considered her own ailments "unheard-of suffering, dear! —I could never make any one feel!" &c. &c.—and assured you, with mild disdain, that the other's malady was "purely nervous, entirely exaggerated, but she *will* dwell on it so much, poor darling!" Each related to you how admirably they would have travelled if *her* counsel had been followed, and described how the other *would* take the direction of everything, *would* confuse poor Chanderlos, the courier, till he hardly knew where he was, and *would* take the night express out of pure unkindness, just because she knew how ill it always made her (the speaker) feel to be torn across any country the whole night at that dreadful pace; each was dissatisfied with everything, pleased with nothing, and bored, as became ladies of good degree; each found the sun too hot or the wind too cold, the mists too damp or the air too dry, and both combined their forces to worry their ladies'-maids, find fault with the viands, drive their lords to the registering of an oath never to travel with women again, welcome us benignly, since they thought we might amuse them, and smile their sunniest on Dunbar—he's heir-prospective to the Gwynne Marquisate, and Lady Marqueterie, the Saint, is not above keeping one eye open for worldly distinctions, while Mrs. Albany Protocol, though a Radical, is, like certain others of the ultra-Liberal party, not above a personal kow-towing before those "ridiculous and ought-to-be exploded conservative institutions"—Rank and Title.

At the Toison d'Or, I say, when, after knocking over izzards *ad libitum* in another part of the district, we descended one evening into the valley where Vicq d'Azyr lies nestled in the sunset light, with the pretty vendangeuses trooping down from the sloping vineyards, and the cattle winding homewards down the hill-side paths, and the vesper-bells softly chiming from the convent-tower rising yonder above its woods of linden and acacia—at the Toison d'Or, just alighting with the respective suites aforesaid, and all those portable embarrassments of books, tiger-skin rugs, flacons of bouquet, travelling-bags warranted to carry any and everything that the most fastidious can require en route from Piccadilly to Peru, with which ladies do love to encumber and embitter their own persons and their companions' lives, we met, as I have told you, mesdames mes sœurs.

"What! Dear me, how very singular! Never should have dreamt of meeting *you;* so much too quiet a place, I should have thought. No Kursaal *here?* Come for sport —oh! Take Spes, will you! Poor little dear, he's been barking the whole way because he couldn't see out of the window. Ah, Major Dunbar, charmed to see you! What an amusing rencontre, is it not?" and Lady Maréchale, slightly out of temper for so eminent a Christian at the commencement of her greeting, smoothed down her ruffled feathers and turned smilingly on Dunbar. I have said he will be one day Marquis of Gwynne.

"By George, old fellow! *you* in this out-of-the-way place! That's all right. Sport good, here? Glad to hear it. The deuce take me, if ever I am lured into travelling in a *partie carrée* again."

And Maréchale raised his eyebrows, and whispered confidentially to me stronger language than I may commit to print, though, considering his provocation, it was surely as pardonable as Uncle Toby's.

"The thing I dislike in this sort of hotels and places is the admixture of people with whom one is obliged to come in contact," said Constance, putting up her glass as she entered the long low room where the humble table d'hôte of the Toison d'Or was spread. Lady Maréchale talks sweetly of the equality of persons in the sight of Heaven, but I never heard her recognise the same upon the soil of earth.

"Exactly! One may encounter such very objectionable characters! *I* wished to dine in our own apartments, but Albany said no; and he is so positive, you know! This place seems miserably primitive," responded Agneta. Mrs.

Protocol pets Rouges and Republicans of every country, talks liberalism like a feminine Sièyes or John Bright, projects a Reform Bill that shall bear the strongest possible family resemblance to the Décrets du 4 Août, and considers "social distinctions *odious* between man and man;" but her practice is scarcely consistent with her theory, seeing that she is about as tenacious and resentful of objectionable contact as a sea-anemone.

"Who is that, I wonder?" whispered Lady Maréchale, acidulating herself in readiness, after the custom of English ladies when catching sight of a stranger whom they "don't know."

"I wonder! All alone—how very queer!" echoed Mrs. Protocol, drawing her black lace shawl around her, with that peculiar movement which announces a woman's prescience of something antagonistic to her, that is to be repelled *d'avance*, as surely as a hedgehog's transfer of itself into a prickly ball denotes a sense of a coming enemy, and a need of caution and self-protection.

"Who is that deucedly handsome woman?" whispered Maréchale to me.

"What a charming creature!" echoed Dunbar.

The person referred to was the only woman at the table d'hôte besides my sisters—a sister-tourist, probably; a handsome—nay more, a beautiful woman, about eight-and-twenty, distinguished-looking, brilliant, with a figure voluptuously perfect as was ever the Princess Borghese's. To say a woman looks a lady, means nothing in our day. "That young lady will wait on you, sir," says the shopman, referring to the shopwoman who will show you your gloves. "Hand the 'errings to that lady, Joe," you hear a fishmonger cry, as you pass his shop door, referring by his epithet to some Mrs. Gamp or Betsy Prigg in search of that piscatory cheer at his stall. Heaven forbid we should give the abused and degenerate title to any woman deserving of the name! Generalise a thing, and it is vulgar. "A gentleman of my acquaintance," says Spriggs, an auctioneer and house-agent, to Smith a collector of the water-rate. "A man I know," says Pursang, one of the Cabinet, to Greville Tempest, who is heir to a Dukedom, and has intermarried with a royal house. The reason is plain enough. Spriggs thinks it necessary to inform Smith, who otherwise might remain ignorant of so signal a fact, that he actually does know a gentleman, or rather what he terms such. Pursang knows that Tempest would never suspect him of being *lié* with men who were anything else; the one is proud of the fine English, the other is content with the simple phrase! Heaven forbid, I say, we should, now-a-days, call any woman a lady who is veritably such; let us fall back on the dignified, definitive, courtly last-century-name of gentlewoman. I should be glad to see that name revived; it draws a line that snobbissimi cannot pass, and has a grand simplicity about it that will not attract Spriggs, Smith, and Spark, and Mesdames S., leurs femmes!

Our sister-tourist, then, at the Toison d'Or, looked, to my eyes at the least, much more than a "lady," she looked an *aristocrate jusqu'au bout des ongles*, a beautiful, brilliant, dazzling brunette, with lovely hazel eyes, flashing like a tartaret falcon's under their arched pencilled eyebrows, quite an unhoped godsend in Vicq d'Azyr, where only stragglers resort as yet, though—alas for my Arcadia—my sister's pet physician, who sent them thither, is about, I believe, to publish a work, entitled "The Water-Spring in the Wilderness; or, A Scamper through Spots Unknown," which will do a little advertising of himself opportunely, and send hundreds next season to invade the wild woodlands and sunny valleys he inhumanly drags forth into the gas-glare of the world. The brilliant hazel eyes were opposite to me at dinner, and were, I confess, more attractive to me than the stewed pigeons, the crisp frog-legs, and the other viands prepared by the (considering we were in the heart of one of the most remote provinces) really not bad cook of the Toison d'Or. Lady Maréchale and Mrs. Protocol honoured her with that stare by which one woman knows so well how to destroy the reputation of another without speech; they had taken her measurement by some method of feminine geometry unknown to us, and the result was apparently not favourable to her, for over the countenances of the two ladies gathered that expression of stiff dignity and virtuous disdain, in the assuming of which, as I have observed before, they are inimitable proficients. "Evidently not a proper person!" was written on every one of their lineaments. Constance and Agneta had made up their minds with celerity and decision as to her social status, with, it is to be presumed, that unerring instinct which leads their sex to a conclusion so instantaneously, that, according to a philosopher, a woman will be at the top of the staircase of Reasoning by a single spring, while a man is toiling slowly up the first few steps.

"You are intending to remain here some days, madame?" asked the fair stranger, with a charming smile, of Lady Maréchale—a pleasant little overture to chance ephemeral acquaintance, such as a table d'hôte surely well warrants.

But the pleasant little overture was one to which Lady Maréchale was far too English to respond. With that inimitable breeding for which our countrymen and women are continentally renowned, she bent her head with stately stiffness, indulged herself with a haughty stare at the offender, and turned to Agneta, to murmur in English her disgust with the *cuisine* of the really unoffending Toison d'Or.

"Poor Spes would eat nothing. Fenton must make him some panada. But perhaps there was nothing better than goat's milk in the house! What could Dr. Berkeley be thinking of? He described the place quite as though it were a second Meurice's or Badischer Hof!"

A look of amusement glanced into the sparkling, yet languid eyes of my opposite neighbour.

"English!" she murmured to herself, with an almost imperceptible but sufficiently scornful elevation of her arched eyebrows, and a slight smile, just showing her white teeth, as I addressed her in French; and she answered me with the ease, the aplomb, the ever suave courtesy of a woman of the world, with that polish which gives the most common subjects a brilliance never their own, and that vivacity which confers on the merest trifles a spell to amuse and to charm. She was certainly a very lovely creature, and a very charming one, too; frank, animated, witty, with the tone of a woman who has seen the world and knows it. Dunbar adored her, at first sight; he is an inflammable fellow, and has been ignited a thousand times at far less provocation. Maréchale prepared for himself fifty conjugal orations by the recklessness with which, under the very eyes of madame, he devoted himself to another woman. Even Albany Protocol, dull, somnolent, and superior to such weaknesses, as becomes a president of many boards and a chairman of many committees, opened his eyes and glanced at her; and some young Cantabs and artists at the other end of the table stopped their own conversation, envying Dunbar and myself, I believe,' for our juxtaposition with the *belle inconnue;* while my sisters sat trifling with the wing of a pigeon, in voluntary starvation (they would have had nothing to complain of, you see, if they had suffered themselves to dine well!), with strong disapprobation marked upon their lineaments, of this lovely vivacious unknown, whoever she might be, talking exclusively to each other, with a certain expression of sarcastic disdain and offended virtue, hinting far more forcibly than words that they thought already the "very worst" of her.

So severe, indeed, did they look, that Dunbar, who is a good-natured fellow, and thinks—and thinks justly—that Constance and Agneta are very fine women, left me to discuss Hoffmann, Heine, and the rest of Germany's satirical poets, with my opposite neighbour, and endeavoured to thaw my sisters; a very difficult matter when once those ladies are iced. He tried Paris, but only elicited a monosyllabic remark concerning its weather; he tried Vicq d'Azyr, and was rewarded for his trouble by a withering sarcasm on the unlucky Toison d'Or; he tried chitchat on mutual acquaintances, and the unhappy people he chanced to name were severally dismissed with a cutting satire appended to each. Lady Maréchale and Mrs. Protocol were in one of those freezing and unassailable moods in which they sealed a truce with one another, and, combining their forces against a common foe, dealt out sharp, spherical, hard-hitting little bullets of speech from behind the abatis in which they entrenched themselves.

At last he, in despair, tried Lemongenseidlitz, and the ladies thawed slightly—their anticipations from that fashionable little quarter were couleur de rose. They would meet there people of the best *monde*, all their dearest—that is of course their most fashionable—friends; the dear Duchess of Frangipane, the Millamonts those charming people, M. le Marquis de Croix-et-Cordon, Sir

Henry Pullinger, Mrs. Merivale-Delafield, were all there; that delightful person, too, the Graf von Rosenläu, who amused them so much at Baden last year, was, as of course Dunbar knew, Master of the Horse to the Prince of Lemongenseidlitz-Phizzstrelitz; they would be well received at the Court. Which last thing, however, they did not *say*, though they might imply, and assuredly fully thought it; since Lady Maréchale already pictured herself gently awakening his Serene Highness to the spiritual darkness of his soul in legitimatising gaming-tables in his duchy, and Mrs. Protocol already beheld herself closeted with his First Minister, giving that venerable Metternich lessons in political economy, and developing to him a system for filling his beggared treasury to overflowing, without taxing the people a kreutzer—a problem which, though it might have perplexed Kaunitz, Colbert, Pitt, Malesherbes, Talleyrand, and Palmerston put together, offered not the slightest difficulty to *her* enterprising intellect. Have I not said that Sherlock states women are at the top of the staircase while we are toiling up the first few steps?

"The Duchess—Princess Hélène—is a lovely woman, I think. Winton saw her at the Tuileries last winter, and raved about her beauty," said Dunbar, finding he had hit at last on an acceptable subject, and pursuing it with more zeal than discretion; for if there be one thing, I take it, more indiscreet than another, it is to praise woman to woman.

Constance coughed and Agneta smiled, and both assented. "Oh yes—very lovely, they believed!"

"And very lively—up to everything, I think I have heard," went on Dunbar, blandly, unconscious of the meaning of cough, smile, and assent.

"Very lively!" sighed the Saint.

"*Very* lively!" smiled the Politician.

"As gay a woman as Marie Antoinette," continued Dunbar, too intent on the truffles to pay en même temps much heed to the subject he was discussing. "She's copied the Trianon, hasn't she?—has fêtes and pastorals there, acts in comedies herself, shakes off etiquette and ceremonial as much as she can, and all that sort of thing, I believe?"

Lady Maréchale leaned back in her chair, the severe virtue and dignified censure of a British matron and a modern Lucretia expressed in both attitude and countenance.

"A second Marie Antoinette?—too truly and unfortunately so, I have heard! Levity in *any* station is sufficiently reprehensible, but when exhibited in the persons of those whom a higher power has placed in exalted positions, it is most deeply to be deplored. The evil and contagion of its example become incalculable; and even when, which I believe her excusers are wont to assert of Princess Hélène, it is merely traceable to an over-gaiety of spirit and an over-carelessness of comment and censure, it should be remembered that we are enjoined to abstain from every *appearance* of evil!"

With which Constance shook out her phylacteries, represented by the thirty-guinea brocade-silk folds of her skirt (a dress I heard her describe as "very plain!—serviceable for travelling"), and glanced at my opposite neighbour with a look which said, "You are evidently not a proper person, but you hear for once what a proper person thinks!"

Our charming companion did hear it, for she apparently understood English very well. She laughed a little—a sweet, low, ringing laugh—(I was rather in love with her, I must say—I am still)—and spoke with a slight pretty accent.

"True, madame! but ah! what a pity your St. Paul did not advise, too, that people should not go by appearances, and think evil where evil is not!"

Lady Maréchale gave stare number two, with a curl of her lip, and bent her head stiffly.

"What a very strange person!" she observed to Agneta, in a murmur, meant, like a stage aside, to be duly heard, and appreciated by the audience. And yet my sisters are thought very admirably-bred women, too! But then, a woman alone—a foreigner, a stranger—surely no one would exact courtesy to such, from "ladies of position"?

"Have you ever seen Princess Hélène, the Duchess of Lemongenseidlitz, may I ask?" Maréchale inquired, hastily, to cover his wife's sneer. He's a very good fellow, and finds the constant and inevitable society of a saint slightly trying, and a very heavy chastisement for a few words sillily said one morning in St. George's.

"I have seen her, monsieur—yes!"

"And is she a second Marie Antoinette?"

She laughed gaily, showing her beautiful white teeth.

"Ah, bah, monsieur! many would say that is a great deal too good a comparison for her! A second Louise de Savoie—a second Duchesse de Chevreuse—nay, a second Lucrezia Borgia, some would tell you. She likes pleasure—who does not, though, except those with whom 'les raisins sont trop verts et bons pour des goujats?'"

"What an insufferably bold person!" murmured Constance.

"Very disagreeable to meet this style of people!" returned Agneta.

And both stiffened themselves with a little more starch; and we know that British wheats produce the stiffest starch in the world!

"Who, indeed!" cried Maréchale, regardless of madame's frown. "You know this for truth, then, of Princess Hélène?"

"Ah, bah, monsieur! who knows anything for truth?" laughed the lovely brunette. "The world dislikes truth so much, it is obliged to hide itself in out-of-the-way corners, and very rarely comes to light. Nobody knows the truth about her. Some think her, as you say, a second Marie Antoinette, who is surrendered to dissipation and levity, cares for nothing, and would dance and laugh over the dead bodies of the people. Others judge her as others judged Marie Antoinette; discredit the gossip, and think she is but a lively woman, who laughs at forms, likes to amuse herself, and does not see why a court should be a prison! The world likes the darker picture best; let it have it! I do not suppose it will break her heart!"

And the fair stranger laughed so sweetly, that every man at the dinner-table fell in love with her on the spot; and Lady Maréchale and Mrs. Protocol sat throughout the remainder of the meal in frozen dignity and unbreakable silence, while the lovely brunette talked with and smiled on us all with enchanting gaiety, wit, and abandon, chatting on all sorts of topics of the day.

Dinner over, she was the first to rise from the table, and bowed to us with exquisite grace and that charming smile of hers, of which the sweetest rays fell upon *me*, I swear, whether you consider the oath an emanation of personal vanity or not, my good sir. My sisters returned her bow and her good evening to them with that pointed stare which says so plainly, "You are not my equal, how dare you insult me by a courtesy?"

And scarcely had we begun to sip our coffee upstairs in the apartments Chanderlos had secured for the miladies Anglaises, than the duo upon her began as the two ladies sat with Spes between them on a sofa beside one of the windows opening on the balcony that ran round the house. A chance inadvertent assent of Dunbar's, à propos of—oh, sin unpardonable!—the beauty of the incognita's eyes, touched the valve and unloosened the hot springs that were seething below in silence. "A handsome woman!—oh yes, a gentleman's beauty, I dare say!—but a very odd person!" commenced Mrs. Protocol. "A very strange person!" assented Lady Maréchale. "Very free manners!" added Agneta. "Quite French!" chorused Constance. "She has diamond rings—paste, no doubt!" said the Politician. "And rouges—the colour's much too lovely to be natural!" sneered the Saint. "Paints her eyebrows, too!" "Not a doubt—and tints her lashes!" "An adventuress, I should say!" "Or worse!" "Evidently not a proper person!" "Certainly not!"

Through the soft mellow air, hushed into evening silence, the words reached me, as I walked through the window on to the balcony, and stood sipping my coffee and looking lazily over the landscape, wrapped in sunset haze, over the valley where the twilight shadows were deepening, and the mountains that were steeped yet in a rose-hued golden radiance from the rays that had sunk behind them.

"My dear ladies," I cried, involuntarily, "can't you find anything a little more kindly to say of a stranger who has never done you any harm, and who, fifty to one, will never cross your path again?"

"Bravo!" echoed Maréchale, who has never gone as quietly in the matrimonial break as Protocol, and indeed will never be thoroughly broken in—"bravo! women are always studying to make themselves attractive; it's a pity they don't put down among the items a trifle of generosity and charity, it would embellish them wonderfully."

Lady Maréchale beat an injured tattoo with the spoon on her saucer, and leaned back with the air of a martyr, and drawing in her lips with a smile, whose inimitable sneer any lady might have envied—it was quite priceless!

"It is the first time, Sir George, I should presume, that a husband and a brother were ever heard to unite in upbraiding a wife and a sister with her disinclination to associate with, or her averseness to countenance, an improper person!"

"An improper person!" I cried. "But, my dear Constance, who ever told you that this lady you are so desperately bitter upon has any fault at all, save the worst fault in her own sex's eyes—that of beauty? I see nothing in her; her manners are perfect; her tone——"

"You must pardon me if I decline taking your verdict on so delicate a question," interrupted Lady Maréchale, with withering satire. "Very possibly you see nothing objectionable in her—nothing at least, that *you* would call so! Your views and mine are sufficiently different on every subject, and the women with whom I believe you have chiefly associated are not those who are calculated to give you very much appreciation for the more refined classes of our sex! Very possibly the person in question is what *you* and Sir George too, perhaps, find charming; but you must excuse me if I really cannot, to oblige you, stoop to countenance any one whom my intuition and my knowledge of the world both declare so very evidently what she should not be. She will endeavour, most probably, if she remain here, to push herself into our acquaintance, but if you and my husband should choose to insult us by favouring her efforts, Agneta and I, happily, can guard ourselves from the objectionable companionship into which those who *should* be our protectors would wish to force us!"

With which Lady Maréchale, with a little more martyrdom and an air of extreme dignity, had recourse to her *flacon* of Viola Montana, and sank among the soft cushions, a model of outraged and Spartan virtue. I set down my coffee-cup, and lounged out again to the peace of the balcony; Maréchale shrugged his shoulders, rose, and followed me. Lo! on the part of the balcony that ran under *her* windows, leaning on its balustrade, her white hand, white as the flowers, playing with the clematis tendrils, the "paste" diamond flashing in the last rays of the setting sun, stood our "dame d'industrie—or worse!" She was but a few feet farther on; she must have heard Lady Maréchale's and Mrs. Protocol's duo on her demerits; she *had* heard it, without doubt, for she was laughing gaily and joyously, laughter that sparkled all over her *riante* face and flashed in her bright falcon eyes. Laughing still, she signed me to her. I need not say that the sign was obeyed.

"Chivalrous knight, I thank you! You are a Bayard of chivalry; you defend the absent! What a miracle, mon Dieu! Tell your friends from me not to speak so loudly when their windows are open; and for yourself, rest assured your words of this evening will not be forgotten."

"I am happy, indeed, if I have been fortunate enough to obtain a chance remembrance, but do not give me too much praise for so simple a service; the clumsiest Cimon would be stirred into chivalry under such inspiration as I had——"

The beautiful hazel eyes flashed smilingly on me under their lashes. (*Those* lashes tinted! Heaven forgive the malice of women!) She broke off a sprig of the clematis, with its long slender leaves and fragrant starry flowers, and gave it to me:

"*Tenez, mon ami*, if ever you see me again, show me that faded flower, and I shall remember this evening at Vicq d'Azyr. Nay, do not flatter yourself—do not thrust it in your breast; it is no gage d'amour! it is only a reward for loyal service, and a souvenir to refresh my own memory, which is treacherous sometimes, though not in gratitude to those who serve me. Adieu, mon Bayard —et bonsoir!"

But I retained the hand that had given me my clematis-spray.

"Meet you again! But will not that be to-morrow? If I am not to see you, as your words threaten, till the clematis be faded and myself forgotten, let me at least, I beseech you, know where, who, by what name——"

She drew her hand away with something of a proud surprised gesture; then she laughed again, that sweet, ringing, mocking laugh:

"No, no, Bayard, it is too much to ask! Leave the future to hazard; it is always the best philosophy. Au revoir! Adieu—perhaps for a day, perhaps for a century!"

And the bewitching mystery floated away from me and through the open window of her room. You will imagine that my "intuition" did not lead me to the conclusion to which Lady Maréchale's led her, or assuredly should I have followed the donor of the clematis, despite her prohibition. Even with my "intuition" pointing where it did, I am not sure what I might have done if, in her salon, I had not caught sight of a valet and a lady's-maid in waiting with her coffee, and they are not such spectators as one generally selects.

The servants closed her windows and drew down their Venetian blinds, and I returned to my coffee. Whether the two ladies within had overheard her conversation as she had heard theirs, I cannot say, but they looked trebly refrigerated, and congealed themselves into the chilliest human ice that is imaginable, and comported themselves towards me fully as distantly as though I had brought a dozen ballet-girls in to dinner with them, or introduced them to my choicest acquaintance from the Château des Fleurs.

"A man's taste is so pitiably low!" remarked Lady Maréchale, in her favourite stage aside to Mrs. Protocol; to which that other lady responded, "Disgracefully so!"

Who *was* my lovely unknown with the bright falcon eyes and the charming laugh, with her strange freedom that yet was *not*, somehow, free, and her strange fascination? I bade my man ask Chanderlos her name—couriers know everything generally—but neither Mills nor Chanderlos gave me any information. The people of the house did not know, or said they did not; they only knew she had servants in attendance who came with her, who revealed nothing, and paid any price for the best of everything. Are impertinent questions ever asked where money is plentiful?

I was dressing the next morning something later than usual, when I heard the roll of a carriage in the courtyard below. I looked through the half-open persiennes with a semi-presentiment that it was my sweet foreigner who was leaving ere I could presume on my clematis or improve our acquaintance. True enough, she it was, leaving Vicq d'Azyr in a travelling-carriage, with handsome roans and servants in imperial-blue liveries. Who the deuce could she be?

"Well, Constance," said I, as I bade Lady Maréchale

good morning, "your *bête noire* won't 'press herself into your acquaintance,' as you were dreading last night, and won't excite Maréchale and me to any more high treason. Won't you chant a Te Deum? She left this morning."

"So I perceived," answered Lady Maréchale, frigidly; by which I suppose *she* had not been above the weakness of looking through *her* persiennes.

"What a pity you and Agneta agitated yourselves with such unnecessary alarm! It must have cost you a great deal of eau-de-cologne and sal-volatile, I am afraid, last night. Do you think she contaminated the air of the salle-à-manger, because I will order Mills to throw some disinfectant about before you go down."

"I have no inclination to jest upon a person of that stamp," rejoined Lady Maréchale, with immense dignity, settling her turquoise wristband-studs.

"'That stamp of persons!' What! Do you think she is an adventuress, an intrigante, or 'worse' still, then? I hoped her dashing equipage might have done something towards cleansing her character. Wealth *is* a universal purifier generally."

"Flippant impertinence!" murmured Lady Maréchale, disgustedly, to Mrs. Protocol, as she swept onwards down the staircase, not deigning me a glance, much less a response, stiffening herself with a little extra starch of Lucretian virtue and British-matronly dignity, which did not grow limp again throughout breakfast, while she found fault with the chocolate, considered the *petits pains* execrable, condemned the sardines as uneatable, petted Spes, kept Maréchale and me at Coventry, and sighed over their enforced incarceration, by Dr. Berkeley's orders, in Vicq d'Azyr, that kept them in this stupid place away from Lemongenseidlitz.

Their anticipations from Lemongenseidlitz were charmingly golden and rose-tinted. They looked forward to consolidating their friendship with the dear Duchess in its balmy air, to improving a passing acquaintance into an intimate one with that charming person the Baroness Liebenfrauenmilch, Mistress of the Robes to Princess Hélène, and to being very intimate at the Court, while the Pullingers (their bosom friends and very dear rivals) would be simply presented, and remain in chagrin, uninvited to the state balls and palace festivities. And what more delightful than that last clause? for what sauce invented, from Carême to Soyer, flavours our own *plats* so deliciously, I should like to know, as thinking that our beloved next-door neighbour is doomed to a very dry cutlet.

As Pérette, in a humbler fashion, built visions from the pot of milk, so mesdames mes sœurs, from the glittering court and capital of Lemongenseidlitz, erected brilliant châteaux en Espagne of all their sayings and doings in that fashionable little city whither they were bound, and into which they had so many invaluable passports. They were impatient to be journeying from our humble, solitary valley, and after a month of Vicq d'Azyr, they departed for their golden land, and I went with them, as I had slain izzards almost *ad nauseam*, and Dunbar's expiration of leave had taken him back to Dublin.

It was five o'clock when we reached its Reidenscher Hof, nine when we had finished dinner. It was stupid work yawning over coffee and *Galignani*. What was to be done? Maréchale proposed the Opera, and for the first time in his life was unopposed by his wife. Constance was in a suave, benignant mood; she was thinking of her Graf von Rosenläu, of the Pullingers, and of the sweet, adroit manner in which she would—when she had captivated him and could proffer such hints—awaken his Serene Highness to a sense of his moral guilt in not bringing to instant capital punishment every agent in those Satanus-farmed banks that throve throughout his duchy. Lady Maréchale and Mrs. Protocol assented, and to the little miniature gaily-decorated Opera House we drove. They were in the middle of the second act of "Ernani." "Ernani" was stale to us all, and we naturally lorgné'd the boxes in lieu of the stage. I had turned my glass on the left-hand stage-box, and was going steadily round, when a faint cry of dismay, alarm, amazement, horror, broke, muffled and low, from mesdames mes sœurs. Their lorgnons were riveted on one spot; their cheeks were blanched; their hands were tremulous; if they had beheld a spiritual visitant, no consternation more profound, more intense, could have seized both with its iron hand. *My* sisters too! the chilliest, the calmest, the most impenetrable, the most unassailable of mortals!

"And we called her, in her hearing, not a proper person!" gasped Lady Maréchale.

"We thought her a lorette! an intrigante! a dame d'industrie?" echoed Mrs. Protocol.

"Who wore paste jewels!"

"Who came from the Rue Bréda!"

"Who wanted to know us!"

"Whom we wouldn't know!"

I turned my Voightlander where their Voightlanders turned; there, in the royal box, leaning back in the fauteuil that marked her rank, there, with her lovely hazel eyes, her witching smile, her radiant beauty, matchless as the pearls gleaming above her brow, there sat the "adventuress—or worse!" of Vicq d'Azyr; the "evidently a not proper person" of my discerning sisters—H.S.H.

Princess Hélène, Grand-Duchess of Lemongenseidlitz-Phizzstrelitz! Great Heavens! how had we never guessed her before? How had we never divined her identity? How had we never remembered all we had heard of her love of laisser-aller, her taste for adventure, her delight in travelling, when she could, unattended and incognita? How had we never put this and that together, and penetrated the metamorphosis?

"*And I called her not a proper person!*" gasped Lady Maréchale, again shrinking back behind the azure curtains; the projectiles she had shot with such vindictive severity, such delighted acrimony, from the murderous mortar of malice, recoiling back upon her head for once, and crushing her to powder. What reception would they have *now* at the Court? Von Rosenlāu would be powerless; the Pullingers themselves would be better off! Pérette's pot of milk was smashed and spilt! "Adieu, veau, vache, cochon, couvée!"

When the pitcher lies shivered into fragments, and the milk is spilt, you know, poor Pérette's dreams are shivered and spilt with them. "I have not seen you at the palace yet?" asked her Grace of Frangipane. "We do not see you at the Court, mesdames?" asked M. de la Croix-et-Cordons. "How did it happen you were not at the Duchess's ball last night?" asked "those odious Pullingers." And what had my sister to say in reply? My clematis secured *me* a charming reception—how charming I don't feel called upon to reveal—but Princess Hélène, with that calm dignity which easily replaced, when she chose, her witching *abandon*, turned the tables upon her detractors, and taught them how dangerous it may be to speak ill—of the wrong people.

A LINE IN THE "DAILY:"

WHO DID IT, AND WHO WAS DONE BY IT.

"LIEUTENANT-COLONEL FAIRLIE'S troop of Horse Artillery is ordered to Norwich to replace the 12th Lancers, en route to Bombay." Those three lines in the papers spread dismay into the souls of Norfolk young ladies, and no less horror into ours, for we were very jolly at Woolwich, could run up to the Clubs and down to Epsom, and were far too material not to prefer ball-room belles to bluebells, strawberry-ice to fresh hautboys, the sparkle of champagne-cup to all the murmurs of the brooks, and the flutter of ballet-girls' wings to all the rustle of forest leaves. But, unhappily, the Ordnance Office is no more given to considering the feelings of their Royal Gunners than the Horse Guards the individual desires of the two other Arms; and off we went to Norwich, repining bitterly, or, in modern English, swearing hard at our destinies, creating an immense sensation with our 6-pounders, as we flatter ourselves the Royals always contrive to do, whether on fair friends or fierce foes, and were looked upon spitefully by the one or two young ladies whose hearts were gone eastwards with the Twelfth, smilingly by the one or two hundred who, having fruitlessly laid out a great deal of tackle on the Twelfth, proceeded to manufacture fresh flies to catch us.

We soon made up, I think, to the Norwich girls for

the loss of the Twelfth. They set dead upon Fairlie, our captain, a Brevet Lieutenant-Colonel, and a C.B. for "services in India," where he had rivalled Norman Ramsay's ancient fame at Fuentes d'Onor, had had a ball put in his hip, and had come home again to be worshipped by the women for his romantic reputation. They made an immense deal, too, of Levison Courtenay, the beauty of the troop, and called Belle in consequence; who did not want any flummery or flirtation to increase his opinion of himself, being as vain of his almond eyes as any girl just entered as the favourite for the season. There were Tom Gower, too, a capital fellow, with no nonsense about him, who made no end of chaff of Belle Courtenay; and Little Nell, otherwise Harcourt Poulteney Nelson, who had by some miracle escaped expulsion both from Carshalton and the College; and *votre humble serviteur* Phil Hardinge, first lieutenant, and one or two other fellows, who having cut dashing figures at our Woolwich reviews, cantering across Blackheath Common, or waltzing with dainty beauties down our mess-room, made the Artillery welcome in that city of shawls and oratorios, where, according to the Gazetteer, no virtuous person ought to dwell, that volume, with characteristic lucidity, pronouncing its streets "ill disposed."

The Clergy asked us to their rectories—a temptation we were often proof against, there being three noticeable facts in rectories, that the talk is always slow, "the Church" being present, and having much the same chilling effect as the presence of a chaperone at a tête-à-tête; the daughters generally ugly, and, from leading the choir at morning services, perfectly convinced that they sing like Clara Novello, and that the harmonium is a most delightful instrument; and, last and worst, the wines are almost always poor, except the port which the reverend host drinks himself, but which, Dieu merci! we rarely or never touch.

The County asked us, too; and there we went for good hock, tolerable-looking women, and first-rate billiard-tables. For the first month we were in Norfolk we voted it unanimously the most infernally slow and hideous county going; and I dare say we made ourselves uncommonly disagreeable, as people, if they are not pleased, be they ever so well bred, have a knack of doing.

Things were thus quiescent and stagnant, when Fairlie one night at mess told us a bit of news.

"Old fellows, whom do you think I met to-day?"

"How should we know? Cut along."

"The Swan and her Cygnets."

"The Vanes? Oh, bravo!" was shouted at a chorus, for the dame and demoiselles in question we had known in town that winter, and a nicer, pleasanter, faster set of women I never came across. "What's bringing them down here, and how's Geraldine?"

"Vane's come into his baronetcy, and his place is close by Norwich," said Fairlie; "his wife's health has been bad, and so they left town early; and Geraldine is quite well, and counting on haymaking, she informed me."

"Come, that is good news," said Belle, yawning. "There'll be one pretty woman in the county, thank Heaven! Poor little Geraldine! I must go and call on her to-morrow."

"She has existed without your calls, Belle," said Fairlie, dryly, "and don't look as if she'd pined after you."

"My dear fellow, how should you know?" said Belle, in no wise disconcerted. "A little rouge soon makes 'em look well, and as for smiles, they'll smile while they're dying for you. Little Vane and I were always good friends, and shall be again—if I care."

"Conceited owl!" said Fairlie, under his moustaches. "I'm sorry to hurt your feelings, then, but your pretty 'friend' never asked after you."

"I dare say not," said Belle, complacently. "Where a woman's most interested she's always quietest, and Geraldine——"

"Lady Vane begged me to tell you you will always be welcome over there, old fellows," said Fairlie, remorselessly cutting him short. "Perhaps we shall find something to amuse us better than these stiltified Chapter dinners."

The Vanes of whom we talked were uncommonly pleasant people whom we had known at Lee, where Vane, a Q.C., then resided, his prospective baronetcy being at that time held by a third or fourth cousin. Fairlie had known the family since his boyhood; there were four daughters, tall graceful women, who had gained themselves and mother the nickname of The Swan and her Cygnets; and then there were twins, a boy of eighteen, who'd just left Eton; and the girl Geraldine, a charming young lady, whom Belle admired more warmly than that dandy often admired anybody besides himself, and whom Fairlie liked cordially, having had many a familiar bit of fun with her, as he had known her ever since he was a dashing cadet, and she made her *début* in life in the first column of the *Times*. Her sisters were handsome women; but Geraldine was bewitching. A very pleasant family they were, and a vast acquisition to us. Miss Geraldine flirted to a certain extent with us all, but chiefly with the Colonel, whenever he was to be had, those two having a very free-and-easy, familiar style of intercourse, owing to old acquaintance; and Belle spent two hours every evening on his toilette when we were going to dine there, and vowed she was a "deuced pretty little puss. Perhaps she might—he wasn't sure, but perhaps (it would be a horrid sacrifice), if he was with her much longer, he wasn't sure she mightn't persuade him to take compassion upon her, he *was* so weak where women were concerned!"

"What a conceit!" said Fairlie thereat, with a contemptuous twist of his moustaches and a shrug of his shoulders to me. "I must say, if I were a woman, I shouldn't feel over-flattered by a lover who admired his own beauty first, and mine afterwards. Not that I pretend to understand women."

By which speech I argued that his old playmate Geraldine hadn't thrown hay over the Colonel, and been taught billiards by him, and ridden his bay mare over the park in her evening dress, without interesting him slightly; and that—though I don't think he knew it—he was deigning to be a trifle jealous of his Second Captain, the all-mighty conqueror Belle.

"What fools they must be that put in these things!" yawned Belle one morning, reading over his breakfast coffee in the *Daily Pryer* one of those "advertisements for a wife" that one comes across sometimes in the papers, and that make us, like a good many other things, agree with Goldsmith:

> Reason, they say, belongs to man,
> But let them prove it if they can:
> Wise Aristotle and Smiglicious,
> By ratiocinations specious,
> Have strove to prove with great precision,
> With definition and division,
> Homo est ratione præditum,
> But for my soul I cannot credit 'em.

"What fools they must be!" yawned Belle, wrapping his dressing-gown round him, and coaxing his perfumy whiskers under his velvet smoking-cap. Belle was always inundated by smoking-caps in cloth and velvet, silk and beads, with blue tassels, and red tassels, and gold tassels, embroidered and filigreed, rounded and pointed; he had them sent to him by the dozen, and pretty good chaff he made of the donors. "Awful fools! The idea of advertising for a wife, when the only difficulty a man has is to keep from being tricked into taking one. I bet you, if I did like this owl here, I should have a hundred answers; and if it were known to be I——"

"Little Geraldine's self for a candidate, eh?" asked Tom Gower.

"Very possible," said Belle, with a self-complacent smile. "She's a fast little thing, don't check at much, and she's deucedly in love with me, poor little dear— almost as much trouble to me as Julia Sedley was last season. That girl all but proposed to me; she did, indeed. Never was nearer coming to grief in my life. What will you bet me that, if I advertise for a wife, I don't hoax lots of women?"

"I'll bet you ten pounds," said I, "that you don't hoax one!"

"Done!" said Belle, stretching out his hand for a dainty memorandum-book, gift of the identical Julia Sedley aforesaid, and entering the bet in it—"done! If I'm not asked to walk in the Close at noon and look out for a pink bonnet and a black lace cloak, and to loiter up the market-place till I come across a black hat and blue muslin dress; if I'm not requested to call at No. 20, and to grant an interview at No. 84; if I'm not written to by Agatha A. with hazel, and Belinda B. with black, eyes—all coming after me like flies after a sugar-cask, why you shall have your ten guineas, my boy, and my colt into the bargain. Come, write out the advertisement, Tom—I can't, it's too much trouble; draw it mild, that's all, or the letters we shall get will necessitate an additional Norwich postman. By George, what fun it will be to do the girls! Cut along, Tom, can't you?"

"All right," said Gower, pushing away his coffee-cup, and drawing the ink to him. "Head it 'MARRIAGE,' of course?"

"Of course. That word's as attractive to a woman as the belt to a prize-fighter, or a pipe of port to a college fellow."

"'MARRIAGE.—A Bachelor——'"

"Tell 'em a military man; all girls have the scarlet fever."

"Very well—'an Officer in the Queen's, of considerable personal attractions'."

"My dear fellow, pray don't!" expostulated Belle, in extreme alarm; "we shall have such swarms of 'em!"

"No, no! we must say that," persisted Gower—"'personal attractions, aged eight-and-twenty——'"

"Can't you put it, 'in the flower of his age,' or his 'sixth lustre?' It's so much more poetic."

"'—the flower of his age" then (that'll leave 'em a wide range from twenty to fifty, according to their taste), 'is desirous of meeting a young lady of beauty, talent, and good family,'—eh?"

"Yes. All women think themselves beauties, if they're as ugly as sin. Milliners and confectioner girls talk Anglo-French, and rattle a tin-kettle piano after a fashion, and anybody buys a 'family' for half-a-crown at the Heralds' Office—so fire away."

"'—who, feeling as he does the want of a kindred heart and sympathetic soul, will accord him the favour of a letter or an interview, as a preliminary to the greatest step in life.'"

"A step—like one on thin ice—very sure to bring a

man to grief," interpolated Belle. "Say something about property; those soul-and-spirit young ladies generally keep a look-out for tin, and only feel an elective affinity for a lot of debentures and consols."

"'The advertiser being a man of some present and still more prospective wealth, requires no fortune, the sole objects of his search being love and domestic felicity.' Domestic felicity—how horrible! Don't it sound exactly like the end of a lady's novel, where the unlucky hero is always brought to an untimely end in a 'sweet cottage on the banks of the lovely Severn'?"

"'Domestic felicity'—bah! What are you writing about?" yawned Belle. "I'd as soon take to teetotalism; however, it'll tell in the advertisement. Bravo, Tom, that will do. Address it to 'L. C., care of Mrs. Greene, confectioner, St. Giles-street, Norwich.' Miss Patty 'll take the letters in for me, though not if she knew their errand. Tip seven-and-sixpence with it, and send it to the *Daily Pryer*."

We did send it to the *Daily*, and in that broadsheet we all of us read it two mornings after.

MARRIAGE.—A Bachelor, an Officer of the Queen's, of considerable personal attractions, and in the flower of his age, is desirous of meeting a young lady of beauty, accomplishments, and good family, who, feeling as he does the want of a kindred heart and sympathetic soul, will accord him the favour either of a letter or an interview, as a preliminary to the greatest step in life. The advertiser being a man of some present and still more prospective wealth, requires no fortune, the sole objects of his search being love and domestic felicity. Address, L. C., care of Mrs. Greene, confectioner, St. Giles-street, Norwich.

"Whose advertisement do you suppose that is?" said Fairlie, showing the *Daily* to Geraldine, as he sat with her and her sisters under some lilac and larch trees in one of the meadows of Fern Chase, which had had the civility, Geraldine said, to yield a second crop of hay expressly for her to have the pleasure of making it. She leaned down towards him as he lay on the grass, and read the advertisement, looking uncommonly pretty in her dainty muslin dress, with its fluttering mauve ribbons, and a wreath she had just twisted up, of bluebells and pinks and white heaths which Fairlie had gathered as he lay, put on her bright hair. We called her a little flirt, but I think she was an unintentional one; at least her agaceries were, all as unconscious as they were—her worst enemies (*i.e.* plain young ladies) had to allow—unaffected.

"How exquisitely sentimental! Is it yours?" she asked, with demure mischief.

"Mine!" echoed Fairlie, with supreme scorn.

"It's some one's here, because the address is at Mrs. Greene's. Come, tell me at once, monsieur."

"The only fool in the Artillery," said Fairlie, curtly: "Belle Courtenay."

"Captain Courtenay!" echoed Geraldine, with a little flush on her cheeks, caused, perhaps, by the quick glance the Colonel shot at her as he spoke.

"Captain Courtenay!" said Katherine Vane. "Why, what can he want with a wife? I thought he had *l'embarras de choix* offered him in that line; at least, so he makes out himself."

"I dare say," said Fairlie, dryly, "it's for a bet he's made, to see how many women he can hoax, I believe."

"How can you tell it is a hoax?" said Geraldine, throwing cowslips at her greyhound. "It may be some medium of intercourse with some one he really cares for, and who may understand his meaning."

"Perhaps you are in his confidence, Geraldine, or perhaps you are thinking of answering it yourself?"

"Perhaps," said the young lady, waywardly, making the cowslips into a ball; "there might be worse investments. Your *bête noire* is strikingly handsome; he is the perfection of style; he is going to be Equerry to the

Prince; his mother is just married again to Lord Chevenix; he did not name half his attractions in that line in the *Daily*."

With which Geraldine rushed across the meadow after the greyhound and the cowslip ball, and Fairlie lay quiet plucking up the heaths by the roots. He lay there still, when the cowslip ball struck him a soft fragrant blow against his lips, and knocked the Cuba from between his teeth.

"Why don't you speak?" asked Geraldine, plaintively. "You are not half so pleasant to play with as you were before you went to India, and I was seven or eight, and you had La Grace, and battledore and shuttlecock, and cricket, and all sorts of games with me in the old garden at Charlton."

He might have told her she was much less dangerous then than now; he was not disposed to flatter her, however. So he answered her quietly,

"I preferred you as you were then."

"Indeed!" said Geraldine, with a hot colour in her cheeks. "I do not think there are many who would indorse your complimentary opinion."

"Possibly," said Fairlie, coldly.

She took up her cowslips, and hit him hard with them several times.

"Don't speak in that tone. If you dislike me, you can say so in warmer words, surely."

Fairlie smiled *malgré lui*.

"What a child you are, Geraldine! but a child that is a very mischievous coquette, and has learned a hundred tricks and *agaceries* of which my little friend of seven or eight knew nothing. I grant you were not a quarter so charming, but you were, I am afraid—more true."

Geraldine was ready to cry, but she was in a passion,

nevertheless; such a hot and short-lived passion as all women of any spirit can go into on occasion, when they are unjustly suspected.

"I you choose to think so of me you may," she said, with immeasurable hauteur, sweeping away from him, her mauve ribbons fluttering disdainfully. "I, for one, shall not try to undeceive you."

The next night we all went up to the ball at the Vanes', to drink Rhenish, eat ices, quiz the women, flirt with the pretty ones in corners, lounge against doorways, criticise the feet in the waltzing as they passed us, and do, in fact, anything but what we went to do—dance—according to our custom in such scenes.

The Swan and her Cygnets looked very stunning; they "made up well," as ladies say when they cannot deny that another is good-looking, but qualify your admiration by an assurance that she is shockingly plain in the morning, and owes all to her milliner and maids. Geraldine, who, by the greatest stretch of scepticism, could not be supposed "made up," was bewitching, with her sunshiny enjoyment of everything, and her untiring waltzing, going for all the world like a spinning-top, only a top tires, and she did not. Belle, who made a principle of never dancing except under extreme coercion by a very pretty hostess, could not resist her, and Tom Gower, and Little Nell, and all the rest, not to mention half Norfolk, crowded round her; all except Fairlie, who leaned against the doorway, seeming to talk to her father or the members, or anybody near, but watching the young lady for all that, who flirted not a little, having in her mind the scene in the paddock of yesterday, and wishing, perhaps, to show him that if he did not admire her more than when she was eight, other men had better taste.

She managed to come near him towards the end of the evening, sending Belle to get her an ice.

"Well," she said, with a comical *pitié d'elle-même*, "do you dislike me so much that you don't mean to dance with me at all? Not a single waltz all night?"

"What time have you had to give me?" said Fairlie, coldly. "You have been surrounded all the evening."

"Of course I have. I am not so disagreeable to other gentlemen as I am to you. But I could have made time for you if you had only asked for it. At your own ball last week you engaged me beforehand for six waltzes."

Fairlie relented towards her. Despite her flirting, he thought she did not care for Belle after all.

"Well," he said, smiling, "will you give me one after supper?"

"You told me you shouldn't dance, Colonel Fairlie," said Katherine Vane, smiling.

"One can't tell what one mayn't do under temptation," said Fairlie, smiling too. "A man may change his mind, you know."

"Oh yes," cried Geraldine; "a man may change his mind, and we are expected to be eminently grateful to him for his condescension; but if *we* change our minds, how severely we are condemned for vacillation: 'So weak!' 'Just like women!' 'Never like the same thing two minutes, poor things!'"

"You don't like the same thing two minutes, Geraldine," laughed Fairlie; "so I dare say you speak feelingly."

"I changeable! I am constancy itself!"

"Are you? You know what the Italians say of azure eyes?"

"But I don't believe it, monsieur!" cried Geraldine:

"Blue eyes beat black fifty to seven,
For black's of hell, but blue's of heaven!"

"I beg your pardon, mademoiselle," laughed Fairlie:

"Done, by the odds, it is not true!
One devil's black, but scores are blue!"

He whirled her off into the circle in the midst of our laughter at their ready wit. Soon after he bid her good night, but he found time to whisper as he did so,

"You are more like *my* little Geraldine to-night!"

The look he got made him determine to make her his little Geraldine before much more time had passed. At least, he drove us back to Norwich in what seemed very contented silence, for he smoked tranquilly, and let the horses go their own pace—two certain indications that a man has pleasant thoughts to accompany him.

I do not think he listened to Belle's, and Gower's, and my conversation, not even when Belle took his weed out of his mouth and announced the important fact: "Hardinge! my ten guineas, if you please. I've had a letter!"

"What! an answer? By Jove!"

"Of course, an answer. I tell you all the pretty women in the city will know my initials, and send after me. I only hope they *will* be pretty, and then one may have a good deal of fun. I was in at Greene's this morning having mock-turtle, and talking to Patty (she's not bad looking, that little girl, only she drops her 'h's' so. I'm like that fellow—what's his name?—in the 'Peau de Chagrin;' I don't admire my loves in cotton prints), when she gave me the letter. I left it on my dressing-table, but you can see it to-morrow. It's a horrid red daubed-looking seal, and no crest; but that she mightn't use for fear of being found out, and the writing is disguised, but that it would be. She *says* she has the three requisites; but where's the woman that don't think herself Sappho and Galatea combined? And she was nineteen last March. Poor little devil! she little thinks how she'll be done. I'm to meet her on the Yarmouth road at two, and to look out for a lady standing by the first milestone. Shall we go, Tom? It may lead to something amusing, you know, though certainly it won't lead to marriage."

"Oh! we'll go, old fellow," said I. "Deuce take you, Belle! what a lucky fellow you are with the women."

"Luckier than I want to be," yawned Belle. "It's a horrid bore to be so set upon. One may have too much of a good thing, you know."

At two the day after, having refreshed ourselves with a light luncheon at Mrs. Greene's of lobster-salad and pale ale, Belle, Gower, and I buttoned our gloves and rode leisurely up the road.

"How my heart palpitates!" said Belle, stroking his moustaches with a bored air. "How can I tell, you know, but what I may be going to see the arbiter of my destiny? Men have been tricked into all sorts of tomfoolery by their compassionate feelings. And then—if she should squint or have a turn-up nose! Good Heavens! what a fearful idea! I've often wondered when I've seen men with ugly wives how they could have been cheated into taking 'em; they couldn't have done it in their senses, you know, nor yet with their eyes open. You may depend they took 'em to church in a state of coma from chloroform. 'Pon my word I feel quite nervous. You don't think the girl will have a parson and a register hid behind the milestone, do you?"

"If she should, it won't be legal without a license, thanks to the fools who turn Hymen into a tax-gatherer, and won't let a fellow make love without he asks leave of the Archbishop of Canterbury," said Gower. "Hallo, Belle, here's the milestone, but where's the lady?"

"Virgin modesty makes her unpunctual," said Belle, putting up his eye-glass.

"Hang modesty!" swore Tom. "It's past two, and we left a good quarter of that salad uneaten. Confound her!"

"There are no signs of her," said I. "Did she tell you her dress, Belle?"

"Not a syllable about it; only mentioned a milestone, and one might have found a market-woman sitting on that."

"Hallo! here's something feminine. Oh, good gracious! this can't be it, it's got a brown stuff dress on, and a poke straw bonnet and a green veil. No, no, Belle. If you married her, that *would* be a case of chloroform."

But the horrible brown stuff came sidling along the road with that peculiar step belonging to ladies of a certain age, characterised by Patty Greene as "tipputting," sweeping up the dust with its horrible folds, making straight *en route* for Belle, who was standing a little in advance of us. Nineteen! Good Heavens! she must have been fifty if she was a day, and under her green veil was a chesnut front—yes, decidedly, a front—and a face yellow as a Canadian's, and wrinkled as Madame Pipelet's, made infinitely worse by that sweet maiden simper and assumed juvenility common to *vieilles filles*. Up she came towards poor Belle, who involuntarily retreated step by step till he had backed against the milestone, and could get no further, while she smiled up in his handsome face, and he stared down in her withered one, with the most comical expression of surprise, dismay, and horror that had ever appeared on our "beauty's" impassive features.

"Are you—the—the—L. C.?" demanded the maiden of ten lustres, casting her eyes to the ground with virgin modesty.

"L. C. ar——My dear madam, I don't quite understand you," faltered Belle, taken aback for once in his life.

"Was it not you," faltered the fair one, shaking out a pocket-handkerchief that sent a horrible odour of musk to the olfactory nerves of poor Belle, most fastidious connoisseur in perfume, "who advertised for a kindred heart and sympathetic soul?"

"Really, my good lady," began Belle, still too aghast by the chesnut front to recover his self-possession.

"Because," simpered his inamorata, too agitated by her own feelings to hear his horrible appellative, keeping him at bay there with the fatal milestone behind him and the awful brown stuff in front of him—"because I, too, have desired to meet with some elective affinity, some spirit-tie that might give me all those more subtle sympathies which can never be found in the din and bustle of the heartless world; I, too, have pined for the objects of your search—love and domestic happiness. Oh, blessed words, surely we might—might we not?——"

She paused, overcome with maidenly confusion, and buried her face in the musk-scented handkerchief. Tom and I, where we stood *perdus*, burst into uncontrollable shouts of laughter. Poor Belle gave one blank look of utter terror at the *tout ensemble* of brown stuff, straw poke, and chesnut front. He forgot courtesy, manners, and everything else; his lips were parted, with his small white teeth glancing under his silky moustaches, his sleepy eyes were open wide, and as the maiden lady dropped her handkerchief, and gave him what she meant to be the softest and most tender glance, he turned straight round, sprang on his bay, and rushed down the Yarmouth road as if the whole of the dignitaries of the church and law were tearing after him to force him *nolens volens* into carrying out the horrible promise in his cursed line in the *Daily*. What was Tom's and my amazement to see the maiden lady seat herself astride on the milestone, and join her cachinnatory shouts to ours, fling her green veil into a hawthorn-tree, jerk her bonnet into our faces, kick off her brown stuff into the middle of the road, tear off her chesnut front and yellow mask, and perform a frantic war-dance on the roadside turf. No less a person than that mischievous monkey and inimitable mimic Little Nell!

"You young demon!" shouted Gower, shrieking with laughter till he cried. "A pretty fellow you are to go tricking your senior officer like this. You little imp, how can you tell but what I shall court-martial you to-morrow?"

"No, no, you won't!" cried Little Nell, pursuing his frantic dance. "Wasn't it prime? wasn't it glorious? wasn't it worth the Kohinoor to see? You won't go and peach, when I've just given you a better farce than all old Buckstone's? By Jove! Belle's face at my chesnut front! This'll be one of his prime conquests, eh? I say, old fellows, when Charles Mathews goes to glory, don't you think I might take his place, and beat him hollow, too?"

When we got back to barracks we found Belle prostrate on his sofa, heated, injured, crestfallen, solacing himself with Seltzer-and-water, and swearing away anything but mildly at that "wretched old woman." He bound us over to secrecy, which, with Little Nell's confidence in our minds, we naturally promised. Poor Belle! to have been made a fool of before two was humiliation more than sufficient for our all-conquering *lion*. For one who had so often refused to stir across a ball-room to look at a Court beauty, to have ridden out three miles to see an old maid of fifty with a chesnut front! The insult sank deep into his soul, and threw him into an abject melancholy, which hung over him all through mess, and was not dissipated till a letter came to him from Mrs. Greene's, when we were playing loo in Fairlie's room. That night Fairlie was in gay spirits. He had called at Fern Chase that morning, and though he had not been able to see Geraldine alone, he had passed a pleasant couple of hours there, playing pool with her and her sisters, and had been as good friends as ever with his old playmate.

"Well, Belle," said he, feeling good-natured even with him that night, "did you get any good out of your advertisement? Did your lady turn out a very pretty one?"

"No; deuced ugly, like the generality," yawned poor Belle, giving me a kick to remind me of my promise. Little Nell was happily about the city somewhere with Pretty Face, or the boy would scarcely have kept his countenance.

"What amusement you can find in hoaxing silly women," said Fairlie, "is incomprehensible to me. However, men's tastes differ, happily. Here comes another epistle for you, Belle; perhaps there's better luck for you there."

"Oh! I shall have no end of letters. I shan't answer any more. I think it such a deuced trouble. Diamonds trumps, eh?" said Belle, laying the note down till he should have leisure to attend to it. "Poor old fellow! I dare say he was afraid of another onslaught from maiden ladies.

"Come, Belle," said Glenville; "come, Belle, open your letter; we're all impatience. If you won't go, I will in your place."

"Do, my dear fellow. Take care you're not pounced down upon by a respectable papa for intentions, or called to account by a fierce brother with a stubbly beard," said Belle, lazily taking up the letter. As he did so, the melancholy indolence on his face changed to eagerness.

"The deuce! the Vane crest!"

"A note of invitation, probably!" suggested Gower.

"Would they send an invitation to Patty Greene's? I tell you it's addressed to L. C.," said Belle, disdainfully, opening the letter, leaving its giant deer couchant intact. "I thought it very likely; I expected it, indeed—poor little dear! I oughtn't to have let it out. Ain't you jealous, old fellows? Little darling! Perhaps I may be tricked into matrimony after all. I'd rather a presentiment that advertisement would come to something. There, you may all look at it, if you like."

It was a dainty sheet of scented cream-laid, stamped with the deer couchant, such as had brought us many an invitation down from Fern Chase, and on it was written, in delicate caligraphy:

"G. V. understands the meaning of the advertisement, and will meet L. C. at the entrance of Fern Wood, at eleven o'clock to-morrow morning."

There was a dead silence as we read it; then a tremendous buzz. Cheaply as we held women, I don't think there was one of us who wasn't surprised at Geraldine's doing any clandestine thing like this. He sat with a look of indolent triumph, curling his perfumed moustaches, and looking at the little autograph, which gave us evidence of what he often boasted—Geraldine Vane's regard,

"Let me look at your note," said Fairlie, stretching out his hand.

He soon returned it, with a brief, "Very complimentary indeed!"

When the men left, I chanced to be last, having mislaid my cigar-case. As I looked about for it, Fairlie addressed me in the same brief, stern tone between his teeth with which he spoke to Belle.

"Hardinge, you made this absurd bet with Courtenay, did you not? Is this note a hoax upon him?"

"Not that I know of—it doesn't look like it. You see there is the Vane crest, and the girl's own initials."

"Very true." He turned round to the window again, and leaned against it, looking out into the dawn, with a look upon his face that I was very sorry to see.

"But it is not like Geraldine," I began. "It may be a trick. Somebody may have stolen their paper and crest —it's possible. I tell you what I'll do to find out; I'll follow Belle to-morrow, and see who does meet him in Fern Wood."

"Do," said Fairlie, eagerly. Then he checked himself, and went on tapping an impatient tattoo on the shutter. "You see, I have known the family for years —known her when she was a little child. I should be sorry to think that one of them could be capable of such——"

Despite his self-command he could not finish his sentence. Geraldine was a great deal too dear to him to be treated in seeming carelessness, or spoken lightly of, however unwisely she might act. I found my cigar-case. His laconic "Good night!" told me he would rather be alone, so I closed the door and left him.

The morning was as sultry and as clear as a July day could be when Belle lounged down the street, looking the perfection of a gentleman, a trifle less bored and *blasé* than ordinary, *en route* to his appointment at Fern Wood (a sequestered part of the Vane estate), where trees and lilies of the valley grew wild, and where the girls were accustomed to go for pic-nics or sketching. As soon as he had turned a corner, Gower and I turned it too, and with perseverance worthy a better cause Tom and I followed Belle in and out and down the road which led to Fern Wood—a flat, dusty, stony two miles —on which, in the blazing noon of a hot midsummer day, nothing short of Satanic coercion, or love of Geraldine Vane, would have induced our beauty to immolate himself, and expose his delicate complexion.

"I bet you anything, Tom," said I, confidently, "that this is a hoax, like yesterday's. Geraldine will no more meet Belle there than all the Ordnance Office."

"Well, we shall see," responded Gower. "Somebody might get the note-paper from the bookseller, and the crest seal through the servants, but they'll hardly get Geraldine there bodily against her will."

We waited at the entrance of the wood, shrouded ourselves in the wild hawthorn hedges, while we could still see Belle—of course we did not mean to be near enough to overhear him—who paced up and down the green alleys under the firs and larches, rendered doubly dark by the evergreens, brambles, and honeysuckles,

which, ripened by the sun,
Forbade the sun to enter.

He paced up and down there a good ten minutes, prying about with his eye-glass, but unable to see very far in the tangled boughs, and heavy dusky light of the untrimmed wood. Then there was the flutter of something azure among the branches, and Gower gave vent to a low whistle of surprise.

"By George, Hardinge! there's Geraldine! Well! I didn't think she'd have done it. You see they're all alike if they get the opportunity."

It *was* Geraldine herself—it was her fluttering muslin, her abundant folds, her waving ribbons, her tiny sailor hat, and her little veil, and under the veil her face, with its delicate tinting, its pencilled eyebrows, and its undulating bright-coloured hair. There was no doubt about it; it was Geraldine. I vow I was as sorry to have to tell it to Fairlie as if I'd had to tell him she was dead, for I knew how it would cut him to the heart to know not only that she had given herself to his rival, but that his little playmate, whom he had thought truth, and honesty, and daylight itself, should have stooped to a clandestine interview, arranged through an advertisement! Their retreating figures were soon lost in the dim woodland, and Tom and I turned to retrace our steps.

"No doubt about it now, old fellow!" quoth Gower.

"No, confound her!" swore I.

"Confound her? *Et pourquoi?* Hasn't she a right to do what she likes?"

"Of course she has, the cursed little flirt; but she'd no earthly business to go making such love to Fairlie. It's a rascally shame, and I don't care if I tell her so myself."

"She'll only say you're in love with her too," was Gower's sensible response. "I'm not surprised myself. I always said she was an out-and-out coquette."

I met Fairlie coming out of his room as I went up to mine. He looked as men will look when they have not been in bed all night, and have watched the sun up with painful thoughts for their companions.

"You have been——" he began; then stopped short, unwilling or unable to put the question into words.

"After Belle? Yes. It is no hoax, Geraldine met him herself."

I did not relish telling him, and therefore told it, in all probability, bluntly, and blunderingly—tact, like talk, having, they say, been given to women. A spasm passed over his face. *"Herself!"* he echoed. Until then I do not think he had realised it as even possible.

"Yes, there was no doubt about it. What a wretched little coquette she must have been; she always seemed to make such game of Belle———"

But Fairlie, saying something about his gloves that he had left behind, had gone back into his room again before I had half done my sentence. When Belle came back, about half an hour afterwards, with an affected air of triumph, and for once in his life of languid sensations really well contented, Gower and I poured questions upon him, as, done up with the toil of his dusty walk, and horrified to find himself so low bred as to be hot, he kicked off his varnished boots, imbibed Seltzer, and fanned himself with a periodical before he could find breath to answer us.

"Was it Geraldine?"

"Of course it was Geraldine," he said, yawning.

"And will she marry you, Belle?"

"To be sure she will. I should like to see the woman that wouldn't," responded Belle, shutting his eyes and nestling down among the cushions. "And what's more, I've been fool enough to let her make me ask her. Give me some more sherry, Phil; a man wants support under such circumstances. The deuce if I'm not as hot as a ploughboy! It was very cruel of her to call a fellow out with the sun at the meridian; she might as well have chosen twilight. But, I say, you fellows, keep the secret, will you? she don't want her family to get wind

Madame la Marquise, etc.

of it, because they're bothering her to marry that old cove, Mount Trefoil, with his sixty years and his broad acres, and wouldn't let her take anybody else if they knew it; she's under age, you see."

"But how did she know you were L. C.?"

"Fairlie told her, and the dear little vain thing immediately thought it was an indirect proposal to herself, and answered it; of course I didn't undeceive her. She *raffoles* of me—it'll be almost too much of a good thing, I'm afraid. She's deuced prudish, too, much more than I should have thought *she*'d have been; but I vow she'd only let me kiss her hand, and that was gloved."

"I hate prudes," said Gower; "they've always much more devilry than the open-hearted ones. Videlicet— here's your young lady stiff enough only to give you her hand to kiss, and yet she'll lower herself to a clandestine correspondence and stolen interviews—a condescension I don't think I should admire in *my* wife."

"Love, my dear fellow, oversteps all—what dy'e call 'em—boundaries," said Belle, languidly. "What a bore! I shall never be able to wear this coat again, it's so ingrained with dust; little puss, why didn't she wait till it was cooler?"

"Did you fix your marriage-day?" asked Tom, rather contemptuously.

"Yes, I was very weak!" sighed Belle; "but you see she's uncommonly pretty, and there's Mount Trefoil and lots of men, and, I fancy, that dangerous fellow Fairlie, after her; so we hurried matters. We've been making love to one another all these three months, you know, and fixed it so soon as Thursday week. Of course she blushed, and sighed, and put her handkerchief to her eyes, and all the rest of it, *en règle;* but she consented, and I'm to be sacrificed. But not a word about it, my dear fellows! The Vanes are to be kept in profoundest darkness, and to lull suspicion, I'm not to go there scarcely at all until then, and when I do, she'll let me know when she will be out, and I'm to call on her mother then. She'll write to me, and put the letters in a hollow tree in the wood, where I'm to leave my answers, or, rather, send 'em; catch me going over that road again! Don't give me joy, old boys. I know I'm making a holocaust of myself, but deuce take me if I can help it—she is so deuced pretty!"

Fairlie was not at mess that night. Nobody knew where he was. I learnt, long months afterwards, that as soon as I had told him of Geraldine's identity, he, still thirsting to disbelieve, reluctant to condemn, catching at straws to save his idol from being shattered as men in love will do, had thrown himself across his horse and torn off to Fern Dell to see whether or no Geraldine was at home.

His heart beat faster and thicker as he entered the drawing-room than it had done before the lines of Ferozeshah, or in the giant semicircle at Sobraon; it stood still as in the far end of the room, lying back on a low chair, sat Geraldine, her gloves and sailor hat lying on her lap. She sprang up to welcome him with her old gay smile.

"Good God! that a child like that can be such an accomplished actress!" thought Fairlie, as he just touched her hand.

"Have you been out to-day?" he asked suddenly.

"You see I have."

"Prevarication is conviction," thought Fairlie, with a deadly chill over him.

"Where did you go, love?" asked mamma.

"To see Adela Ferrers; she is not well, you know, and I came home through part of the wood to gather some of the anemones; I don't mean anemones, they are over—lilies of the valley."

She spoke hurriedly, glancing at Fairlie all the time, who never took his iron gaze off her, though all the beauty and glory was draining away from his life with every succeeding proof that stared him in the face with its cruel evidence.

At that minute Lady Vane was called from the room to give some directions to her head gardener about some flowers, over which she was particularly choice, and Fairlie and Geraldine were left in dead silence, with only the ticking of the timepiece and the chirrup of the birds outside the open windows to break its heavy monotony.

Fairlie bent over a spaniel, rolling the dog backwards and forwards on the rug.

Geraldine stood on the rug, her head on one side, in her old pretty attitude of plaintiveness and defiance, the bright sunshine falling round her and playing on her gay dress and fair hair—a tableau lost upon the Colonel, who, though he had risen too, was playing sedulously with the dog.

"Colonel Fairlie, what is the matter with you? How unkind you are to-day!"

Fairlie was roused at last, disgusted that so young a girl could be so accomplished a liar and actress, sick at heart that he had been so deceived, mad with jealousy, and that devil in him sent courtesy flying to the winds.

"Pardon me, Miss Vane, you waste your coquetries on me. Unhappily, I know their value, and am not likely to be duped by them."

Geraldine's face flushed as deep a rose hue as the geraniums nodding their heads in at the windows.

"Coquetries?—duped? What do you mean?"

"You know well enough what. All I warn you is,

never try them again on me—never come near me any more with your innocent smiles and your lying lips, or, by Heaven, Geraldine Vane, I may say what I think of you in plainer words than suit the delicacy of a lady's ears!"

Geraldine's eyes flashed fire; from rose-hued as the geraniums she changed to the dead white of the Guelder roses beside them.

"Colonel Fairlie, you are mad, I think! If you only came here to insult me——"

"I had better leave? I agree with you. Good morning."

Wherewith Fairlie took his hat and whip, bowed himself out, and throwing himself across his horse, tore away many miles beyond Norwich, I should say, and rode into the stable-yard at twelve o'clock that night, his horse with every hair wringing and limb trembling at the headlong pace he had been ridden; such a midnight gallop as only Mazeppa, or a Border rider, or Turpin racing for his life, or a man vainly seeking to leave behind him some pursuing ghost of memory or passion, ever took before.

We saw little of him for the next few days. Luckily for him, he was employed to purchase several strings of Suffolk horses for the corps, and he rode about the country a good deal, and went over to Newmarket, and to the Bury horse fair, inspecting the cattle, glad, I dare say, of an excuse to get away.

"I feel nervous, terribly nervous; do give me the Seltzer and hock, Tom. They wonder at the fellows asking for beer before their execution. I don't; and if a fellow wants it to keep his spirits up before he's hanged, he may surely want it before he's married, for one's a swing and a crash, and it's all over and done most likely before you've time to know anything about it; but the other you walk into so deliberately, superintend the sacrifice of yourself, as it were, like that old cove Seneca; feel yourself rolling down-hill like Regulus, with all the horrid nails of the 'domesticities' pricking you in every corner; see all the sunshine of life, as poets have it, fading, sweetly but surely, from your grasp, and Death, *alias* the Matrimonial Black Cap, coming down ruthlessly on your devoted heads. I feel low—shockingly low. Pass me the Seltzer, Tom, do!"

So spake Geraldine's *sposo* that was to be, on the evening before his marriage-day, lying on his sofa in his Cashmere dressing-gown, his gold embroidered slippers, and his velvet smoking-cap, puffing largely at his meerschaum, and unbosoming his private sentiments and emotions to the (on this score) sufficiently sympathetic listeners, Gower and I.

"I don't pity you!" said Tom, contemptuously, who had as much disdain for a man who married as for one who bought gooseberry for champagne, or Cape for comet hock, and did not know the difference—"I don't pity you one bit. You've put the curb on yourself; you can't complain if you get driven where you don't like."

"But, my dear fellow, *can* one help it?" expostulated Belle, pathetically. "When a little winning, bewitching, attractive little animal like that takes you in hand, and traps you as you catch a pony, holding out a sieve of oats, and coaxing you, and so-ho-ing you till she's fairly got the bridle over your head, and the bit between your teeth, what is a man to do?"

"Remember that as soon as the bit *is* in your mouth, she'll never trouble herself to give you any oats, or so-ho you softly any more, but will take the whip hand of you, and not let you have the faintest phantom of a will of your own ever again," growled the misogamistic Tom.

"Catch a man's remembering while it's any use," was Belle's very true rejoinder. "After he's put his hand to a little bill, he'll remember it's a very green thing to do, but he don't often remember it before, I fancy. No, in things like this, one can't help oneself; one's time is come, and one goes down before fate. If anybody had told me that I should grow as spoony about any woman as I have about that little girl Geraldine, I'd have given 'em the lie direct; I would, indeed! But then she made such desperate love to me, took such a deuced fancy to me, you see; else, after all, the woman I might have chosen—— By George! I wonder what Lady Con, and the little Bosanquet, and poor Honoria, and all the rest of 'em will say?"

"What?" said Gower; "say 'Poor dear fellow!' to you, and 'Poor girl, I pity her!' to your wife. So you're going to elope with Miss Geraldine? A man's generally too ready to marry his daughters, to force a fellow to carry them off by stealth. Besides, as Bulwer says somewhere, '*Gentlemen* don't run away with the daughters of gentlemen.'"

"Pooh, nonsense! all's fair in love or war," returned Belle, going into the hock and Seltzer to keep up his spirits. "You see, she's afraid, her governor's mind being so set on old Mount Trefoil and his baron's coronet; they might offer some opposition, put it off till she was one-and-twenty, you know—and she's so distractedly fond of me, poor little thing, that she'd die under the probation, probably—and I'm sure I couldn't keep faithful to her for two mortal years. Besides, there's something amusing in eloping; the excitement of it keeps up one's spirits; whereas, if I were marched to church with so many mourners—I mean groomsmen—I should feel I was rehearsing my own obsequies like Charles V., and should funk it, ten to one I should. No! I like eloping: it gives the certain flavour of forbidden fruit, which many things, besides pure water, want to 'give them a relish.'"

"Let's see how's the thing to be managed?" asked Gower. "Beyond telling me I was to go with you, consigned ignominiously to the rumble, to witness the ceremony, I'm not very clear as to the programme."

"Why, as soon as it's dawn," responded Belle, with leisurely whiffs of his meerschaum, "I'm to take the carriage up to the gate at Fern Wood—this is what she tells me in her last note; she was coming to meet me, but just as she was dressed her mother took her to call on some people, and she had to resort to the old hollow tree. The deuce is in it, I think, to prevent our meeting; if it weren't for the letters and her maid we should have been horribly put to it for communication—I'm to take the carriage, as I say, and drive up there, where she and her maid will be waiting. We drive away, of course, catch the 8.15 train, and cut off to town, and get married at the Regeneration, Piccadilly, where a fellow I know very well will act the priestly Calcraft. The thing that bothers me most of all is getting up so early. I used to hate it so awfully when I was a young one at the college. I like to have my bath, and my coffee, and my paper leisurely, and saunter through my dressing, and get up when the day's *warmed* for me. Early parade's one of the crying cruelties of the service; I always turn in again after it, and regard it as a hideous nightmare. I vow I couldn't give a greater test of my devotion than by getting up at six o'clock to go after her—deuced horrible exertion! I'm quite certain that my linen won't be aired, nor my coffee fit to drink, nor Perkins with his eyes half

open, nor a quarter of his wits about him. Six o'clock!
By George! nothing should get me up at that unearthly
hour except my dear, divine, delicious little demon
Geraldine! But she's so deuced fond of me, one must
make sacrifices for such a little darling."

With which sublimely unselfish and heroic sentiment
the bridegroom-elect drank the last of his hock and Seltzer,
took his pipe out of his lips, flung his smoking-cap lazily
on to his Skye's head, who did not relish the attention,
and rose languidly to get into his undress in time for
mess.

As Belle had to get up so frightfully early in the
morning, he did not think it worth while to go to bed
at all, but asked us all to vingt-et-un in his room, where,
with the rattle of half-sovereigns and the flow of rumpunch, he kept up his courage before the impending doom
of matrimony. Belle was really in love with Geraldine,
but in love in his own particular way, and consoled himself for his destiny and her absence by what I dare say
seems to mademoiselle, fresh from her perusal of "Aurora
Leigh" or "Lucille," very material comforters indeed.
But, if truth were told, I am afraid mademoiselle would
find, save that from one or two fellows here and there,
who go in for love as they go in for pig-sticking or tiger-
hunting, with all their might and main, wagering even
their lives in the sport, the Auroras and Lucilles are very
apt to have their charms supplanted by the points of a
favourite, their absence made endurable by the aroma of
Turkish tobacco, and their last fond admonishing words,
spoken with such persuasive caresses under the moonlight
and the limes, against those "horrid cards, love," forgotten that very night under the glare of gas, while the
hands that lately held their own so tenderly, clasp well-

nigh with as much affection the unprecedented luck "two honours and five trumps!"

<small>Man's love is of man's life a thing apart.</small>

Byron was right; and if we go no deeper, how can it well be otherwise, when we have our stud, our pipe, our Pytchley, our Newmarket, our club, our coulisses, our Mabille, and our Epsom, and they—oh, Heaven help them!—have no distraction but a needle or a novel! The Fates forbid that our *agrémens* should be *less*, but I dare say, if they had a vote in it, they'd try to get a trifle *more*. So Belle put his "love apart," to keep (or to rust, whichever you please) till six A.M. that morning, when, having by dint of extreme physical exertion got himself dressed, saw his valet pack his things with the keenest anxiety relative to the immaculate folding of his coats and the safe repose of his shirts, and at last was ready to go and fetch the bride his line in the *Daily* had procured him.

As Belle went down the stairs with Gower, who should come too, with his gun in his hand, his cap over his eyes, and a pointer following close at his heels, but Fairlie, going out to shoot over a friend's manor.

Of course he knew that Belle had asked for and obtained leave for a couple of months, but he had never heard for what purpose; and possibly, as he saw him at such an unusual hour, going out, not in his usual travelling guise of a wide-awake and a Maude, but with a delicate lavender tie and a toilet of the most unexceptionable art, the purport of his journey flashed fully on his mind, for his face grew as fixed and unreadable as if he had had on the iron mask. Belle, guessing as he did that Fairlie would not have disliked to have been in his place that morning, was both too kind-hearted and infinitely too much of a gentleman to hint at his own triumph. He laughed, and nodded a good morning.

"Off early, you see, Fairlie; going to make the most of my leave. 'Tisn't very often we can get one: our corps is deuced stiff and strict compared to the Guards and the Cavalry."

"At least our strictness keeps us from such disgraceful scenes as some of the other regiments have shown up of late," answered Fairlie between his teeth.

"Ah! well, perhaps so; still, strictness ain't pleasant, you know, when one's the victim."

"Certainly not."

"And, therefore, we should never be hard upon others."

"I perfectly agree with you."

"There's a good fellow. Well, I must be off; I've no time for philosophising. Good-bye, Colonel."

"Good-bye—a safe journey."

But I noticed that he held the dog's collar in one hand and the gun in the other, so as to have an excuse for not offering that *poignée de main* which ought to be as sure a type of friendship, and as safe a guarantee for good faith, as the Bedouin Arab's salt.

Belle nodded him a farewell, and lounged down the steps and into the carriage, just as Fairlie's man brought his mare round.

Fairlie turned on to me with unusual fierceness, for generally he was very calm, and gentle, and impassive in manner.

"Where is he gone?"

I could not help but tell him, reluctant though I was, for I guessed pretty well what it would cost him to hear it. He did not say one word while I told him, but bent over Marquis, drawing the dog's leash tighter, so that I might not see his face, and without a sign or a reply he was out of the barracks, across his mare's back, and rushing away at a mad gallop, as if he would leave thought, and memory, and the curse of love for a worthless woman behind him for ever.

His man stood looking at the gun Fairlie had thrown to him with a puzzled expression.

"Is the Colonel gone mad?" I heard him say to himself. "The devil's in it, I think. He used to treat his things a little carefuller than this. As I live, he's been and gone and broke the trigger!"

The devil wasn't in it, but a woman *was*, an individual that causes as much mischief as any Asmodeus, Belphégor, or Mephistopheles. Some fair unknown correspondents assured me the other day, in a letter, that my satire on women was "a monstrous libel." All I can say is, that if it *be* a libel, it is like many a one for which one pays the highest, and which sounds the blackest—a libel that is *true!*

While his rival rode away as recklessly as though he was riding for his life, the gallant bridegroom—as the *Court Circular* would have it—rolled on his way to Fern Wood, while Gower, very amiably occupying the rumble, smoked, and bore his position philosophically, comforted by the recollection that Geraldine's French maid was an uncommonly good-looking, coquettish little person.

They rolled on, and speedily the postilion pulled up, according to order, before the white five-bar gate, its paint blistering in the hot summer dawn, and the great fern-leaves and long grass clinging up round its posts, still damp with the six o'clock dew. Five minutes passed —ten minutes—a quarter of an hour. Poor Belle got impatient. Twenty minutes—five-and-twenty—thirty. Belle couldn't stand it. He began to pace up and down the turf, soiling his boots frightfully with the long wet grass, and rejecting all Tom's offers of consolation and a cigar-case.

"Confound it!" cried poor Belle, piteously, "I thought women were always ready to marry. I know, when I went to turn off Lacquers of the Rifles at St. George's, his bride had been waiting for him half an hour, and was in an awful state of mind, and all the other brides as well, for you know they always marry first the girl that gets there first, and all the other poor wretches were kept on tenterhooks too. Lacquers had lost the ring, and found it in his waistcoat after all! I say, Tom, devil take it, where *can* she be? It's forty minutes, as I live. We shall lose the train, you know. She's never prevented coming, surely. I think she'd let me hear, don't you? She could send Justine to me if she couldn't come by any wretched chance. Good Heavens, Tom, what shall I do?"

"Wait, and don't worry," was Tom's laconic and common-sense advice; about the most irritating probably to a lover's feelings that could pretty well be imagined. Belle swore at him in stronger terms than he generally exerted himself to use, but was pulled up in the middle of them by the sight of Geraldine and Justine, followed by a boy bearing his bride's dainty trunks.

On came Geraldine in a travelling-dress: Justine following after her, with a brilliant smile, that showed all her white teeth, at "Monsieur Torm," for whom she had a very tender friendship, consolidated by certain half-sovereigns and French phrases whispered by Gower after his dinners at Fern Chase.

Belle met Geraldine with all that tender *empressement* which he knew well how to put into his slightest actions; but the young lady seemed already almost to have begun repenting her hasty step. She hung her head down, she held a handkerchief to her bright eyes, and to Belle's tenderest and most ecstatic whispers she only answered by a convulsive pressure of the arm, into which he had drawn her left hand, and a half-smothered sob from her heart's depths.

Belle thought it all natural enough under the circumstances. He knew women always made a point of impressing upon you that they are making a frightful sacrifice for your good when they condescend to accept you, and he whispered what tender consolation occurred to him as best fitted for the occasion, thanked her, of course, for all the rapture, &c. &c., assured her of his life-long devotion—you know the style—and lifted her into the carriage, Geraldine only responding with broken sighs and stifled sobs.

The boxes were soon beside Belle's valises, Justine soon beside Gower, the postilion cracked his whip over his outsider, Perkins refolded his arms, and the carriage rolled down the lane.

Gower was very well contented with his seat in the rumble. Justine was a very dainty little Frenchwoman, with the smoothest hair and the whitest teeth in the world, and she and "Monsieur Torm" were eminently good friends, as I have told you, though to-day she was very coquettish and wilful, and laughed à propos de bottes at Gower, say what Chaumière compliments he might.

"Ma chère et charmante petite," expostulated Tom, "tes moues mutines sont ravissantes, mais je t'avoue que je préfère tes——"

"Tais-toi, bécasse!" cried Justine, giving him a blow with her parasol, and going off into what she would have called éclats de rire.

"Mais écoute-moi, Justine," whispered Tom, piqued

by her perversity; "je raffole de toi! jet t'adore, sur ma parole! je——Hallo! what the devil's the matter? Good gracious! Deuce take it!"

Well might Tom call on his Satanic Majesty to explain what met his eyes as he gave vent to all three ejaculations and maledictions. No less a sight than the carriage door flying violently open, Belle descending with a violent impetus, his face crimson, and his hat in his hand, clearing the hedge at a bound, plunging up to his ankles in mud on the other side of it, and starting across country at the top of his speed, rushing frantically straight over the heavy grass-land as if he had just escaped from Hanwell, and the whole hue and cry of keepers and policemen was let loose at his heels.

"Good Heavens! By Jove! Belle, Belle, I say, stop! Are you mad? What's happened? What's the row? I say —the devil!"

But to his incoherent but very natural exclamations poor Tom received no answer. Justine was screaming with laughter, the postilion was staring, Perkins swearing, Belle, flying across the country at express speed, rapidly diminishing into a small black dot in the green landscape, while from inside the carriage, from Geraldine, from the deserted bride, peals of laughter, long, loud, and uproarious, rang out in the summer stillness of the early morning.

"By Jupiter! but this is most extraordinary. The deuce is in it. Are they both gone stark staring mad?" asked Tom of his Cuba, or the blackbirds, or the hedgecutter afar off, or anything or anybody that might turn out so amiable as to solve his problem for him.

No reply being given him, however, Tom could stand it no longer. Down he sprang, jerked the door open again, and put his head into the carriage.

"Hallo, old boy, done green, eh? Pity 'tisn't the 1st of April!" cried Geraldine, with renewed screams of mirth from the interior.

"Eh? What? What did you say, Miss Vane?" ejaculated Gower, fairly staggered by this extraordinary answer of a young girl, a lady, and a forsaken bride.

"What did I say, my dear fellow? Why, that you're done most preciously, and that I fancy it'll be a deuced long time before your delectable friend tries his hand at matrimony again, that's all. Done! oh, by George, he *is* done, and no mistake. Look at me, sir, ain't I a charming bride?"

With which eloquent language, Geraldine took off her hat, pulled down some false braids, pushed her hair off her forehead, shook her head like a water-dog after a bath, and grinned in Gower's astonished eyes—*not* Geraldine, but her twin-brother, Pretty Face!

"Do you know me now, old boy?" asked the Etonian, with demoniacal delight—"do you know me now? Haven't I chiselled him—haven't I tricked him—haven't I done him as green as young gooseberries, and as brown as that bag? Do you fancy he'll boast of his conquests again, or advertise for another wife? So you didn't know how I got Cary Clements, of the Ten Bells, to write the letters for me? and Justine to dress me in Geraldine's things? You know they always did say they couldn't tell her from me; I've proved it now, eh?—rather! Oh, by George, I never had a better luck! and not a creature guesses it, not a soul, save Justine, Nell, and I! By Jupiter, Gower, if you'd heard that unlucky Belle go on swearing devotion interminable, and enough love to stock all Mudie's novels! But I never dare let him kiss me, though my beard *is* down, confound it! Oh! what jolly fun it's been, Gower, no words can tell. I always said he shouldn't marry her; he'll hardly try to do it now, I fancy! What a lark it's been! I couldn't have done it, you know, without that spicy little French girl—she did my hair, and got up my crinoline, and stole Geraldine's dress, and tricked me up altogether, and carried my notes to the hollow oak, and took all my messages to Belle. Oh, Jupiter! what fun it's been! If Belle isn't gone clean out of his senses, it's very odd to me. When he was going to kiss me, and whispered, 'My dearest, my darling, my wife!' I just took off my hat and grinned in his face, and said, 'Ain't this a glorious go?' Oh! by George, Gower, I think the fun will kill me!"

And the wicked little dog of an Etonian sank back among the carriage cushions stifled with his laughter. Gower staggered backwards against a roadside tree, and stood there with his lips parted and his eyes wide open, bewildered, more than that cool hand had ever been in all his days, by the extraordinary finish of poor Belle's luckless wooing; the postilion rolled off his saddle in cachinnatory fits at the little monkey's narrative; Perkins, like a soldier as he was, utterly impassive to all surrounding circumstances, shouldered a valise and dashed at quick march after his luckless master; Justine clapped her plump French-gloved fingers with a million ma Fois! and mon Dieus! and O Ciels! and far away in the grey distance sped the retreating figure of poor Belle, with the license in one pocket and the wedding-ring in the other, flying, as if his life depended on it, from the shame, and the misery, and the horror of that awful sell, drawn on his luckless head by that ill-fated line in the *Daily*.

While Belle drove to his hapless wooing, Fairlie galloped on and on. Where he went he neither knew nor cared. He had ridden heedlessly along, and the grey, left to her own devices, had taken the road to which her head for the last four months had been so often turned —the road leading to Fern Chase,—and about a mile from the Vane estate lost her left hind shoe, and came to a dead stop of her own accord, after having been ridden for a couple of hours as hard as if she had been at the Grand Military. Fairlie threw himself off the saddle, and, leaving the bridle loose on the mare's neck, who he knew would not stray a foot away from him, he flung himself on the grass, under the cool morning shadows of the roadside trees, no sound in the quiet country round him breaking in on his weary thoughts, till the musical ring of a pony's hoofs came pattering down the lane. He never heard it, however, nor looked up, till the quick trot slackened and then stopped beside him.

"Colonel Fairlie!"

"Good Heavens! Geraldine!"

"Well," she said, with tears in her eyes and petulant anger in her voice, "so you have never had the grace to come and apologise for insulting me as you did last week?"

"For mercy's sake do not trifle with me."

"Trifle! No, indeed!" interrupted the young lady. "Your behaviour was no trifle, and it will be a very long time before I forgive it, if ever I do."

"Stay—wait a moment."

"How can you ask me, when, five days ago, you bid me never come near you with my cursed coquetries again?" asked Geraldine, trying, and vainly, to get the bridle out of his grasp.

"God forgive me! I did not know what I said. What I had heard was enough to madden a colder man than I. Is it untrue?"

"Is what untrue?"

"You know well enough. Answer me, is it true or not?"

"How can I tell what you mean? You talk in enigmas. Let me go."

"I will never let you go till you have answered me."

"How can I answer you if I don't know what you mean?" retorted Geraldine, half laughing.

"Do not jest. Tell me, yes or no, are you going to marry that cursed fool?"

"What 'cursed fool'? Your language is not elegant, Colonel Fairlie!" said Geraldine, with demure mischief.

"Belle! Would you have met him? Did you intend to elope with him?"

Geraldine's eyes, always large enough, grew larger, and a darker blue still, in extremest astonishment.

"Belle!—elope with him? What, are you dreaming? Are you mad?"

"Almost," said Fairlie, recklessly. "Have you misled him, then—tricked him? Do you care nothing for him? Answer me, for Heaven's sake, Geraldine!"

"I know nothing of what you are talking!" said Geraldine, with her surprised eyes wide open still. "Oblige me by leaving my pony's head. I shall be too late home."

"You never answered his advertisement, then?"

"The very question insults me! Let my pony go."

"You never met him in Fern Wood—never engaged yourself to him—never corresponded with him?"

"Colonel Fairlie, you have no earthly right to put such questions to me," interrupted Geraldine, with her hot geranium colour in her cheeks and her eyes flashing fire. "I honour the report, whoever circulated it, far more than it deserves, by condescending to contradict it. Have the kindness to unhand my pony, and allow me to continue my ride."

"You shall *not* go," said Fairlie, as passionately as she, "till you have answered me one more question: Can you, will you ever forgive me?"

"No," said Geraldine, with an impatient shake of her head, but a smile nevertheless under the shadow of her hat.

"Not if you know it was jealousy of him which maddened me, love for you which made me speak such unpardonable words to you?—not if I tell you how perfect was the tale I was told, so that there was no link wanting, no room for doubt or hope?—not if I tell you what tortures I had endured in losing you—what bitter punishment I have already borne in crediting the report that you were secretly engaged to my rival—would you not forgive me then?"

"No," whispered the young lady perversely, but smiling still, the geraniums brighter in her cheeks, and her eyes fixed on the bridle.

Fairlie dropped the reins, let go her hand, and left her free to ride, if she would, away from him.

"Will you leave me, Geraldine? Not for this morning only, remember, nor for to-day, nor for this year, but —for ever?"

"No!" It was a very different "No" this time.

"Will you forgive me, then, my darling?"

Her fingers clasped his hand closely, and Geraldine looked at him under her hat; her eyes, so like an April day, with their tears, and their tender and mischievous smile, were so irresistibly provocative that Fairlie took his pardon for granted, and thanked her in the way that seemed to him at once most eloquent and most satisfactory.

If you wish to know what became of Belle, he fled across the country to the railway station, and spent his leave Heaven knows where—in sackcloth and ashes, I suppose—meditating on his frightful sell. *We* saw nothing more of him; he could hardly show in Norwich again with all his laurels tumbled in the dust, and his trophies of conquest laughing-stocks for all the troop. He exchanged into the Z battery going out to India, and I never saw or heard of him till a year or two ago, when he landed at Portsmouth, a much wiser and pleasanter man. The lesson, joined to the late campaign under Sir Colin, had done him a vast amount of good; he had lost his conceit, his vanity, his affectation, and was what Nature meant him to be—a sensible, good-hearted fellow. As luck would have it, Pretty Face, who had joined the Eleventh, was there too, and Fairlie and his wife as well, and Belle had the good sense to laugh it over with them, assuring Geraldine, however, that no one had eclipsed the G. V. whom he had once hoped had answered his memorable advertisement. He has grown wiser, and makes a jest of it now; it may be a sore point still, I cannot say—nobody sees it; but, whether or no, in the old city of Norwich, and in our corps, from Cadets to Colonels, nobody forgets THE LINE IN THE "DAILY;" WHO DID IT, AND WHO WAS DONE BY IT.

FITZ'S ELECTION;

OR,

BLUE AND YELLOW.

THERE was to be an Election. The Lords and Commons hadn't hit it; one hon. gentleman had blackguarded another hon. gentleman; the big schoolboys of St. Stephen's had thrown stones at each other, and as they all lived in glass houses, the practice was dangerous; the session had not benefited the country—so far as the country could see—one bit; the *Times* opined that the nation was going to the dogs, and suggested that parliament should dissolve. The *Times* is Cæsar now-a-days, so parliament obeyed, broke itself up, and appealed to the country—*i. e.* set the Carlton and Reform counting up their money, the lawyers quarrelling for all the dirty work, and the 10*l.* voters looking out for XXX and fivers; and the country responded promptly, loving a tussle as dearly as a beagle, by sharpening its bowie-knives for the contest, wondering who would buy its votes the highest, and hunting up its stock of Blue and Yellow banners.

"So the governor wants me to stand for Cantitborough. I'm not sure I won't. I'm confoundedly tired of this life year after year. Perhaps the election will give me a little fun. What do you say?" began my cousin Fitz one morning, lying reading the *Field* and drinking strong coffee with brandy in it by way of breakfast, when I called on him in his chambers in the Albany. "I want something to do. The town's so confoundedly Tory, there'll be no end of opposition. We shall set them all together by the ears, the Blues and Yellows won't speak for years, and I shall be written up in the *Cantilborough Post* as a Leveller, a Socialist, a Sceptic, a Democrat, and all the delicious names that the slow coaches call anybody who's a little wide awake and original. Yes, I think I'll put up for it."

"Who contests it with you?"

"There are three of 'em," answered Fitz; "one an old Indian, Tory out-and-out, worth a million, and consequently worshipped by his neighbours, at whom, I believe, when heated with overmuch curry and cognac, he swears more than is customary in these polite times. The next is a boy, just one-and-twenty—you know him, Cockadoodle's son. He was in petticoats the other day, but, as his father's an Earl, he's to be transplanted from the nursery to the Commons without any intermediate education. The other is that sneaking thing, that compromise between right and wrong, that hybrid animal, a Liberal Conservative. You know him, too, Le Hoop Smith; that creature who made his tin by wool, or something horrid, and bought Foxley, and set up as the patriarchal father of his people, in the new-fangled country squire style, with improved drainage, model cottages, prize labourers, and all the rest of it. Two of us must go to the wall. I shall like the fight, and you'll do the chief of the canvassing, mind. All I engage to do is to kiss any pretty women there may be in the place."

"You're very kind, taking the fun and giving me the work. I suppose you know you'll have to shake hands with every one of the Great Unwashed?"

"Brutes!" rejoined Fitz, who was popularly supposed to be a Socialist and Democrat; "I'll see them all hanged first!"

"And you must joke with the butchers, and have a glass with the coalheavers, and make friends with the sweeps."

"I'd sooner lose my election," rejoined the Republican.

"And you must kiss a baby or two."

The horror, loathing, and disgust expressed on Fitz's face were as good to see as "Box and Cox."

"Not to get the premiership! Faugh! I'd lose my seat fifty times over. Of all the loathsome ideas! If you've nothing pleasanter to suggest, you'd better get out of the room, if you please."

"Thank you. Don't you remember the sensation Mr. Samuel Slumkey produced by like caresses in Pickwick?"

"Pickwick go to the devil, and you too! I shall do nothing more than give them my tin, as everything is bought and sold now-a-days, and tell them I shall vote for free trade, cheap divorces, marriage with whoever one likes, religious toleration—in fact, for liberty, for everything and everybody. Then, if they don't like my opinions, they can have the Liberal Conservative instead. *I* shan't care two straws."

"Admirably philosophic! It's lucky you're not going to try the county. The farmers and clericals wouldn't have you at any price. You cut at the root of their monopoly—corn-laws and tithes, church-rates and protection. However, the more fight the more fun. We shall be like a couple of terriers in a barn full of rats. When shall we go down?"

"Tuesday. I shall go to Hollywood, it's a snug little

box, and so much closer the town than the governor's; and as he's so ill, he won't want the bother of us. I mean to have little Beauclerc as my agent; he was with me at Eton, and is the sharpest dog in Lincoln's Inn. That's enough business for to-day. I'm now going to Tattersall's to look at a roan filly to run tandem with Rumpunch; then I'm to meet my Lady Frisette in the Square Gardens at two; and at seven dine at the Castle with Grouse and some other men. So ring the bell for Soames, and order the cab round, there's a good boy."

My cousin (Randolph Fitzhardinge, according to the register and his visiting cards, but to us and to everybody briefly Fitz) is a fine, tall, handsome fellow, a trifle bronzed, and more than a trifle blasé, aquiline features, a devil-may-care expression, and a figure not beat in the Guards. He has been amusing himself about in the world ever since he left Christ Church, ten years ago, and as he will come into 12,000l. a year whenever his father leaves him to reign in his stead, has not thought himself necessitated to do more than live in the Albany, hunt with the Pytchley, lounge in the "bay-window," habituate the coulisses, and employ all the other ingenious methods for killing time invented by men about town. He is a good old fellow; the best oar in the Blue-Jersey B. C., the firmest seat and the lightest hand in the county, as good a batsman as any in the Zingari Eleven (and these cover a multitude of sins), the cleverest sailor in the whole R. V. Y. Squadron, quite able to be his own captain were he not too lazy to so far exert himself, and, moreover, is as clear-headed, generoushearted, and high-spirited a man as any on earth.

Tuesday came, and Fitz (leaving Lady Frisette dissolved in tears in her boudoir, which tears, no doubt, were dried as soon as his back was turned, as being no longer necessary, and destructive to rouge and beauty), with Beauclerc and myself—and Rumpunch and the new filly in a horse-box—put himself in the express for Pottle-shire.

We had a carriage to ourselves, and of course, as soon as we were out of Paddington, took out our pipes and began to enjoy a quiet smoke.

"I do wish," began Fitz, opening the window and taking off his cap, for it was a hot June afternoon, "they'd keep a carriage, as they do in Venice, for the muffs that can't stand the sweet odours of regalia, and not sacrifice us by boxing us up without a weed for four, six, perhaps twelve hours, or else making us pay 5*l.* for other people's olfactory fancies. I wonder somebody don't take it up. They write a lot of nonsense about this nuisance and that evil, that they're great idiots to notice at all; but if they would write up the crying injustice to smokers on British railways, there'd be something like a case—the Woolwich flogging's nothing to it."*

"Wait till we've got the election, and then send a letter to the *Times* about it, signed 'M.P.,' or a 'Lover of Justice,'" said Beauclerc, the barrister, a cute little fellow, fast as a telegraph, and sharp as a ferret's bite.

"I'll get up a petition rather, signed by all smokers, and addressed to all the directors. I think we're pretty safe for to-day. I don't fancy the express stops at more than a couple of stations between this and Cantitborough so we are not likely to have any women to bore us. I detest travelling with women," said Fitz, looking out of

---

* This has been done since Fitz suggested it. But the smokers' grievance is little abated. Perhaps ladies fear smoking-carriages like smoking-rooms will be too often preferred to their fair selves, and they will have to travel from Dan to Beersheba in miserable solitude !

the window as if he dreaded an advent of feminines along the telegraph wires. "You have to put out your pipe, offer them your *Punch*, and squeeze into nothing to make room for their skirts. Let's look at the Bradshaw. No! we only stop twice: thought so. It will certainly be odd if we can't keep the carriage to ourselves."

With which unchivalrous sentiment Fitz poked up his pipe, cut the paper with his ticket, and settled himself comfortably. Twenty minutes after, the engine gave a shriek, which woke him out of his serenity.

"Here's Bottleston, confound it!" cried Fitz. "I know the place—there's never anybody but a farmer or two for the second class. No fear of crinoline out of these wilds."

Fitz made rather too sure. As we hissed, and whistled, and panted, and puffed into the station, what should we see on the platform but six women—absolutely six— talking and laughing together, with a maid and a lot of luggage cased up, after the custom of females, in brown holland, as if the boxes had put on smock-frocks by mistake. Fitz swore mildly, puffed an enormous cloud to frighten them, and leaned forward to show as if the carriage was full. Not a bit of use was it—with the instinctive obstinacy of her sex, up to our very door came one of the fatal half dozen.

"There's room in here, Timbs," she said, with the supremest tranquillity, motioning to her maid to put in the hundred things—bouquet, dressing-case, book, travelling-bag, and Heaven knows what, with which young ladies will cumber themselves on a journey of half an hour.

"The perfume is extremely like that of a tobacco-shop, where there is license to smoke on the premises," whispered the intruder to one of her companions, with a significant glance at us.

The whistle screamed—the young ladies bid each other good-bye with frantic haste and great enthusiasm—the train started, throwing the maid into Beau's arms, who (as she was thirty and red-haired) was not grateful for the accident, and her mistress seated herself opposite Fitz and began to pay great attention to a poodle imprisoned in a basket, and very prone to rebel against his incarceration.

"That little brute will yap all the way, I suppose?" muttered Fitz, looking supremely haughty and stiltified.

The dog's owner glanced up quickly. "Dauphin never annoys any one."

Fitz, cool as he was, looked caught, bent his head, and putting his pipe in his pocket with a sigh, stuck his glass in his eye and calmly criticised the young lady. She was decidedly good style, with large bright hazel eyes and hair to match, beautifully dressed, too, in black laces and dark azure silks. She was pretty enough to console Beau for the loss of his smoke, and even Fitz thawed a little, and actually went the length of offering her (with his grandest air, though) the *Saturday* he was reading. After a time he dropped a monosyllable or two about the weather; she was ready enough to talk—I hate that "silent system" of John Bull and his daughters—and in half an hour Fitz had examined and admired the poodle, and was forgetting his lost pipe in chatting with the poodle's mistress, when he somehow or other got upon the general election.

"We are all excitement," laughed the young lady. "It is quite delightful to have anything to stir up this unhappy county. I have only lived in it six months, but I am sure it is the dullest place in the world—the North Pole couldn't be worse."

"Is it indeed?" said Fitz. "Pray can you tell me who are the candidates?"

"General Salter, Mr. Fitzhardinge, Lord Verdant, and a Mr. Smith—Le Hoop Smith, I mean; I beg his pardon!"

"May I ask whom you favour with your good wishes?"

"They are none of them worth much, I fancy," she answered. "Mr. Fitzhardinge, I understand, is the only clever one; but everybody says he is good for nothing."

"Not exactly the man to be a member, then," observed Fitz, gravely, stroking the poodle. "What is said against him?"

"I don't know. They call him extravagant, sceptic, socialist, republican—in fact, there is no name they don't give him. I think he would do the Shire good for that very reason; it wants something original."

"Then you are a Radical," smiled Fitz.

She smiled too.

"It is treason for me to say so; we are all Blue à outrance. Ah! here is Cantitborough."

It *was* Cantitborough; that neat, clean, quiet, antiquated town, that always puts me in mind of an old maid dressed for a party; that slowest and dreariest of boroughs, where the streets are as full of grass as an acre of pasture-land, and the inhabitants are driven to ring their own door-bells lest they should rust from disuse.

The train stopped, and Fitz looked as disgusted at losing his travelling companion as he had done at her first appearance, and stared with "Who the devil are you?" plainly written on his face, at a young fellow who met her on the platform. Fitz was before him, though, in handing her and the poodle out, and went to look after her luggage, for motives of his own, as you may guess. He was very graciously thanked for his trouble, had a pretty bow to repay him, and saw the poodle and its mistress off with her unknown cavalier (a brother, probably, from the don't carish way that he met her) before he got on a dog-cart and tooled us down the road to Hollywood, a snug little box two miles from Cantitborough, left him by Providence, impersonated by a godfather, with eight or nine hundred a year.

"Of course you improved the occasion, Fitz, and saw the name on the boxes?" said Beau, as we drove along.

"Of course. It's Barnardiston. I never heard of it in the county, did you, Fan? She ought to be a lady, by her style and her voice; what a touchstone of birth voice is! I wonder who that young fool was who met her?"

"Why of necessity a fool because he chanced to be in your way?" laughed Beau. "He was a Cantab, I guess, by his cut; Cambridge is always stamped on those little straw hats and fast coats, as Balmoral boots indicate a strong-minded young woman, earrings out of their bonnets, girls that want one to look at 'em, Quaker colours and sunshades, girls who can't go in for the attractive line, so have sought refuge in the district visiting. Bless your heart, I always know a woman by her dress."

"What do you say to Dauphin's owner, then?"

"Possibly coquettish; fast enough to be pleasant; not fast enough to be bold; good taste, but not a notion of economy; knows she's pretty feet, and is too wise to disfigure them," promptly responded little Beau.

"Bravo!" said Fitz, "that's just my style. We'll fish the girl up, and show her that if I'm 'good for nothing' in all the other capacities of life, I'm first-rate at a flirtation; can't live without one, indeed, and I don't see why one should try, since, as the women are never easy but when we're making love to them, it would be a want of charity not to oblige them. Here we are. By Jove! I hope they'll have iced the wine properly."

"Soames," said Fitz to his man, when he had discussed the champagne, which *was* iced as cold as a "wallflower's" answer when you ask if she has enjoyed her ball—"Soames, go over this evening to Cantitborough, and find out for me if there are any people called Barnardiston living anywhere there, and bring me word all about them."

"Certainly, sir."

And that night, when we were smoking out on the lawn, Soames, who had often sped on like errands, made his report. There was a Barnardiston *père*, a gentleman of independent fortune, living at the Larches; a Barnardiston *mère*, over whom he tyrannised greatly; a son, who was at John's; two small boys, and two daughters, one, Glencora, who was engaged to the perpetual curate of St. Hildebrande's, and one, Caroline, who, as far as Soames could hear, was not engaged to anybody at all.

"Now, by George!" said Fitz, puffing his regalia in the moon's face, "Dauphin's mistress is a vast lot too good for that pursy little Low Church fellow at St. Hildebrande's. I wonder if it *is* she? Glencora sounds more like her than Caroline."

"Calm your mind, old fellow," said Beau; "our beauty isn't engaged to a parson, take my word for it. I always know the betrothed of the Church at a glance. They're getting in training to take interest in the distribution of flannel petticoats and brown-papered tracts; they cast their eyes away from good-looking fellows, for fear they should be tempted to compare blue ties with white chokers; they wear already the Lady Bountiful head of the parish air; they try to inflate themselves with big talk on the duties of a clergyman's wife, but in their secret souls are already weighed down by the dreadful decree that 'deacons' wives must be grave, not slanderous; 'sober, faithful in all things;' as if women would not just as soon be put in Newgate for life as denied their natural food—scandal and flirtation. No! take comfort, Fitz, your love of the railway carriage is no parson's fiancée, I'll swear."

Upon my honour I never knew a funnier contrast in my life than the candidates for the borough; and when I saw them all four on the Market Hill, I never laughed more at old Buckstone. There was first, of course, little Verdant, long, lanky, and meek-looking, like all the Cockadoodles, sitting forward on his horse's neck, as if he were afraid of tumbling off. There was his brother Conservative, Le Hoop Smith, bland, sweet smiling, and for all the world like a tabby cat on its best behaviour, in a gorgeous turnout, with his arms, fished up by the Heralds'-office, blazoned on the panels as big as a signpost. Then, on a fat, white shooting pony was Salter, the old fellow of the H.E.I.C.S., as round as a pumpkin and as yellow as a buttercup, who'd have thought nothing of lashing the independent electors as he'd flogged his Sepoys, and who, not being able to do that, swore at them vigorously; and then, last of all, was Fitz, haughty, dashing, "*distingué*" (as the shop people say of a 2s. 6d. cotton print), and sitting down on his thorough-bred as if they were both cast together in bronze. There was no doubt of Verdant's coming in; the fact of his being the son of the only live Earl near Cantitborough secured *that*. The tradesmen were for Salter, because he eat much and paid well. The clergy and professions were for Le Hoop Smith, because he was such a pious, poetical, spotless creature; and for Fitz——Well, poor Fitz had the women, and one or two enlightened individuals, on his side. A very small-hap'orth of bread to a whole ocean of sack were all the constituents he seemed likely to gain, though Beau and other agents set to work as hard as steam-engines, and I canvassed perseveringly:—the Socialist had a profound contempt in practice for the Canaille, whom in theory he dignified into the People; and despite his opinion that all men were equal, was not at all prepared to suffer familiarity from his unwashed brethren. If you have ever had the ill luck, as I have had, to be in a small spiteful country town in election time, when everybody is spitting and swearing like cats on the tiles, you can fancy what Cantitborough was at this period of its history. We stirred its utmost depths. The best hotel was a Blue committee-room; its second best was a Yellow committee-room. Bigwigs talked loud of their principles; *gamins* flaunted rag flags in the gutters; mysterious strangers haunted its tap-rooms. Mr. Brown cut Mr. Green because he was Yellow. Mrs. A. dropped her bosom friend, Mrs. B., because she was Blue. The Town Council was divided against itself, and, consequently, couldn't stand straight on its legs (a charge, by the way, often brought against its members individually). Mary, the kitchen-maid, would no longer "walk along" with James the milk-man, because he was all for that "hugly Smith." Cobblin, the shoemaker, was surprised by seeing two fivers lying snug in the heel of a Wellington; and Chalice, the rector, was startled by a gentle hint that the Deanery of Turtle-fat might be vacant.

"Who do you think I'm going to solicit the vote from this morning?" said Fitz at breakfast two or three mornings after.

"Pottler, of the Three Kings, I hope," said Beau, helping himself to a devil, "if you do what you ought."

"The Three Kings be shot!" said Fitz. "The barmaid there is as ugly as sin, and forty, I'm certain. He's not an eye to trade to keep her; a pretty face at a bar disposes of numberless shilling glasses."

"Old Hops, then; and *do* remember to tell him his beer is better than Bass's," said Beau, whose refractory client gave him no end of trouble.

"What! that stuff, full of jack? Oh! confound it, I can't humbug like that; 'tisn't in my line, especially with those riffraff."

"The devil take your pride!" retorted Beau. "How do you expect to get along with your election, when it's such a piece of work to make you shake hands with even a respectable butcher or——"

"Pah! hold your tongue!" cried the Radical, glancing at his own white fingers. "I like the hydra-headed to have all the bread he wants, but I can't bear touching his dirty hands. I'm sure I make love to the women, Beau, though, with most exemplary perseverance——"

"Rather too perseveringly," growled the exigeant Beau. "I don't think it tells well with the fathers, and I'm quite sure it influences husbands the wrong way. You're unexceptionable with your equals, but Rumpunch himself isn't more unmanageable than you are with your inferiors. I always notice if a gentleman—I mean a thorough-bred one—takes up democracy, and all that, opinions, the more exclusive, as sure as a gun, does he grow in his actions. He may put on the *bonnet rouge* with the people, but he'll always expect the people to doff theirs to him. Well, it's human nature, I suppose; we're all anomalies——"

"For Heaven's sake, don't begin to moralise, Beau," said Fitz. "Of all the abominations that pester the earth, the didactic style is the worst. Well! will you come with me to the Larches?"

"The where?" shouted Beau, in amazement.

"The Larches; the Barnardiston's place."

Beau dropped some cutlet, en route to his lips, off his fork, in staring at Fitz. "Are you mad? Why he's on Verdant's committee."

"What of that? I've walked about ten entire days to meet his daughter, and haven't met her: sequitur, I shall call there."

Beau gave a grunt of wonder and disgust. "Of all the cool hands, I *do* think you're the very coolest."

"Of course I am. Have you only now found it out? Ring the bell, and order the horses."

"Well," said Beau, with a touching air of resignation, "if you'd keep quiet, and do as you're told, I'd bring you in as sure as this beer's Brighton Tipper; but since you *will* act for yourself, why, if you lose your election, *I* wash my hands of it."

Up to the Larches rode Fitz and I, a pretty house of very white stone, and with very green Venetians—that tried hard to look like an Italian villa on a small scale, and failed signally—standing in its grounds at the west end of Cantitborough.

"There she is," whispered Fitz, as we paced up the carriage drive. True enough, stooping over a bed of verbena, gardening sedulously, with Dauphin barking furiously round her, in ecstatic delight, was our late travelling companion. At the sound of our horses' hoofs the poodle rushed at us after the manner of small dogs, and his mistress turned round to see the cause of his irritation. Off went Fitz's hat, and he bowed to his saddle-bow. At the same moment a young lady came out of a French window, and called "Coral!" Dauphin's mistress threw down her trowel, obeyed the summons, and went into the house; not without a bow to Fitz, though.

"The devil! she *is* Glencora, and engaged to that owl, then," swore Fitz. "I say, she hasn't one bit the cut of a parson's *future*, has she? Upon my word it's a pity—horrid waste of good material—to throw *her* into the Church's arms! Never mind, though; it will be the more fun for me. I shan't only have a flirtation, but the fun of making him jealous."

"Glad you take it so philosophically, but it won't do you much good in the borough to flirt with their pet preacher's fiancée."

"Hold your tongue. If I prefer a flirtation to a seat in the Commons, mayn't I indulge my preference?" said the candidate for Cantitborough, throwing his bridle to Soames, as a Buttons, that one wanted a microscope to see clearly, opened the door, and ushered us into the library of the hottest out-and-out Tory in the county.

There sat old Barnardiston in state, a tall, plethoric-looking fellow, the very embodiment of conservatism, orthodoxy, and British prejudice. It was as good as a play to see his face when the Radical candidate was shown in, and to see Fitz, with his most nonchalant yet most courtly air, address him, and solicit his vote, as if in perfect ignorance that Lord Verdant's proposer, the Bluest of Blues, Barnardiston, who looked on free trade as treason to the commonwealth, and on the ballot as a device of Satan, was not perfectly *d'accord* with himself upon politics. The old gentleman, of course, proceeded to bow us out with a good deal of grandiloquent bosh about his principles, which he was evidently very injured to think had not been too widely known to have prevented Fitz's intrusion. Fitz was nonplussed; his call did not promise to be very productive. The old Tory was unpropitious, and there was no sign of the girls whatever. He was just going to take his leave in despair, when, as luck would have it, down came all at once such a shower of hailstones, such claps of thunder, such a conflict of the elements, as the novel-writers say, that, out of common courtesy, the old boy, though it was plain to see that he looked on us as a brace of the most impudent scoundrels he had ever come across, was obliged to ask us if we would wait till it was over. Fitz thanked him, and said he would, in his pleasant, easy manner, as if he and the great Tory were the best possible friends; and (very stiffly, though) Barnardiston, fairly let in for the entertainment of the dangerous sceptic and socialist, asked us to go into the drawing-room.

"Bravo! brass and pluck always win," whispered Fitz aside to me, as the door was opened, and we saw the identical Cora feeding a brace of love-birds in the window, her sister, quite unlike her—a stout, square, business-looking girl—writing district papers, with a lot of tracts round her, and their mamma reading in a dormeuse.

Breathing an inward prayer for the continuance of the thunderstorm, Fitz sat himself down (just under the love-birds), and proceeded to make himself agreeable—especially to the betrothed of the incumbent of St. Hildebrande's. You would have thought him the *enfant de la maison* for the last ten years at least, to hear him talk news and literature with madame, fun and ornithology with mademoiselle, utterly regardless that Barnardiston was keeping a gloomy silence, and the district collector looking glum on her sister's vivacious chat, probably with the eye of a belle-sœur to the absent Whitechurch's interests. He amused them so well, and was so well amused himself, that the sun had stared him in the face for full twenty minutes, and the birds were telling everybody the storm was gone, before Fitz thought proper to find out that it was "beginning to clear up"—a fact so undeniable that he had nothing for it but to make his adieux, after offering to lend Mrs. Barnardiston some book or other she wanted; and when the lodge gates closed behind us, Fitz had a good shout of laughter.

"Now, then, didn't I manage that gloriously?"

"Yes! I never doubted your powers of impudence yet; but whether your election——"

"Confound my election! It was worth losing fifty votes only to see that old boy's face when I asked for his support; and, by George! isn't she pretty? To see all that going to Whitechurch is rather a trial of one's patience. What in the world was she thinking of to throw herself away on him? A little flirtation will be only common humanity to her. Did you see how mischievous she looked when she saw me? The 'good for nothing' was lurking in her mind, I bet you."

"In pleasant contrast with the good in everything of her future sposo. The cardinal virtues ain't relished by women."

Fitz laughed as he pricked Rumpunch into a gallop. "I must have some fun with her. I won't quite spoil her matrimonial speculations, though, for I shan't be inclined to put it *au sérieux*, like the Rev. Augustine. Confound it, there's Jimmy! What in the world is he doing here?"

"Hallo, old boy! how are you?" said the man thus apostrophised, Jimmy Villars, a friend of Fitz's. "I've heard lots about you, Randolph. You're turning Cantitborough upside down, and I'm come to help you."

"That's right. Nobody more welcome. Where are you staying?"

"At the Levisons'—you know them. No? Then you shall immediately. Levison is a great yachting man. Yes to be sure; *Bonniebelle's* owner; thought you knew him by name. Western of Ireland Club, you remember. He's married now; a very pleasant girl hooked and finished him. They're county people and thorough-going Liberals, so you won't frighten 'em, though they *are* connected with that Arch-Blue old Barnardiston."

"By Jove!" thought Fitz, "'if a man take luck by the horns, don't it always favour him!' Introduce me, then, Jimmy," he said, aloud; "I want a little fun. I'm bored to death with committees, canvassing, meetings, dinners, speechifying, and letter-writing. Then the Cantitburghers are such awful owls, and one's aims and ends do seem so small when one's mixed up with the bigotry of prejudice and the tomfoolery of party, that I'm growing heartily sick of the whole thing already."

Poor Beau was distracted. Fitz had been a refractory client enough before, so far as obstinately speaking his mind, telling the truth, tilting against his voters' opinions, and entirely refusing to "butter" anybody, went; but after he met Jimmy Villars, Beau had ten times more trouble, for while little Verdant was calling at every house and conquering them all with his title, and Le Hoop Smith was giving to all the charities, and quoting the "Christian Year" largely to the clergy, and Salter was delighting the ten-pound men with coarse jokes, and flinging guineas and stout away recklessly, Fitz, ten to one, was either bothering poor Beau not to bribe, instead of letting things go on quietly; or talking rationalism and liberalism high over the head of some startled constituent (who came off from the interview with the decision that Mr. Fitzbardinge was eminently "dangerous"); or playing billiards, and going eel-netting with Villars and the Levisons; or sitting in Edith Levison's drawing-room with her and her cousin, Glencora Barnardiston. Nevertheless, Beau, the sharpest-witted, neatest-handed agent that ever lived, worked away with the settled despair of a man baling water out of a leaking ship with a teacup, and really grew quite worried and anxious in his personal appearance, toiling for the devil-may-care Radical, for whom, ever since Fitz pounded him on their first introduction at Eton, he had always entertained a sort of dogged attachment, something, he used to say, like that of an aged grandmother for the "poor dear boy" who plagues her life out with crackers, and goes more wrong than all his brothers put together.

The Levisons were, as Jimmy had promised, very pleasant people; and as soon as we were introduced to them, made Fitz and me, and Beau too, if he had had time for such puerilities, welcome to Elm Court, Levison's place, just four miles from Cantitborough, whenever we liked to go there. We went pretty often, for Levison's wife was a merry little thing, and generally had one or two choice spirits like herself driven over to spend the day; among them, her cousin and favourite, the fiancée of the Rev. Augustine Whitechurch, a fat, sleek man of large Easter offerings, and touching testimonials; of good family, and wide (Cantitborough) fame, whom everybody praised, though nobody liked, as a sort of voucher for their own religion. I have seen a good many serpents and rabbits, rats and beagles, doves and tiger-cats chained together, but I never saw any pair who seemed to be more uncongenial than Cora and her prétendu. She was lively, witty, high-spirited, and loved mischief as much as she hated Dorcas meetings, missionary reports, and interesting converted beggars, while he was Low Church—*i.e.*, looked upon life as a miserable pilgrimage that it was our duty to make with the hardest possible peas in our shoes; wanted a wife the embodiment of that dreadful individual, Hannah More's "Lucilla," and worried poor Cora's very life out with animadversions on her pursuits, amusements, and friends. He came sometimes with her to Elm Court, where he and Fitz took an instantaneous dislike to each other, and kept each other at bay like a cat and a spaniel.

"Do you think you will win your election, Fitz?" asked Villars one evening after dining there, and we were strolling over the grounds afterwards in the twilight.

"Haven't an idea, my dear fellow," responded Fitz, cheerfully, "and am not sure that I wish; for the Cantitburghers are such awful idiots, that to represent them faithfully I should be compelled to buy a pair of ass's ears, like Bottom, which might produce a peculiar sensation in the House."

"Especially," smiled Cora, "as the cap would fit so many of its members."

"Those that are 'good for nothing' included."

She laughed and coloured.

"Oh, I had hoped you had not recognised me. What a shame to keep it secret all this time. I might have been begging your pardon in a long oration every time we met. I shall take care how I talk to strangers again in a train."

"Pray don't. I'm exceptional in my taste, I know, but I do like truths sometimes, even if they hit hard. Don't you?"

"Yes; but I fancy my truth didn't hit you severely at all. I think I told you you were condemned as a sceptic, a socialist, and a republican; and, since all clever men have been classed into one of the three, you should be super-excellent to combine the trio."

Fitz laughed.

"I am quite content to be condemned by Cantitborough to any amount, so long as *you* don't find me utterly 'good for nothing.'"

She looked up at him merrily.

"Certainly; you are good for waltzing, billiards, and German songs; those are all the duties I require of you, so I don't ask any further."

"I only wish you required more," said Fitz, softly. "I am sorry you think of me as a passing acquaintance, chatted with in a ball-room, and parted from without regret, to meet no more in the eddies of society."

"I never said that I considered you so," interrupted Cora, hurriedly, snapping the roses off their stems as they walked along.

"But you implied it; and if you knew the pain your light words cause, you would not speak them."

She was silent, so was he. It was part of Fitz's code of warfare to leave his sentences to bear their fruit.

"Glencora, you are extremely imprudent to be out in this damp atmosphere in such a light evening dress," said the Rev. Augustine at her elbow.

"This exquisite evening! Thank you for your care, but I don't belong to the sanitary-mad individuals," replied Miss Glen, impatiently. "I never cloak up, so never take cold; if I do, I will apply to you for some of those extraordinary little hundreds and thousands you carry in the morocco case, and physic the parish with, in alternate doses of texts and globules."

"Ah! *do* you believe in those little comfits, Mr. Whitechurch?" said Fitz, taking up the warfare. "You save the souls and the bodies en même temps—a very nice arrangement, I dare say. It must be delightful to practise the two healing arts at once; and then, if you *should* ever chance to mistreat a case, it wouldn't so much matter, because you'd have made sure your patient was 'fit' to die, whether he were willing or not. Homœopathy's a capital thing for trade. I'm very glad to see it spreading; they say the undertakers bid fair to be some of the wealthiest men in the kingdom through it, and the sugar-bakers thrive amazingly."

"It requires no wit to jest upon deep subjects," said Whitechurch, loftily. "The holiest topic, the gravest matter, can of course be turned into ridicule."

"If it is weak, certainly."

"No, sir! Not if it is weak, but if its opponents are bigoted and coarse-mouthed. Ridicule was thrown upon Moses's divining-rod——"

"And he turned it into a serpent, and made it eat up all the other rods, which was ingenious, if not Christian."

"All the borough are acquainted with your latitudinarian opinions, Mr. Fitzhardinge."

"Are they?" laughed Fitz. "They must be rather a treat to Cantitborough, after all the Conservative oratory it has expended on it. By the way, Mr. Whitechurch, that election sermon of yours last Sunday was an admirable hit. I heard Lord Cockadoodle say that he wished old Ewen would kick off, and leave Dunslope in his gift."

Whitechurch coloured. The sermon was a gross piece of toadyism, and though he did keep his affections on things above, he couldn't help sometimes taking a glance downwards, where the fat living of Dunslope was among the prominent points that caught his eye.

Cora sighed quickly, turned round, and said something about going into the house.

"Do," said Fitz, bending towards her. "Let us go and try those German airs."

Go they did, and Fitz's cornet, which he played as well as Kœnig, sent out its mellow notes in a concert of sweet sounds, which was anything but harmonious to the ears of the incumbent of St. Hildebrande as he walked up and down before the drawing-room windows, listening to Caroline, who, regarding him already as a brother, took the liveliest interest in his parochial business affairs, doubtless with the kindly view of covering her sister's shortcomings in that line.

"Poor dear Cora!" I heard her sigh, as she passed me when I was smoking on the terrace with Jimmy. "Don't be annoyed with her, Augustine. She *does* flirt a little, perhaps, but they say all pretty women do. I'm not tempted, you know; I am plain and unpretending; but, thank Heaven! my thoughts are not fixed on this world, or on men's idle admiration. Don't be vexed with her; she is thoughtless, I am afraid."

"But I am extremely annoyed," said the parson's dictatorial tones. "I spoke to her the other day about fixing the time for our marriage. I require a wife; I cannot attend to the schools, and the cook wastes a great deal; but she put me off—would give me no answer. *I* am not to be treated so lightly; and as for her dancing, and singing, and riding with those idle men, especially with that wild dissolute Fitzhardinge, it is intolerable, unbearable, most indecorous——"

"I know it is very sad," chimed in the gentle Cary. "But dear Glen never had any due sense of the responsible position your wife will occupy. She is careless, worldly——"

Here they went out of hearing, and I was no further enlightened, but went into the drawing-room, where they were all playing vingt-et-un, and called to me to join them; and I thought, as I saw Cora, with her large hazel eyes full of animation, Verdant gazing at her sentimentally on her left, and Fitz discoursing with eloquent glances and facile compliment on her right, her light laugh ringing through the room, and her merry talk keeping all going, that it was a thousand pities for her to be imprisoned in the sombre atmosphere of St. Hildebrande's rectory, under the cheerless régime of St. Hildebrande's incumbent, whose gloomy doctrine would infallibly silence the laughter, hush-hush the jest, burn the cards, interdict the waltzing—in short, crush all the native song out of the poor bird he had netted.

"I say, old boy," said I, when we were having a pipe that night in the dining-room at Hollywood, "make hay while the sun shines; you won't have much longer to flirt."

"Why not?" said Fitz, sharply.

"Because Whitechurch wants to get married; not from any particular penchant for the state, or any fresh access of love, but because his girls' schools want looking after, and his cook's ruining him."

"The fool!" ejaculated Fitz, with a giant cloud of Turkish; "why doesn't he go to the register-office, and hire a seamstress and a housekeeper?"

"Possibly because a wife will combine both, and be cheaper. Barnardiston will give his daughters twenty thousand pounds each if he like his sons-in-law. Fancy Cora arming herself with needles and thread, and teaching half a dozen charity-girls to make pocket-handkerchiefs for Ojibbeways, and going into her kitchen to see that dear Augustine's curry is peppered to a T, or that the cook doesn't encourage the policeman——"

"Faugh! Be quiet, can't you?" growled Fitz, in intense disgust. "You might talk with just as much coolness of Rumpunch being set to run in a costermonger's cart. The idea! What on earth could make her accept him?"

"First offer," interrupted Beau; "couldn't tell she'd get another."

"Pooh! nonsense; at her age girls ain't hard up in that way. If she were thirty she might have been desperate; very rusty hooks are snapped up when there's no longer a chance of silver ones; but at nineteen——"

"Hooks of all kinds are snapped at by all ages," interrupted Beau again, "and you've said so scores of times, Fitz, when it suited you, and your perceptions weren't clouded. Heaven knows why the Clergy trouble themselves to tell women at the end of the marriage-service not to be afraid, with any amazement; there never was more heedless waste of words, for I never knew any of the crinolines who didn't catch at a wedding-ring as Rover catches at a mutton-bone."

"I have, though," muttered Fitz. "Some women send away troops of fellows."

"It does puzzle me," said I, "how Glen, with the pick of the county, could choose that parson. She don't like him, I fancy."

"Like him!" cried Fitz, with immeasurable scorn; "how should she? An ugly brute, with the pluck of a chicken."

"Don't call your spiritual pastors and masters bad names, Fitz," said Beau. "You keep me in hourly terror, for if you have a row with the Cantitburghers' pet preacher it'll be all up with your election."

"I shan't have a row with him," sneered Fitz, with much contempt. "I flirt with her because she amuses me, but if she likes the man, she's welcome to him for me."

Though she was so very welcome to him, I heard Fitz in his room (the room is next to mine, and the walls are lath and plaster) mutter to himself as he undressed, "What on earth makes her take that fool?" a question to which I do not suppose either his pipe, or his bed-candle, or Rover, who always sleeps by his bedside, or the harvest moon that was looking through the window, vouchsafed him any reply.

The Larches was, of course, forbidden ground to Fitz. He did call there with the book for Mrs. Barnardiston, and was received very cordially by that lady, but in the evening found a note from the old Tory, thanking him for his courtesy, but saying that at least until the "coming important contest" was decided, he thought acquaintance, since their opinions were so opposite, had better not continue. That was a settler; Fitz could not push himself in after that, especially as Fitz would not make himself cheap for a kingdom. Nevertheless, he would find occasion to ride past the Larches, Cora being given to amateur gardening, which generally consisted in gathering the flowers, or throwing guelder-roses at Dauphin, and a very pretty sight she was when she was so occupied, though Caroline considered it childish, and Whitechurch waste of time. By Jove! if one may not dawdle a little time on the road gathering the flowers one finds in life —and precious few there are!—what earthly use, I wonder, do the flowers grow there for?

Past the Larches we were riding one evening after dinner, having spent all the day in election business that had bored us both to death, and very slowly was Rumpunch pacing under the shadow of the shrubberies that divided that stronghold of "Blue" opinion from the high road. Just opposite a break in the laburnums and hawthorns that gave a view through a white gate into the garden, Rumpunch had, or was supposed to have, a nasty stone in his foot—a stone that a man who adored horseflesh as Fitz did was bound to look after. The stone took some moments to find—indeed, I am uncertain that it *was* found after all—but while Fitz was examining the off hoof, through the trees we perceived Whitechurch and his betrothed. Whitechurch looked more pompous than usual, and the serene brow that the ladies of his parish raved about was certainly contracted. Cora looked excited, and rather ready to cry. They drew near the gate, not being able to see us for the trees, and we caught the clergyman's last words—very stiff and icy they were, too.

"You will think over what I have said, Glencora, and I expect you to pay some attention to it. Good-night."

She gave not the slightest response. Whitechurch swung the gate open, and passed down the road with his back to us. Cora stood still, with her eyes on the ground, in a reverie; then she caught Dauphin up, kissed him, burst into tears as she bent over the dog, and walked away through the trees. I glanced at Fitz. His teeth were set like a mastiff's, and he looked after Whitechurch as if he longed to deliver from his left shoulder and floor the retreating figure.

"You'd have improved the occasion better than that, Fitz?"

"Curse the fellow!" muttered the Radical candidate. "I just wish I had him out for a couple of rounds on a quiet morning—a hypocritical idiot, that'll worry all her young life out of her."

With which disconnected remark, and sundry smothered curses, the sight of the farewell having seemingly stirred him into mighty wrath, Fitz sprang on Rumpunch. When he got home he vented it in pipes and whisky, and Beau looked at him as a man might look on a pet hound, that he feared was going in for hydrophobia.

"Something's come to Fitz," said Beau, anxiously, "for he's just signed me a large cheque without a word; and I know he wouldn't have given it to me to corrupt the people with without some bother, if he'd known what he was doing."

"I'm going over to Levison's, Beau," said he at breakfast next day. "We're to drive to the Chase, for a sketching party; will you come?"

"I?" growled Beau. "I should think I've something better to do; if I hadn't, the figure at your poll would be a o. The idea of a man's coming down to stand for a borough, and then going spending all his time with a set of women! I've no patience with you."

"Haven't you, old fellow?" laughed Fitz. "Patience is a virtue, and as no lawyer has any virtues at all, I suppose we can't wonder at you. I did begin enunciating my opinions, but you stopped my mouth."

"Opinions! Pray what have they to do with an election?" retorted Beau. "One would take you for a boy of twenty, talking as if you didn't know everything going on on the face of the earth was an affair of pounds, shillings, and pence. Who the devil cares two straws what opinions you have? Can't you keep 'em quiet, if you will have such things? They hinder a man shockingly. If he's a taste for 'em, he should lock 'em up in his study. You want to get returned——"

"Don't care a hang about it," cried Fitz.

"—for Cantitborough?" continued Beau, too irate to mind the interruption; "and if you do, you should make up your mind to give your money to me and your agents with your eyes shut, as a verger takes a Christmas-box, and to put the stopper for a time on all that liberalist and rationalist stuff. It's all very sensible, when shared with the *esprits forts;* but it don't sell just now—it must wait another century or two. If you want to get on with the world, you mustn't frighten it by drawing Truth out of her well; for the world, at present, is a very great baby, and Truth is its bogey, and makes it run away. But you're as wilful as an unbroke colt, and one might as well talk to this reindeer tongue as to you. So get along to your sketching party; you're out of mischief there."

With which oration, delivered with the spurt of a champagne cork, Beau pushed his plate away, drank a glass of Bass, and ordered a dog-cart to drive into the town, while his obstinate client put his block and his moist colour-box in his pocket, and took his cap to walk over to Elm Court. A nicer place to flirt in than that Chase, with its soft turfy seats, and its thick shadowy woodlands, and its picturesque distance, as an excuse for sketching, it was impossible to find. Fitz was very great at sketching; he made a sketching tour once with one of the "Associates," but to-day the outline of Dauphin's nose was all achieved, for he was chiefly busy mixing Cora's colours, fetching her water, telling her how to tone down this, and deepen that, till——Well, I didn't envy the Reverend Augustine, as his lady-love sat at the roots of an old beech, a little apart from the rest of us, with Fitz lying full length on the turf beside her, as handsome a dog as ever turned a girl's head with his pretty speeches.

Glencora was very shy and quiet with him that day; she, who generally talked nineteen to the dozen. I was listening to the "Princess," which Villars was reading aloud to Mrs. Levison and another fair one, but it really did bore me to such a degree that I was obliged to get out of sound to where I could light a pipe without offending female nerves. I was near Fitz, who was smoking—permitted the indulgence by Cora, who has no nonsense about her—and I caught the end of his sentence as he lay looking up at her, and gathering the ferns with his left hand. Fitz has a quiet way of flirting, but it's a very effective one.

"No; I don't wish to win the election," he was saying. "My views have changed since I came down here."

"What! has Cantitborough air turned you Blue?"

"Not exactly; but since, when I leave Cantitborough, I shall be forgotten as a mere acquaintance by those who have made the place dear to me, I shall never set foot in it again. Isn't it old North, in the 'Noctes,' who says 'there are places in this earth that we shudder to revisit, haunted by images too beautiful to be endured'? *I* feel the truth of that now."

"By George!" thought I, "Fitz is growing very serious. Won't poor Cora credit it all, and never dream it will be talked in the same strain to some new listener next month!"

"Will you give me that sketch?" Fitz went on, after a pause, in which the ferns had come to considerable grief. "It is much to ask, but I should like some memorial of days that I shall never forget, though you will."

"Do you think I shall ever forget them?"

The temptation to revenge yesterday's scene was too sweet to be resisted. Fitz drew her down towards him. "Will you promise me that——"

But Cora sprang up, scattering her materials to the four winds. "Hush, hush, you must not speak so to me; you do not know——"

What he didn't know never appeared, for Mrs. Levison turned her head over her shoulders, saying,

"Glen, darling, have you any ultramarine? I can't find mine."

Glen went towards her, and Fitz rose with a worried,

anxious look on his face, very different to the fun his love affairs generally brought him.

"Why did your cousin engage herself to Mr. Whitechurch?" asked he, point blank, of Mrs. Levison, finding himself alone with her for two minutes before dinner that night.

"Ah! isn't it a pity? a dreadful man like that, who'll think it sinful for her to waltz or go to the Opera. If Gerald wouldn't let me waltz, or have a box, I would sue for a separation to-morrow."

"But why accept him?" said Fitz, impatiently.

"That was all my uncle's doing," answered Edith. "He's terribly mean, you know, without the slightest reason to be so. Glencora came home from school at seventeen. Augustine proposed for her. My uncle thought it a good match, and ordered her to accept him; her mamma begged her not to go against her papa. Poor Cora, as thoughtless as my canary-bird, never knew the misery she was making for herself, and consented. She has been miserable ever since! They've been engaged two years; and," continued Edith, with immense energy, "Mr. Fitzhardinge, I'd as soon see her joining the Poor Clares as wearing orange-blossoms for *that* man!"

So would Fitz, probably, on the well-known principle of the dog in the manger; a very natural principle, especially when one has a fancy to eat the straw oneself. He did not say so, however.

Whitechurch came to dine that night at Elm Court. The dinner was not so lively as usual, for Fitz and Cora, generally the fastest hitters in the tennis-ball of conversation, might have been Gog and Magog set down at the table for any amusement they afforded the society.

After dinner at Elm Court we were wont to take our cigars about in the grounds instead of over the wine in the glorious sultry August evenings. Levison went after his wife—he was still actually in love with her—Fitz lighted an Havannah and strolled off by himself, and Jimmy and I sat down in a Robinson Crusoe hut to have a chat about the Cambridge Eight, the October meetings, and other subjects we had in common. Villars was just telling me how it was that Long Fortesque happened to make such a pot of money on the Cesarewitch, when, through the thick shrubs and young trees that surrounded our smoking-room, I caught a glimpse of Cora's pink dress as she stood in earnest talk with somebody or other invisible to us.

"Oh! hang it, Jimmy," said I, "there's another love-scene going on; let's get out of the way."

"Keep still, young one, rather," retorted Villars "or you may just walk into the middle of it, and smash all the fun. Is it that dear little pet, and Fitz making a fool of himself about her? It's abominable to listen, but, boxed up here, one can't help it. Fitz would shoot us if we walked out in his face and spoiled sport. Besides, we shan't hear anything new; love-scenes are all alike."

This, however, seemed far from being a love-scene. Cora was speaking impetuously and hurriedly.

"I have acted very wrongly, I know I have. A girl always does, if she engages herself where she cannot give her affection. I beg your pardon for having misled you. I blame myself very much for not having spoken frankly to you long ago, and asked you to release me from an engagement I can never fulfil."

"It is a pity you did not think so long ago," replied Whitechurch, sententiously.

"It *is* a pity. I wish to Heaven I had."

"I dare say you do! You say very justly that we are ill suited to each other; our tastes, and aims, and pursuits are utterly alien. I was lured, I confess, by your personal attractions. I trusted that the good seed, once sown, might flourish in so fair a soil; but I was deceived. You have only forestalled me in the rupture of our engagement. I confess that I dared not take a helpmate out of Philistia, and I have learned that there are treasures elsewhere superior to the ephemeral charms of mere exterior beauty."

"I am rejoiced to hear it," retorted Cora, haughtily. "Our want of congeniality cannot have struck you more forcibly than it has done me. You will, at least, do me the justice to admit that I never simulated an affection I could not feel."

"Certainly; we part in peace, and shall, I trust, meet again on perfectly friendly terms."

"He'll take Cary, mark my word," said Villars, as the incumbent of St. Hildebrande's raised his hat, and left her. "All her district visiting and ragged school teaching hasn't been without an eye to business, I'll bet."

Cora, fancying herself alone, threw herself down on a turf seat under a mountain-ash, looking pretty enough, with the sunset lighting up her bright dress and uncovered hair, while she sat in thought, out of which Dauphin, by the application of a cold nose, the wagging of a short tail, and many impatient barks, vainly tried to rouse her.

"Pretty she looks, don't she?" whispered Villars. "Do for the Sleeping Beauty, if her eyes were shut. Why don't Fitz play the Knight's part?"

He'd scarcely spoken when the scent of an Havannah floated to us on the evening wind, and along the shrubbery path came Fitz, with his arms folded, and his eyes on the ground. Dauphin ran up to him in an ecstatic state of welcome. Cora started up, her cheeks flushing as bright-hued as the sky, and said something highly unintelligible about its going to rain, which, seeing there wasn't a cloud in the heavens, seemed looking far into futurity indeed. Fitz didn't answer her with regard to her atmospheric prophecies, but, throwing away his cigar into the middle of an oleander, he began where he had left off in the morning.

"Cora, my darling," he murmured, "I beseech you listen to me! I seem never to have hated or to have loved till now. For Heaven's sake, free yourself from those accursed ties, and give yourself to me——"

"The deuce!" muttered Jimmy, when Glencora had whispered that she was free, and the Radical candidate had pledged himself with every vow under the sun to the great Blue's daughter, and they had strolled away among the shrubberies, "since Fitz has got up the steam and come it *au sérieux* like this, a spavined 'bus horse may enter itself for the Derby. A pretty fellow he is to come canvassing; but one might have been sure what sort of an election *he*'d try for when hazel eyes like those were in the way."

I suppose Fitz found this style of canvassing more to his taste, for the harvest moon was high in the heavens, and the nightingale was jug-jugging in the cool woodlands, and the ladies had sung two or three songs after the coffee, before he and Cora walked in through the bay-window.

To see Beau's face when Fitz told him he had turned out Whitechurch!

"Well, I *do* think you're gone clean mad, Randolph," he began, when he recovered his first breathless horror. "To fly in the face of the borough like that—to steal their pet parson's fiancée—to outwit their most influential householder—to get yourself called every name they can lay their tongues to—how the deuce do you think that's likely to forward your election?"

Fitz lay back and laughed without stopping for five minutes.

"You may laugh," growled Beau. "You won't laugh when you see four thousand five hundred pounds six shillings and eightpence gone, and nothing to show for it."

"That's your fault," put in Fitz, "for spending such a lot on unholy purposes. What sort of a face would you show before an Election Committee?"

"I should like to know," continued Beau, more furious every word he uttered, "what a *woman* is worth to lose an election for? Women are as cheap as green peas, but you won't find free boroughs as easy to come by. A pretty row we shall have in the town! Won't the Blues print placards about you! Won't there just be choice epithets chalked after your name on the walls! Won't the *Cantilborough Post* catch hold of it, and rake up every one of your love affairs; and pretty nice ones some of 'em are, as *I* know, since I was called in to settle 'em! Won't old Blue Bar move heaven and earth to keep you out! Well, all I can say is, that you're more fit for a private asylum than a rational hustings."

With which final philippic Beau flung himself out of the room, too irate to hear Fitz call after him:

"Take my compliments to the editor of the *Cantilborough Post*, and ask him to be so kind as to print, next week, in the biggest capitals he has, that I consider a touch of Cora's lips worth a premiership! Don't forget, Beau! And, I say, you may add, too, that Blue and Yellow are two of the primary colours, and intended to unite from earliest memory."

Beau was quite right. The Blues were frantic with delight at being able to damage the Yellow member, who, somehow, had been making ground in spite of them; and Barnardiston was furious, not because Whitechurch was thrown over, for Whitechurch had turned his affections towards the good working qualities of Caroline, but because the man he hated worst in the whole county—handsome, reckless, bold, republican Fitz—had cheated him out of the chance of a coronet. The very day Cora accepted Randolph she refused little Lord Verdant, and so enraged was the great Tory, that he told Cora to leave his roof, and sent Fitz's letters back unopened. Cora, who, having her mamma on her side, however, did not mind it much, took refuge with Edith Levison, Levison himself being indignant with Barnardiston for his folly; and in the sultry summer days and the long summer evenings Fitz and Miss Glen passed many a pleasant hour under the shady trees of Elm Court, while in the little bigoted, quarrelling, peppery town, four miles off, the Cantitborough men were blackening his name in committee-rooms, and the Cantitborough women were pulling her to smithereens at their tea-fights.

The day that beats the Derby for stirring English phlegm into mad excitement—the day when Blue and Yellow ride rampant against each other—the day when the demon of Party breaks loose—when the Unwashed smash each other's heads to their full satisfaction, when voters are locked up in durance vile and plied with hocussed grog, and torn hither and thither by distracted cabs—when men work, and wear, and quarrel, and growl, and swear by a bit of blue ribbon, as if it were the sole stay of the country, and grasp at a yellow banner as though it were the mainstay of liberty—the election-day dawned on Cantitborough, the sun shining extra bright, as if laughing with its jolly round face at the baby play these little pigmies below fancied of such universal importance.

The nomination day arrived, and each separate Cantitburgher uprose from his bed with the solemn conviction that the destinies of England hung on his own individual hands. Beau splashed through his bath with the rapidity of a water-dog, brushed his whiskers as hastily as a Cantab too late for chapel, and dressed himself in much the same eager excitement as a Cornet harnessing for his first parade.

"Seven o'clock, and that fellow not up!" growled Beau, performing a fanfaronade on his candidate's door.

"What the devil are you making that row for?" responded Fitz. "Why *can't* you take things quietly?"

"If I had, I wonder how you'd stand," swore Beau, "on the poll to-day! Not up! when Smith, and Salter, and Verdant will be in the town by nine full fig, and all your committee will be looking out for you at half-past at the Ten Bells!"

Fitz laughed.

"You get your breakfast, and go into Cantitborough, whether I'm up or not. And, I say, Beau, send Soames to me, and order some one to saddle Rumpunch, will you?"

"Go into Cantitborough without *him!* He's certainly mad," muttered Beau, in soliloquy. Being, however, of a philosophic turn of mind, he and I ate a good breakfast, though ungraced by the presence of our host. "Why is that fellow so late?" he asked fifty times to each cup of coffee. "Eight o'clock, by Jove! and we shall be a mortal hour getting into procession and going to the town. Do ring the bell—ring it loud. Thank you. James, go and see if your master is up."

"Can't make anybody hear, sir," said James, returning.

"Not hear? Bless my soul, it's very extraordinary!" said Beau, looking the picture of unutterable worry and woe. "Fitz must have taken an overdose of opium. Confound him! What did he get in love for? I'll call him myself."

Up went Beau and battered at the door, with not the slightest success.

"I say, Fitz! Fitz! are you deaf, or dead, or what?" shouted Beau, forgetting that in the event of either hypothesis Fitz would be the last person calculated to give him an answer.

"God bless me!" cried Beau, bursting the door open, "where *are* you? If ever there was a wayward, obstinate, provoking——" Beau stopped in astonishment too great for speech. The room was empty, the bed empty, Fitz, Rover, and Soames departed, all the drawers open, a portmanteau on the floor, and shirts, and coats, and brushes, and boots tossed about as when a man has packed in a hurry and left behind all the things he will not want.

"Bolted, by Heaven!" cried Beau. "Where's he gone? What's he done? He is mad—he must be mad! Send the servants off everywhere! Where, in the devil's name, can he be flown? Oh, curse it, what *is* to be done?"

That was more than I could tell him. We did send the men everywhere, but they could not find their master, nor Soames either. Beau had a faint idea of dragging the pond, in case Fitz had thrown himself into a watery grave; but then it was not probable that Soames was immolated as well. Nine o'clock struck; there were the Yellow men with the Yellow banners, and the Yellow ribbons, and the Yellow agents, and the Yellow band, and no Yellow candidate! In that half-hour I am sure poor Beau lost as much flesh as a jockey before the Derby. "Well we must go," said he, in sheer desperation. "Perhaps he'll turn up in the town; if not, we must tell 'em he's seriously ill. By George! I wish he'd been at York before he brought me on such a fool's errand."

Into Cantitborough we rode, with many shouts and enthusiastic rushes out from the cottages we passed; and into the market-place we went with great row and glory, save that we were a procession without a head. There was little Verdant, meeker than ever after Cora's rejection, looking like a noodle, with his father and a galaxy of titles at the head of his procession; and there was Le Hoop Smith, bland and smiling, at the head of his; and fat, yellow old Salter at the head of his. But where was Fitz—the handsome, dashing Fitz, whom the women were crowded to admire and the mob to cheer?—who, thanks to untiring Beau was grown popular even in Blue Cantitborough? And when the Blues saw not Rumpunch and his rider, were they not frantic with triumph? and were not Fitz's committee in an agony of wonder and dread, and the women in a state of bemoaning agony and woe, and the mob in a frantic fit of excitement and indignation, after the custom of mobs from all ages downwards? And was not Beau—poor Beau—distracted in his own mind, and worried like a fox with fifty packs after him —more inimitably cool, and confident, and matchless, than any man could possibly be pictured, when he set the mayor's hair straight upon end with an account of the frightful attack of cholera that had seized poor Fitz in the morning; distracted the committee with assurances that he had left their candidate as blue as the lapis-lazuli ring on his finger, and in mortal danger of his life; appealed so touchingly to the enlightened men of Cantitborough not to allow the unfortunate invalid's cause to be injured; and conducted himself altogether so brilliantly, that the Blues whispered in knots in dismay?

Yes, Beau was magnificent that day, I confess, though he did push me aside as a thundering muff when I made a mistake, and told one of the committee my cousin had broken his ankle the night before—yes, Beau was glorious, I admit.

The proceedings began with the crier's bell and the mayor's oration, which was entirely unheard from calls from the crowd of "Go it, old Baldhead!" "Speak up, old Malt-and-Hops!" "How many nine gallons did Salter order?" and like personal allusions to his occupation. Then uprose old Barnardiston, who was not very cordially received, for the simple reason that he was the hardest magistrate on the bench; however, the Blues cheered him to the skies when he proposed as a fitting representative for the free, loyal, honourable, enlightened, and all the rest of it borough, the son of the noble and generous House of Cockadoodle, the benefactors and patrons of Cantitborough. After his seconder came two out-and-out Blues, who proposed the gentle and intellectual Le Hoop Smith, of Hooping Hall, Pottleshire; and two more, who put forward that public-spirited, benevolent, and large-hearted gentleman, Curry Salter, late of the Bengal Infantry; and then two Liberals arose, in a wild storm of mad cheers and savage yells, to offer to the borough, as a member, Ralph Fitzhardinge, Esq., of Hollywood and Evensdale, who had been most unhappily stricken down by illness at the very moment he was mounting his horse, to come and have the honour of addressing them in person.

And now up got little Beau, as plucky as a gamecock, and began to tell them how it was that he was compelled to take their candidate's place. So ingeniously did he apologise for Fitz; so delightfully did he set the crowd screaming at his witticisms; so mercilessly did he show up his opponents' weak points; so admirably did he describe Fitz's opinions much better than Fitz would have done himself, who would have talked Mill and Comte and frightened them with his daring; so pathetically did he implore them not to let the great Liberal cause be prejudiced by an unavoidable accident, that the mob cheered him, as if he had been the Queen and they Etonians, hurrahed for Fitzhardinge till their throats were hoarse, and even some determined Blues were caused to waver in their minds. The hands clad in kid, doeskin, silk, cashmere, or dirt, as it might chance, that lifted themselves out from the tumultuous sea of shouting, struggling, fighting Blues and Yellows, were declared in favour of Lord Verdant and Randolph Fitzhardinge! Beau's triumph was magnificent; it smashed hollow all the mural crowns that ever were manufactured; and it was worth a guinea to see him in it, mercurial as quicksilver, rapid as a champagne cork, sharp as a ferret on his foes, and winning as a widow bent on conquest to his friends, haranguing these, arguing with those, thanking a fat councilman, and pledging a thin churchwarden, talking up for the Queen and down for the Pope, agreeing with everybody and offending none, telling them poor Fitz was Prussian Blue when he left him, and rapidly progressing towards Indigo, but had now taken a favourable turn, as he had just heard by a messenger, thanks be to, &c. &c.

Yes, Beau was grand on that day, and never more effective than when, at twelve o'clock at night, having shaken the last hand, and drunk the last glass, and talked the last solemn talk with the solemn committee, he sprang on his horse in the Ten Bells yard to tear over to Hollywood to see how his poor friend was. He had just his foot in the stirrup, and I was on my back, receiving no end of condolences for my cousin's most ill-timed attack from three or four of the principal of the committee, when a hand was laid on my knee, and an awful voice, which I knew only too well, said, in tones the fac-simile of the first tragedian's at the Royal Grecian,

"Sir, you are a scoundrel and a liar!"

"Hallo!" said I, "mild language! I am used to gentlemen, not to Billingsgate. What the devil do you mean——"

"What do *you* mean, sir," stormed Mr. Barnardiston, "by daring to come before an assembly of upright, loyal, God-fearing citizens with a lie on your lips? What do *you* mean by joining in a vile plot to trick a whole community, and rob a parent of a child——"

"Take care, old gentleman; you're talking libel," interrupted Beau, pleasantly. "The cognac's been too much for you. Go home and sleep it off, for it don't do for the Romans to see their pet Cincinnatus a little the worse for——"

"Hold your tongue, sir," screamed Barnardiston, purple with rage, "or, by Heaven, I'll find a way to make you! How dared you come here—both of you—and tell the whole borough that the cursed villain you call friend and cousin——"

"Gently, gently, my dear sir; remember how you compromise yourself," put in Beau, with most solicitous courtesy.

"The consummate rascal," pursued Barnardiston, fiercer than ever, waxing into sarcasm—"I mean the honourable gentleman, the noble-hearted, high-spirited Liberal candidate, who has sneaked out of a contest in which he knew he could not win, and ordered his obliging agent and his boy-cousin to chicane a whole town with some garbled folly of the cholera to screen his private marriage with the daughter of one whom her father would sooner see——"

"Eh?—what?—what did you say? *Married!*" cried Beau, nonplussed for once in his life.

"Ay, sir; married. And you know it as well as I, despite your admirable acting, which would do credit to Mr. Fechter," sneered the Arch-Blue.

"By Heaven, if *I had* known!" swore Beau, furiously; then stopped and changed his tone. "Married, you say, and to your daughter?" he yawned, with all the languid insolence in life. "Well, I congratulate you. You must feel uncommonly pleased; it is a much higher match than you could have looked for."

Barnardiston was perfectly black in the face. He turned himself, with his back to us, and began to harangue the committee-men, who looked scared out of their lives:

"Fellow-citizens!——"

"Ah! that's the correct style," said Beau; "it's so beautifully patriotic."

"Men of Cantitborough, I appeal to you. Judge between me and the honourable gentleman you have chosen to represent you. We have been separated by politics, but we are old fellow-townsmen, and you will give me a patient hearing. Mr. Fitzhardinge comes down to canvass a borough which has only heard of him before through wildness and follies which disgrace his name. He meets a girl—a young girl, an innocent girl—who is betrothed of her own will to one of the purest-minded, sweet-natured men that ever breathed, a man whom you have crowned with the honour of your reverence and esteem———"

"And Easter offerings, with which he buys the whisky that makes his inspiration," interpolated Beau.

"A man whom you all revere and love, and whose heart is locked up in this young girl's affections———"

"Or her possible twenty thousand pounds."

"What does this villain—I can use no milder term, gentlemen—do, but seduce these pure and fond affections from the holy man who once held them; woo her, win her, persuade her to break off the ties of her engagement, and fetter herself anew to him. I refuse my consent, because I know Mr. Fitzhardinge's character too well to peril my child's happiness in his keeping———"

"Because you thought Verdant was hanging after her," interrupted Beau.

"I reject his suit. What does he do? He induces her to brave me with all the open disobedience which cuts so keenly to a father's heart———"

"Turn on Lear—a quotation will save you no end of trouble," said Beau, kindly.

"He persuades her to go and reside———"

"When you'd turned her out of your house."

"To reside with people to whom I have the most marked objection———"

"Why did you court Levison so hard, then, to take your pretty niece?"

"The most marked objection. I distinctly forbid her marriage. She wants two years of her majority; and so this scoundrel———Passion gets the better of me, sirs!"

"Or Cockadoodle's comet wine does."

"When I tell you that Mr. Fitzhardinge takes the day of his nomination—the day he knew I should be tied to town endeavouring to serve my country's interests—to marry my poor child privately, with no witnesses but the Levisons, in the church at Elm Court, at ten o'clock this morning, I need comment no further on the miserable trick by which you, gentlemen, and all the rest of Cantitborough, have been duped to-day. I only ask you, as fellow-townsmen, once private friends, and always, I hope, friends in the common cause of truth and honour, to side with me, and never allow this destroyer of home peace, this unprincipled breaker of every public and domestic law, to represent in the senate of our nation this free, loyal, and Protestant borough."

"Gentlemen, hear my version," began Beau.

"Will you listen to a villain's tool?" pursued Barnardiston.

"I give you my honour——" cried Beau.

"What is his honour worth?" shouted Barnardiston.

"Will you hear me?"

"Will you believe him?"

Tumultuous was the scene, frightful the commotion, terrific the tempest of Blue and Yellow which raged over devoted Cantitborough. Blues and Yellows swarmed into the Ten Bells yard; Blues and Yellows surged round mine and Beau's horses; Blues and Yellows asked frantically what was the row, and carrying off but an unintelligible version, proceeded, as the next best plan, to kick up a row on their own account. They screamed, and shouted, and pummelled each others' shoulders, and punched each others' heads, and hissed, and yelled, and swore, and cudgelled, and

> Fought as only men can fight who know no reason why.

In vain the Yellow agent tried to speak. Every elegant missile that the dark night could allow to come to hand was pelted at him and me; in vain the Blue leaders tried to turn the tumult to account; the mob, who being in a mood to pelt, would have pelted the moon could they have got at her, forced them to retreat, covered with much obloquy and still more rotten eggs. Smash, crash went half the windows in the place; ladies rushed from their couches in nightcaps and hysteria; policemen turned and fled, or used their truncheons in some private grudge; not a Town and Gown row, even with Fighting Bob or the first of the Fancy in surplice and mortar-board to help us, ever beat it; and at last, in sheer desperation, having satiated ourselves with enough hard hitting to last a twelvemonth, Beau and I set spurs to our horses, and knocking down, at a low computation, some three hundred men and boys, fought our way out of the town, and galloped on to Hollywood in silence.

"By Heaven!" said Beau, through his set teeth, as he threw himself down at last in the arm-chair of the diningroom, thoroughly done up for the first time in his life—"by Heaven! if I'd known Fitz was such a fool, I'd have seen him at the devil before he'd made one of me too. The election's lost, smashed, ruined. I may as well withdraw his name from the poll. To go and disgrace himself before all the county; to go and offend his constituents, and his county, and everything worth considering, from a ridiculous fancy for a little flirt whom he'll be wishing at Jericho in twelve months' time—four thousand pounds fifteen shillings and eightpence gone for nothing! I'm a cool man—a very cool man, generally—but I confess this does get the better of me. How shall I ever forget, or how will all Cantitborough forget, my being brought down here only to tell a parcel of lies, and not *succeed* through them, even? By Jupiter!" and Beau sprang up from his chair and dashed his hand down on the table with an impetus that made the bottles and glasses on it leap up terrified into the air—"by Jupiter! I swear I'll never speak to your madman of a cousin, or to his confounded wife, as long as I live—never! I, the sharpest dog in all Lincoln's Inn, to be done green like this!"

With which pathetic summary poor Beau fell back again into his chair, and opened his lips no more that night. The morrow dawned; the poll was opened; Beau, like a plucky soldier, sticking to his colours as long as there was a rag of them left, rode into Cantitborough early, and I with him, and made his way to the polling-booth in the midst of the yells, and shouts, and fiendish exclamations, and laughter, and derision of the mob, who swarmed through the streets still strewn with the débris of the midnight conflict. In vain did Beau seek a hearing from his chief constituents; in vain did he try to gather round him the committee; in vain did he try to rally round him even a few straggling troopers to make a stand with him in this Thermopylæan fix. In vain! The Cantitburghers had been duped, and when did ever Christian live with magnanimity enough to pardon that? The news of Fitz's marriage had spread throughout the town; the ladies were furious against Cora for having wedded the only handsome man who had been seen in Cantitborough for the last ten years. They made their husbands, and sons, and fathers solemnly promise to withdraw their vote from such a wicked creature, and the husbands, and sons, and fathers, some liking to buy religious reputation cheap by siding with the pet parson, and others having Fitz's money already in their pockets, determining to hold virtuously aloof from the contest, vowed the required vow, and the tide of public adoration set steadily in for Verdant and Le Hoop Smith.

The committees sat in their respective rooms, the mob round the booth danced, and shouted, and yelled, in utter contempt of police, the Peelers being *hors de combat* from the past night's fray; Beau, and two or three staunch Liberals, stood firm, with anxious visage and hearts sunk to zero. The tower clock struck four—the poll was closed—the votes stood thus:

Verdant	550
Le Hoop Smith	310
Salter	200
Fitzhardinge	6

Great was the exultation, great the clamour, that arose. You do not need to be told how the Blue banners waved, and the Blue band, inflamed with triumph and stout, began to play, and the Blue members bowed down to the ground, and thanked the noble, intelligent, and generous community which had returned them as their representatives; how the Blues insulted the Yellows with frightful contumely, and how the Yellows, few in flesh but strong in spirit, returned the compliment; and how the Yellow banners struck up the Blue banners when the triumphal procession formed, and Blue heads went down under Yellow fists, and Yellow heroes collapsed beneath Blue boots, and the remaining half of the windows were smashed; and how the uproar was at its height, when into the market-place, spurring on Rumpunch, flecked with foam, came the head and root of it, my brother Fitz, as handsome, as devil-may-care, and as cool as ever.

Louder grew the yells, wilder the shouts, fiercer the row; up in the air flew the eggs and the mud and the sticks and the stones, and all the popular missiles of the Great Unwashed; but steady as a rock stood Rumpunch under Fitz's curb, and firm as a rock sat Fitz himself, in the midst of it. There's nothing like pluck for pleasing or awing the canaille; it is the one thing they will appreciate and revere. Their shouts hushed for a second, and they stopped in their onslaught upon him. He took advantage of it, and held up his hand: "Men, listen to me for a minute!"

They did listen to him, and Fitz went on:

"I hear I have lost my election. I am sorry for it, but I could scarcely expect otherwise; and if I have preferred securing an election of another kind, I hope the constituents of Cantitborough are all too gallant and chivalric gentlemen to disagree with me." Here uprose immense cheering from a few, and laughter even from the enraged community. "I can't alter your decision now, but I'll try to merit a different one next time I contend for the honour of representing you. I have no right to ask any favour at your hands; but, nevertheless, I am going to ask two: the first, that you will clear my cousin, and my agent and friend, of any imputation of knowing the true cause of my absence, and any deliberate intention of concealing it by a lie. The other is, that there may be no disunion or blood-shed on my behalf, and no broken heads caused through my fault. Let us all agree to differ; let the victorious go to their homes without insulting the vanquished, and the vanquished without quarrelling with the conquerors for justly earned success. Let us all part in good will, and let my friends go to the Ten Bells and drink my health and that of my bride, if they will be so kind, with three times three!"

It was a queer election speech, and without precedent, certainly, but in the little antiquated borough it told admirably. Never before was seen such an election, without doubt; but, somehow or other, Fitz, going into a new track, and doing such a thing as had never been done, got, all of a sudden, more heartily cheered, applauded, and hurrahed, than the successful candidates themselves. The gentlemen of the town sneered, and ridiculed, and fumed about his speech being most illegal, most unprecedented, most absurd; but the Unwashed, only looking at the pluck, and the manliness of tone, and the flowing taps of the Ten Bells, cheered him vociferously, and would have had the polling done over again if they could.

Beau stood looking on, with his brow knit like a Jupiter Tonans, and turned into the Ten Bells with a grunt.

"That fellow should have lived in the middle ages, with all his confounded folly. And yet, devil take him, why can't one hate him?"

"Will you forgive me, old boy?" laughed Fitz, following him into a private room twenty minutes after.

"Get out!" growled Beau, yet looking lovingly on him nevertheless. "A pretty fellow you are! making yourself look like a fool, and everybody else. I should have thought you more a man of sense than to run mad after a mere pretty face. Four thousand five hundred pounds fifteen shillings and eightpence gone for nothing!"

"Never mind, old fellow," laughed Fitz. "Barnardiston would have scented the ceremony, and forbidden it, on any other day; and as to waiting till she was of age, quite out of the question. If her face is not better to look at than the Speaker's, why——"

"Spare me that, spare me that!" cried Beau. "I'll forgive *you*, but I really can't stand *her* praises."

"Come and look at her, and you'll soon forgive her," said Fitz, taking out his watch. "I've made an immense sacrifice to you, Beau, in leaving her at one o'clock to ride over to this little owl of a town, whose animadversions are much more honour than its praise. She's at Sandslope—you know, that place by the sea, ten miles from here. I took her there yesterday, and now I must gallop back to her, or she'll be thinking the Blues and Yellows have eaten me up; and I say, Beau, don't be vexed, dear old boy. I will canvass for the next election in earnest; and when you come over to Sandslope (we don't want you *just* yet), if you don't say that Cora is excuse enough for anything, why you'll be made of granite."

"Hum!" grunted Beau, "I shall always hate her. But that don't matter; give my compliments to her (not my congratulations, for she'll find out that to have *you* for a husband is no matter for felicitation), and tell her that my sister the other day walked down Regent-street with 'Chaste and Elegant, 2*l*. 10s.' on her cloak, and that I hope she'll ticket herself the same, 'Mrs. Randolph Fitzhardinge, value 4500*l*. 15s. 8d.,' for she has cost you that to a certainty."

Apparently Fitz still thinks her worth it, for he has never regretted his hasty step. She did look excuse enough for anything when we saw her a week or two after, when she asked Beau's pardon so prettily and penitentially for the mischief she had done, that Beau, being the very reverse of a stoic, forgave her her sins, only made her solemnly promise to leave Fitz unmolested when next he stood for a free borough. Beau was made amiable, too, that morning, by hearing that Le Hoop Smith would be petitioned against for bribery, and that Barnardiston was already rumoured to repent having treated so cavalierly such a high match for his daughter.

Caroline married Whitechurch; they quarrel night and day at home, but abroad, administer, in amicable concert enough, very big texts and very small globules to their unlucky parishioners. Beau is supremely happy just at present, Fitz having procured for him a recordership, long the object of his desires. And Fitz? Well, Fitz wrote to me this June that he was going yachting in the Levant, with Cora and "three or four *other* pleasant fellows," that Cora is as bright as a sunbeam, and agrees with him in thinking the sherbet, laughter, and delicious bays of the Ionian Isles much better than the odours of the Thames in the senatorial halls of St. Stephen's.

But though they make a jest of it, and think the one election well won and the other well lost, I doubt if Cantitborough has ever forgotten, or will ever forget, the strangest contest that an enlightened borough of the enlightened nineteenth century ever beheld, and if the Cantitburghers will ever cease discussing in news, and drawing, and tap-room the memorable strife of BLUE AND YELLOW.

"REDEEMED."

AN EPISODE WITH THE CONFEDERATE HORSE.

Bertie Winton had got the Gold Vase.

The Sovereign, one of the best horses that ever had a dash of the Godolphin blood in him, had led the first flight over the ridge-and-furrow, cleared the fences, trying as the shire-thorn could make them, been lifted over the stiffest doubles and croppers, passed the turning-flags, and been landed at the straight run-in with the stay and pace for which his breed was famous, enrapturing the fancy, who had piled capfuls of money on him, and getting the Soldiers' Blue Riband from the Guards, who had stood crackers on little Benyon's mount—Ben, who is as pretty as a girl, with his *petites mains blanches*, riding like any professional.

Now, I take it—and I suppose there are none who will disagree with me—that there are few things pleasanter in this life than to stand, in the crisp winter's morning, winner of the Grand Military, having got the Gold Vase for the old corps against the best mounts in the Service.

Life must look worth having to you, when you have come over those black, barren pastures and rugged ploughed lands, where the field floundered helplessly in grief, with Brixworth brook yawning gaunt and wide beneath you, and the fresh cold north wind blowing full in your teeth, and have ridden in at the distance alone, while the air is rent by the echoing shouts of the surging crowd, and the best riding-men are left "nowhere" behind. Life must look pleasant to you, if it has been black as thunder the night before. Nevertheless, where Bertie Winton sat, having brought the Sovereign in, winner of the G. M., with that superb bay's head a little drooped, and his flanks steaming, but scarce a hair turned, while the men who had won pots of money on him crowded round in hot congratulation, and he drank down some Curaçoa punch out of a pocket pistol, with his habitual soft, low, languid laugh, he had that in his thoughts which took the flavour out of the Curaçoa, and made the sunny, cheery winter's day look very dull and grey to him. For Bertie, sitting there while the cheers reeled round him like mad, with a singularly handsome, reckless face, long tawny moustaches, tired blue eyes, and a splendid length and strength of limb, knew that this was the last day of the old times for him, and that he had sailed terribly near the wind of—dishonour.

He had been brought to *envisager* his position a little of late, and had seen that it was very bad indeed—as bad as it could be. He had run through all his own fortune from his mother, a good one enough, and owed almost as much again in bills and one way and another. He had lost heavily on the turf, gamed deeply, travelled with the most expensive adventuresses of their day, startled town with all its worst crim. cons.; had every vice under heaven, save that he drank not at all; and now, having shot a Russian prince at Baden the August before, about Lillah Lis, had received on the night just passed, from the Horse Guards, a hint, which was a command, that his absence was requested from her Majesty's Service—a mandate which, politely though inexorably couched, would have taken a more forcible and public form but for the respect in which his father, old Lion Winton, as he was called, was held by the Army and the authorities. And Bertie, who for five-and-thirty years had never thought at all, except on things that pleasured him, and such bagatelles as *barrière* duels abroad, delicately-spiced intrigues, bills easily renewed, the *cru* of wines, and the siege of women, found himself pulled up with a rush, and face to face with nothing less than ruin.

"I'm up a tree, Melcombe," he said to a man of his own corps that day as he finished a great cheroot before mounting.

"Badly?"

"Well, yes. It'll be smash this time, I suppose."

"Bother! That's hard lines."

"It's rather a bore," he answered, with a little yawn, as he got into saddle; and that was all he ever said then or afterwards on the matter; but he rode the Sovereign superbly over the barren wintry grass-land, and landed him winner of the Blue Riband for all that, though Black Care, for the first time in his life, rode behind him and weighted the race.

Poor Bertie! nobody would have believed him if he had said so, but he had been honestly and truly thinking, for some brief time past, whether it would not be possible and worth while for him to shake himself free of this life, of which he was growing heartily tired, and make a name for himself in the world in some other fashion than by winging Russians, importing new dancers, taking French women to the Bads, scandalising society, and beggaring himself. He had begun to wonder whether it was not yet, after all, too late, and whether if——when down had come the request from the Horse Guards for him to sell out, and the rush of all his creditors upon him, and away for ever went all his stray shapeless fancies of a possible better future. And—consolation or aggravation, whichever it be—he knew that he had no one, save himself, to thank for it; for no man ever had a more brilliant start in the race of life than he, and none need have better running over the course, had he only kept straight or put on the curb as he went down hill. Poor Bertie! you must have known many such lives, or I can't tell where your own has been spent; lives which began so brilliantly that none could rival them, and which ended—God help them!—so miserably and so pitifully that you do not think of them without a shudder still?

Poor Bertie!—a man of a sweeter temper, a more generous nature, a more lavish kindliness, never lived. He had the most versatile talents and the gentlest manners in the world; and yet here he was, having fairly come to ruin, and very nearly to disgrace.

It was little wonder that his father, looking at him and thinking of all he might have been, and all he might have done, was lashed into a terrible bitterness of passionate grief, and hurled words at him of a deadly wrath, in the morning that followed on the Grand Military. Fiery as his comrades the Napiers, of a stern code as a soldier, and a lofty honour as a man, haughty in pride and swift to passion, old Sir Lionel was stung to the quick by his son's fall, and would have sooner, by a thousand-fold, have followed him to his grave, than have seen him live to endure that tacit dismissal from the service of the country—the deepest shame, in his sight, that could have touched his race.

"I knew you were lost to morality, but I did not know till now that you were lost to honour!" said the old Lion, with such a storm of passion in him that his words swept out, acrid and unchosen, in a very whirlwind. "I knew you had vices, I knew you had follies, I knew you wasted your substance with debtors and gamblers like yourself, on courtesans and gaming-tables, in Parisian enormities, and vaunted libertinage, but I did not think that you were so utterly a traitor to your blood as to bring disgrace to a name that never was approached by shame until *you* bore it!"

Bertie's face flushed darkly, then he grew very pale. The indolence with which he lay back in an écarté-chair did not alter, however, and he stroked his long moustaches a little with his habitual gentle indifferentism.

"It is all over. Pray do not give it that tremendous earnestness," he said, quietly. "Nothing is ever worth that; and I should prefer it if we kept to the language of gentlemen!"

"The language of gentlemen is *for* gentlemen," retorted the old man, with fiery vehemence. His heart was cut to the core, and all his soul was in revolt against the degradation to his name that came in the train of his heir's ruin. "When a man has forgot that he has been a gentleman, one may be pardoned for forgetting it also! You may have no honour left for your career to shame; *I* have—and, by God, sir, from this hour you are no son of mine. I disown you—I know you no longer! Go and drag out all the rest of a disgraced life in any idleness that you choose. If you were to lie dying at my feet, I would not give you a crust!"

Bertie raised his eyebrows slightly.

"*Soit!* But would it not be possible to intimate this quietly? A scene is such very bad style—always exhausting, too!"

The languid calmness, the soft nonchalance of the tone, were like oil upon flame to the old Lion's heart, lashed to fury and embittered with pain as it was. A heavier oath than print will bear broke from him, with a deadly imprecation, as he paced the library with swift, uneven steps.

"It had been better if your 'style' had been less and your decency and your honour greater! One word more is all you will ever hear from my lips. The title must come to you; that, unhappily, is not in my hands to prevent. It must be yours when I die, if you have not been shot in some gambling brawl or some bagnio abroad before then; but you will remember, not a shilling of money, not a rood of the land are entailed; and, by the Heaven above us, every farthing, every acre shall be willed to the young children. *You* are disinherited, sir—disowned for ever—if you died at my feet! Now go, and never let me see your face again."

As he spoke, Bertie rose.

The two men stood opposite to each other—singularly alike in form and feature, in magnificence of stature, and distinction of personal beauty, save that the tawny gold of the old Lion's hair was flaked with white, and that his blue eyes were bright as steel and flashing fire, while the younger man's were very worn. His face, too, was deeply flushed and his lips quivered, while his son's were perfectly serene and impassive as he listened, without a muscle twitching, or even a gleam of anxiety coming into his eyes.

They were of different schools.

Bertie heard to the end; then bowed with a languid grace. "It will be fortunate for Lady Winton's children! Make her my compliments and congratulations. Good day to you."

Their eyes met steadily once—that was all; then the door of the library closed on him; Bertie knew the worst;

he was face to face with beggary. As he crossed the hall the entrance to the conservatories stood open; he looked through, paused a moment, and then went in. On a low chair, buried among the pyramids of blossom, sat a woman reading, aristocrat to the core, and in the earliest bloom of her youth, for she was scarcely eighteen, beautiful as the morning, with a delicate thorough-bred beauty, dark lustrous eyes, arched pencilled brows, a smile like sunshine, and lips sweet as they were proud. She was Ida Deloraine, a ward of Sir Lionel's, and a cousin of his young second wife's.

Bertie went up to her and held out his hand.

"Lady Ida, I am come to wish you good-bye."

She started a little and looked up.

"Good-bye! Are you going to town?"

"Yes—a little farther. Will you give me that camellia by way of *bon voyage?*"

A soft warmth flushed her face for a moment; she hesitated slightly, toying with the snowy blossom; then she gave it him. He had not asked it like a love gage.

He took it, and bowed silently over her hand.

"You will find it very cold," said Lady Ida, with a trifle of embarrassment, nestling herself in her dormeuse in her warm bright nest among the exotics.

He smiled—a very gentle smile.

"Yes, I am frozen out. Adieu!"

He paused a moment, looking at her—the brilliant picture framed in flowers; then, without another word, he bowed again and left her, the woman he had learned too late to love, and had lost by his own folly for ever.

"Frozen out? What could he mean?—there is no frost," thought Lady Ida, left alone in her hothouse warmth among the white and scarlet blossoms, a little startled, a little disappointed, a little excited with some vague apprehension, she could not have told why; while Bertie Winton went on out into the cold grey winter's morning from the old Northamptonshire hall that would know him no more, with no end so likely for him as that which had just been prophesied—a shot in a gambling hell.

Facilis descensus Averni—and he was at the bottom of the pit. Well, the descent had been very pleasant. Bertie set his teeth tight, and let the waters close over his head and shut him out of sight. He knew that a man who is down has nothing more to do with the world, save to quietly accept—oblivion.

* * * * * *

It was a hot summer night in Secessia.

The air was very heavy, no wind stirring the dense woods crowning the sides of the hills or the great fields of trodden maize trampled by the hoofs of cavalry and the tramp of divisions. The yellow corn waved above the earth where the dead had fallen like wheat in harvest-time, and the rice grew but the richer and the faster because it was sown in soil where slaughtered thousands rotted, unsepulchred and unrecorded. The shadows were black from the reared mountain range that rose frowning in the moonlight, and the stars were out in southern brilliancy, shining as calmly and as luminously as though their rays did not fall on graves crammed full with dead, on flaming homesteads, crowded sick-wards, poisonous waters that killed their thousands in deadly rivalry with shot and shell, and vast battalions sleeping on their arms in wheat-fields and by river-swamps, in opposing camps, and before beleaguered cities, where brethren warred with brethren, and Virginia was drenched with blood. There was no sound, save now and then the challenge of some distant picket or the faint note of a trumpet-call, the roar of a torrent among the hills, or the monotonous rise and fall from miles away in the interior, of the negroes' funeral song, "Old Joe"—more pathetic, somehow, when you catch it at night from the far distance echoing on the silence as you sit over a watch-fire, or ride alone through a ravine, than many a grander requiem.

It was close upon midnight, and all was very still; for they were in the heart of the South, and on the eve of a perilous enterprise, coined by a bold brain and to be carried out by a bold hand.

It was in the narrow neck of a valley, pent up between rocky shelving ridges, anywhere you will between Maryland and Georgia—for he who did this thing would not care to have it too particularly drawn out from the million other deeds of "derring-do" that the mighty story of the Great War has known and buried. Eight hundred Confederate Horse, some of Stuart's Cavalry, had got driven and trapped and caged up in this miserable defile, misled and intercepted; with the dense mass of a Federal army marching on their rear, within them by bare fifteen miles, and the forward route through the crammed defile between the hills, by which alone they could regain Lee's forces, dammed up by a deep, rapid, though not broad river; by a bridge strongly fortified and barricaded; and, on the opposite bank, by some Federal corps a couple of thousand strong, well under cover in rifle-pits and earthworks, thrown up by keen woodsmen and untiring trench-diggers. It was close peril, deadly as any that Secessia had seen, here in the hot still midnight, with the columns of the Federal divisions within them by eight hours' march, stretching out and taking in all the land to the rear in the sweep of their semicircular wings; while in front rose, black and shapeless in the deep gloom of the rocks above, the barricades upon the bridge, behind which two thousand rifles were ready to open fire at the first alarm from the Federal guard. And alone, without the possibility of aid, caged in among the trampled corn and maize that filled the valley, imprisoned between the two Federal forces as in the iron jaws of a trap, the handful of Southern troopers stood, resolute to sell their lives singly one by one, and at a costly price, and perish to a man, rather than fall alive into the hands of their foes.

When the morning broke they would be cut to pieces, as the chaff is cut by the whirl of the steam wheels. They knew that. Well, they looked at it steadily; it had no terrors for them, the Cavaliers of Old Virginia, so that they died with their face to the front. There was but one chance left for escape; aid there could be none; and that chance was so desperate, that even to them—reckless in daring, living habitually between life and death, and ever careless of the issue—it looked like madness to attempt it. But one among them had urged it on their consideration—urged it with passionate entreaty, pledging his own life for its success; and they had given their adhesion to it, for his name was famous through the Confederacy.

He had won his spurs at Manasses, at Antietam, at Chancellorsville; he had been in every headlong charge with Stuart; he had been renowned for the most dashing Border raids and conspicuous staff service of any soldier in Secessia; he had galloped through a tempest of the enemy's balls, and swept along their lines to reconnoitre, riding back through the storm of shot to Lee, as coolly as though he rode through a summer shower at a review; and his words had weight with men who would have gone after him to the death. He stood now, the only man dismounted, in true Virginian uniform; a rough riding-coat, crossed by an undressed chamois belt, into which his sabre and a brace of revolvers were thrust, a broad Spanish sombrero shading his face, great Hessians reaching above his knee, and a long silken golden-coloured beard sweeping to his waist—a keen reconnoitrer, a daring raider, a superb horseman, and a soldier heart and soul.

When he had laid before them the solitary chance of the perilous enterprise that he had planned, each man of the eight hundred had sought the post of danger for himself; but there he was, inexorable—what he had proposed he alone would execute. The Federals were ignorant of their close vicinity, for their near approach had been unheard, the trodden maize and rice, and the angry foaming of the torrent above, deadening the sound of their horses' hoofs; and the Union-men, satisfied that the "rebels" were entrapped beyond escape, were sleeping securely behind their earthworks, the passage of the river blockaded by their barricade, while the Southerners were drawn up close to the head of the bridge in sections of threes, screened by the intense shadow of the overhanging rocks; shadow darker from the brilliance of the full summer moon that, shining on the enemy's encampment, and on the black boiling waters thundering through the ravine, was shut out from the defile by the leaning pine-covered walls of granite. It was terribly still, that awful silence, only filled with the splashing of the water and the audible beat of the Federal sentinel's measured tramp, as they were drawn up there by the bridge head; and though they had cast themselves into the desperate effort with the recklessness of men for whom death waited surely on the morrow, it looked a madman's thought, a madman's exploit, to them, as their leader laid aside his sword and pistols, and took up a small barrel of powder, part of some ammunition carried off from some sappers' and miners' stores in the raid of the past day, the sight of which had brought to remembrance a stray, half-forgotten story told him in boyhood of one of Soult's Army—the story on which he was about to act now.

"For God's sake, take care!" whispered the man nearest him; and though he was a veteran who had gone through the hottest of the campaign since Bull's Run, his voice shook, and was husky as he spoke.

The other laughed a little—a slight, soft, languid laugh.

"All right, my dear fellow," he whispered back. "There's nothing in it to be alarmed at; a Frenchman did it in the Peninsula, you know. Only if I get shot, or blown up, and the alarm be given, do you take care to bolt over and cut your way through in the first of the rush, that's all."

Then, without more words, he laid himself down at full length with a cord tied round his ankle, that they might know his progress, and the cask of gunpowder, swathed in green cloth, that it should roll without noise along the ground; and, creeping slowly on his way, propelling the barrel with his head, and guiding it by his hands, was lost to their sight in the darkness. By the string, as it uncoiled through their hands, they could tell he was advancing; that was all.

The chances were as a million to one that his life would pay the forfeit for that perilous and daring venture; a single shot and he would be blown into the air a charred and shapeless corpse; one spark on that rolling mass that he pushed before him, and the explosion would hurl him upwards in the silent night, mangled, dismembered, blackened, lifeless. But his nerve was not the less cool, nor did his heart beat one throb the quicker, as he crept noiselessly along in the black shade cast by the parapet of the bridge, with the tramp of the guard close above on his ear, and rifles ready to be levelled on him from the covered earthworks if the faintest sound of his approach or the dimmest streak of moonlight on his moving body told the Federals of his presence. He had looked death in the teeth most days through the last five years; it had no power to quicken or slacken a single beat of his pulse as he propelled himself slowly forward along the black, rugged, uneven ground, and on to the passage of the bridge, as coolly, as fearlessly, as he would have crept through the heather and bracken after the slot of a deer on the moorside at home.

He heard the challenge and the tramp of the sentinel on the opposite bank; he saw the white starlight shine on the barrels of their breech-loaders as they paced to and fro in the stillness, filled with the surge and rush of the rapid waters beneath him. Shrouded in the gloom, he dragged himself onward with slow and painful movement, stretched out on the ground, urging himself forward by the action of his limbs so cautiously that, even had the light been on him, he could scarcely have been seen to move, or been distinguished from the earth on which he lay. Eight hundred lives hung on the coolness of his own; if he were discovered, they were lost. And, without haste, without excitation, he drew himself along under the parapet until he came to the centre of the bridge, placed the barrel close against the barricades, uncovered the head of the cask, and took his way back by the same laborious, tedious way, until he reached the

Virginian Troopers gathered together under the shelving rocks.

A deep hoarse murmur rolling down the ranks, the repressed cheer they dared not give aloud, welcomed him and the dauntless daring of his act; man after man pressed forward entreating to take his place, to share his peril; he gave it up to none, and three times more went back again on that deadly journey, until sufficient powder for his purpose was lodged under the Federal fortifications on the bridge. Two hours went by in that slow and terrible passage; then, for the last time, he wound a saucisson round his body serpent-wise, and, with that coil of powder curled around him, took his way once more in the same manner through the hot, dark, heavy night.

And those left behind in the impenetrable gloom, ignorant of his fate, knowing that with every instant the crack of the rifles might roll out on the stillness, and the balls pierce that death-snake twisted round his limbs, and the rocks echo with the roar of the exploding powder, blasting him in the rush of its sheet of fire and stones, sat mute and motionless in their saddles, with a colder chill in their bold blood, and a tighter fear at their proud hearts, than the Cavaliers of the South would have known for their own peril, or than he knew for his.

Another half-hour went by—an eternity in its long drawn-out suspense—then in the darkness under the rocks his form rose up amongst them.

"Ready?"—"Ready."

The low whisper passed all but inaudible from man to man. He took back his sabre and pistols and thrust them into his belt, then stooped, struck a slow match, and laid it to the end of the saucisson, whose mouth he had fastened to the barrels on the bridge, and rapidly as the lightning, flung himself across the horse held for him, and fell into line at the head of the troop.

There was a moment of intense silence while the fire crept up the long stick of the match; then the shrill, hissing, snake-like sound, that none who have once heard ever forget, rushed through the quiet of the night, and with a roar that startled all the sleeping echoes of the hills, the explosion followed; the columns of flame shooting upward to the starlit sky, and casting their crimson lurid light on the black brawling waters, on the rugged towering rocks, on the gnarled trunks of the lofty pines, and on the wild, picturesque forms and the bold, swarthy, Spanish-like faces of the Confederate raiders. With a shock that shook the earth till it rocked and trembled under them, the pillar of smoke and fire towered aloft in the hush of the midnight, blasting and hurling upward, in thunder that pealed back from rock to rock, lifeless bodies, mangled limbs, smouldering timbers, loosened stones, dead men flung heavenward like leaves whirled by the wind, and iron torn up and bent like saplings in a storm, as the mass of the barricades quivered, oscillated, and fell with a mighty crash, while the night was red with the hot glare of the flame, and filled with the deafening din.

The Federals, sleeping under cover of their intrenchments, woke by that concussion as though heaven and earth were meeting, poured out from pit and trench, from salient and parallel, to see their fortifications and their guard blown up, while the skies were lurid with the glow of the burning barricades, and the ravine was filled with the yellow mist of the dense and rolling smoke. Confused, startled, demoralised, they ran together like sheep, vainly rallied by their officers, some few hundred opening an aimless desultory fire from behind their works, the rest rushing hither and thither, in that inextricable intricacy, and nameless panic, which doom the best regiments that were ever under arms, when once they seize them.

"Charge!" shouted the Confederate leader, his voice ringing out clear and sonorous above the infernal tempest of hissing, roaring, shrieking, booming sound.

With that resistless impetus with which they had, over and over again, broken through the granite mass of packed squares and bristling bayonets, the Southerners, raising their wild war-whoop, thundered on to the bridge, which, strongly framed of stone and iron, had withstood the shock, as they had foreseen: and while the fiery glare shone, and the seething flame hissed, on the boiling waters below, swept, full gallop, over the torn limbs, the blackened bodies, the charred wood, the falling timbers, the exploding powder, with which the passage of the bridge was strewn, and charged through the hellish din, the lurid fire, the heavy smoke, at a headlong pace, down into the Federal camp.

A thousand shots fell like hail amongst them, but not a saddle was emptied, not even a trooper was touched; and with their line unbroken, and the challenge of their war-shout pealing out upon the uproar, they rode through the confusion worse confounded, and cutting their way through shot and sabre, through levelled rifles, and through piled earthworks, with their horses breathing fire, and the roar of the opening musketry pealing out upon their rear, dashed on, never drawing rein, down into the darkness of the front defile, and into the freshness of the starry summer night, saved by the leader that they loved, and —FREE!

"Tarnation cheeky thing to do. Guess they ain't wise to rile us that way," said a Federal general from

Fremont, as they discussed this exploit of the Eight Hundred at the Federal head-quarters.

"A splendid thing!" said an English visitor to the Northern camp, who had come for a six months' tour to see the war for himself, having been in his own time the friend of Paget and Vivian and Londonderry, the comrade of Picton, of Mackinnon, and of Arthur Wellesley. "A magnificent thing! I remember Bouchard did something the same sort of thing at Amarante, but not half so pluckily, nor against any such odds. Who's the fellow that led the charge? I'd give anything to see him and tell him what I think of it. How Will Napier would have loved him, by George!"

"Who's the d—d rebel, Jed?" said the General, taking his gin-sling.

"Think he's an Englishman. We'd give ten thousand dollars for him, alive or dead: he's fifty devils in one, that *I* know," responded the Colonel of Artillery, thus appealed to, a gentlemanlike, quiet man, educated at West Point.

"God bless the fellow! I'm glad he's English!" said the English visitor, heartily, forgetting his Federal situation and companions. "Who is he? Perhaps I know the name?"

"Should say you would. It's the same as your own —Winton. Bertie Winton, they call him. Maybe he's a relative of yours!"

The blood flushed the Englishman's face hotly for a second; then a stern dark shadow came on it, and his lips set tight.

"I have no knowledge of him," he said, curtly.

"Haven't you now? That's curious. Some said he was a son of yours," pursued the Colonel.

The old Lion flung back his silvery mane with his haughtiest imperiousness.

"No, sir; he's no son of mine."

Lord Winton sat silent, the dark shadow still upon his face. For five years no rumour even had reached him of the man he had disowned and disinherited; he had believed him dead—shot, as he had predicted, after some fray in a gaming-room abroad; and now he heard of him thus in the war-news of the American camp! His denial of him was not less stern, nor his refusal to acknowledge even his name less peremptory, because, with all his wrath, his bitterness, his inexorable passion, and his fierce repudiation of him as his son, a thrill of pleasure stirred in him that the man still lived—a proud triumph swept over him, through all his dark thoughts, at the magnificent dash and daring of a deed wholly akin to him.

Bertie, a listless man about town, a dilettante in pictures, wines, and women, spending every moment that he could in Paris, gentle as any young beauty, always bored, and never roused out of that habitual languid indolent indifferentism which the old man, fiery and impassioned himself as the Napiers, held the most damnable effeminacy with which the present generation emasculates itself, had been incomprehensible, antagonistic, abhorrent to him. Bertie, the Leader of the Eight Hundred, the reckless trooper of the Virginian Horse, the head of a hundred wild night raids, the hero of a score of brilliant charges, the chief in the most daring secret expeditions, and the most intrepid cavalry skirmishes of the South, was far nearer to the old Lion, who had in him all the hot fire of Crawford's school, with the severe simplicity of Wellington's stern creeds. "He is true to his blood at last," he muttered, as he tossed back his silky white hair, while his blue flashing eyes ranged over the far distance where the Southern lines lay, with something of eager restlessness; "he is true to his blood at last!"

There was fighting some days later in the Shenandoah Valley.

Longstreet's corps, with two regiments of cavalry, had attacked Sheridan's divisions, and the struggle was hot and fierce. The day was warm, and a brilliant sun poured down into the green cornland and woodland wealth of the valley as the Southern divisions came up to the attack in beautiful precision, and hurled themselves with tremendous *élan* on the right front of the Federals, who, covered by their hastily thrown-up breastworks, opened a deadly fire that raked the whole Confederate line as they advanced. Men fell by the score under the murderous mitraille, but the ranks closed up shoulder to shoulder, without pause or wavering, only maddened by the furious storm of shot, as the engagement became general and the white rolling clouds of smoke poured down the valley, and hid conflict and combatants from sight, the thunder of the musketry pealing from height to height; while in many places men were fighting literally face to face and hand to hand in a death-struggle—rare in these days, when the duello of artillery and the rivalry of breech-loaders begins, decides, and ends most battles.

On Longstreet's left, two squadrons of Virginian Cavalry were drawn up, waiting the order to advance, and passionately impatient of delay as regiment after regiment were sent up to the attack and were lost in the whirling cloud of dust and smoke, and they were kept motionless in reserve. At their head was Bertie Winton, unconscious that, on a hill to the right, with a group of Federal commanders, his father was looking down on that struggle in the Shenandoah. Bertie was little altered, save that on his face there was a sterner look, and in his eyes a keener and less listless glance; but the old languid grace, the old lazy gentleness, were there still. They were part of his nature, and nothing could kill them in him. In the five years that had gone by none whom he had known in Europe had ever heard a word of him or from him; he had cut away all the moorings that bound him to his old life, and had sought to build up his ruined fortunes, like the penniless soldier that he was, by his sword alone. So far he had succeeded: he had made his name famous throughout the States as a bold and unerring cavalry leader, and had won the personal friendship and esteem of the Chiefs of the Southern Confederacy. The five years had been filled with incessant adventures, with ever-present peril, with the din of falling citadels, with the rush of headlong charges, with daring raids in starless autumn nights, with bivouacs in trackless western forests, with desert-thirst in parching summer heats, with winters of such frozen roofless misery as he had never even dreamed—five years of ceaseless danger, of frequent suffering, of habitual renunciation; but five years of *life* —real, vivid, unselfish—and Bertie was a better man for them. What he had done at the head of Eight Hundred was but a sample of whatever he did whenever duty called, or opportunity offered, in the service of the South; and no man was better known or better trusted in all Lee's divisions than Bertie Winton, who sat now at the head of his regiment, waiting Longstreet's orders. An aide galloped up before long.

"The General desires you to charge and break the enemy's square to the left, Colonel."

Bertie bowed with the old Pall Mall grace, turned, and gave the word to advance. Like greyhounds loosed from leash, the squadrons thundered down the slope, and swept across the plain in magnificent order, charging full gallop, riding straight down on the bristling steel and levelled rifles of the enemy's kneeling square. They advanced in superb condition, in matchless order, coming on with the force of a whirlwind across the plain; midway they were met by a tremendous volley poured direct upon them; half their saddles were emptied; the riderless chargers tore, snorting, bleeding, terrified, out of the ranks; the line was broken; the Virginians wavered, halted, all but recoiled; it was one of those critical moments when hesitation is destruction. Bertie saw the danger, and with a shout to the men to come on, he spurred his horse through the raking volley of shot, while a shot struck his sombrero, leaving his head bare, and urging the animal straight at the Federal front, lifted him in the air as he would have done before a fence, and landed him in the midst of the square, down on the points of the levelled bayonets. With their fierce war-cheer ringing out above the sullen uproar of the firing, his troopers followed him to a man, charged the enemy's line, broke through the packed mass opposed to them, cut their way through into the centre, and hewed their enemies down as mowers hew the grass. Longstreet's work was done for him; the Federal square was broken, never again to rally.

But the victory was bought with a price; as his horse fell, pierced and transfixed by the crossed steel of the bayonets, a dozen rifles covered the Confederate leader; their shots rang out, and Bertie Winton reeled from his saddle and sank down beneath the press as his own Southerners charged above him in the rush of the onward attack. On an eminence to the right, through his race-glass, his father watched the engagement, his eyes seldom withdrawn from the Virginian cavalry, where, for aught he knew, one of his own blood and name might be—memories of Salamanca and Quatre Bras, of Moodkee and Ferozeshah, stirring in him, while the fire of his dead youth thrilled through his veins with the tramp of the opposing divisions, and he roused like a war-horse at the scent of the battle, as the white shroud of the smoke rolled up to his feet, and the thunder of the musketry echoed through the valley. Through his glass, he saw the order given to the troopers held in reserve; he saw the magnificent advance of that charge in the morning light; he saw the volley poured in upon them; and he saw them under that shock reel, stagger, waver, and recoil. The old soldier knew well the critical danger of that ominous moment of panic and of confusion; then, as the Confederate Colonel rode out alone and put his horse at that leap on to the line of steel, into the bristling square, a cry loud as the Virginian battle-shout broke from him. For when the charger rose in the air, and the sun shone full on the uncovered head of the Southern leader, he knew the fair English features that no skies could bronze, and the fair English hair that blew in the hot wind. He looked once more upon the man he had denied and had disowned; and, as Bertie Winton reeled and fell, his father, all unarmed, and non-combatant as he was, drove the spurs into his horse's flanks, and dashing down the steep hillside, rode over the heaps of slain, and through the pools of gore into the thick of the strife.

With his charger dead under him, beaten down upon one knee, his sword-arm shivered by a bullet, while the blood poured from his side where another shot had lodged, Bertie knew that his last hour had come, as the impetus of the charge broke above him—as a great wave may sweep over the head of a drowning man—and left him in the centre of the foe. Kneeling there, while the air was red before his sight, that was fast growing blind from the loss of blood, and the earth seemed to reel and rock under him, he still fought to desperation, his sabre in his left hand; he knew he could not hold out more than a second longer, but while he had strength he kept at bay.

His life was not worth a moment's purchase—when, with a shout that rang over the field, the old Lion rode down through the carnage to his rescue, his white hair floating in the wind, his azure eyes flashing with war-fire, his holster-pistol levelled; spurred his horse through the struggle, trampled aside all that opposed him, dashed untouched through the cross-fire of the bullets, shot through the brain the man whose rifle covered his son who had reeled down insensible, and stooping, raised the senseless body, lifted him up by sheer manual strength to the level of his saddle-bow, laid him across his holsters, holding him up with his right hand, and, while the Federals fell asunder in sheer amazement at the sudden onslaught, and admiration of the old man's daring, plunged the rowels into his horse, and, breaking through the reeking slaughter of the battle-field, rode back, thus laden with his prisoner, through the incessant fire of the cannonade up the heights to the Federal lines.

"If you were to lie dying at my feet!"—his father remembered those words, that had been spoken five years before in the fury of a deadly passion, as Bertie lay stretched before him in his tent, the blood flowing from the deep shot-wound in his side, his eyes closed, his face livid, and about his lips a faint and ghastly foam.

Had he saved him too late? had he too late repented?

His heart had yearned to him when, in the morning light, he had looked once more upon the face of his son, as the Virginian Horse had swept on to the shock of the charge; and all of wrath, of bitterness, of hatred, of dark, implacable, unforgiving vengeance were quenched and gone for ever from his soul as he stooped over him where he lay at his feet, stricken and senseless in all the glory of his manhood. He only knew that he loved the man—he only knew that he would have died for him, or died with him.

Bertie stirred faintly, with a heavy sigh, and his left hand moved towards his breast. Old Sir Lion bent over him, while his voice shook terribly, like a woman's.

"Bertie! My God! don't you know *me?*"

He opened his eyes and looked wearily and dreamily around; he did not know what had passed, nor where he was; but a faint light of wonder, of pleasure, of recognition, came into his eyes, and he smiled—a smile that was very gentle and very wistful.

"I am glad of that — before I die! Let us part friends—*now*. They will tell you I have—redeemed—the name."

The words died slowly and with difficulty on his lips, and as his father's hand closed upon his in a strong grasp of tenderness and reconciliation, his lids closed, his head fell back, and a deep-drawn, laboured sigh quivered through all his frame; and Lion Winton, bowing down his grand white crest, wept with the passion of a woman. For he knew not whether the son he loved was living or dead—he knew not whether he was not at the last too late.

* * * * * * *

Three months further on, Lady Ida Deloraine sat in her warm bright nest among the exotics, gazing out upon the sunny lawns and the green woodlands of Northamptonshire. Highest names and proudest titles had been pressed on her through the five years that had gone, but her loveliness had been unwon, and was but something more thoughtful, more brilliant, more exquisite still than of old. The beautiful warmth that had never come there through all these years was in her cheeks now, and the nameless lustre was in her eyes, which all those who had wooed her, had never wakened in their antelope brilliancy, as she sat looking outward at the sunlight; for in her hands lay a camellia, withered, colourless, and yellow, and eyes gazed down upon the marvellous beauty of her face which had remembered it in the hush of Virginian forests, in the rush of headlong charges, in the glare of bivouac fires, in the silence of night-pickets, and in the din of falling cities.

And Bertie's voice, as he bent over her, was on her ear.

"That flower has been on my heart night and day; and since we parted I have never done that which would have been insult to your memory. I have tried to lead a better and a purer life; I have striven to redeem my name and my honour; I have done all I could to wash out the vice and the vileness of my past. Through all the years we have been severed I have had no thought, no hope, except to die more worthy of you; but now—oh, my God!—if you knew how I love you, if you knew how my love alone saved me——"

His words broke down in the great passion that had been his redemption; and as she lifted her eyes upward to his own, soft with tears that gathered but did not fall, and lustrous with the light that had never come there save for him, he bowed his head over her, and, as his lips met hers, he knew that the redeemed life he laid at her feet was dearer to her than lives, more stainless, but less nobly won.

THE MARQUIS'S TACTICS;

OR,

LORD GLEN'S WAGER.

"My dear Cyril, why don't you marry?" asked the Marquis of Glenallerton of his second son.

St. Albans, lying on his sofa in his rooms in Albemarle-street, smoking a hookah, and drinking hock and Seltzer, looked up, stared, and laughed.

"Why don't I marry? My dear governor, you shouldn't ask point-blank questions like that. Please remember one's nerves. Why don't I? Because, though Pascal says, '*L'homme n'est ni bête ni ange*,' I think he is most irrevocably and undeniably *bête* when he assumes the matrimonial fetters?"

"Of course?" responded the Marquis, familiarly known as Lord Glen. "We all know that: marriage is a social arrangement and inconvenience, like the income-tax, and one conforms to it as such. I'm not asking you to go and fall in love and crown a thousand follies with an irremediable one; God forbid! with all your absurdities you are too much a man of the world to make me fear that. I was merely thinking——You're near thirty, ain't you?"

"Eight-and-thirty, last January."

"Very well. You have *mené la vie* to your heart's content; you are most shockingly indolent; your debts are very heavy; you *will* bet—and on the most unlikely events, too—as if you were a millionnaire like Crowndiamonds. I think, considering you are a younger son, and will get nothing more from me, that a good marriage, far from being a folly, would show greater wisdom than I should give you credit for after your tomfoolery at Wilverton— the idea of losing a borough that your family have had in their pocket for ages, for a pack of rubbish about 'not bribing!' Bacon took bribes, however they try to smoothe it over as 'fees,' and Walpole gave 'em. Do you set yourself above *them*, pray?"

"Certainly not; one was a lawyer, and had the devil to sharpen his wits; the other was a toper, and did very shrewd things in his cups. But don't worry me about it, pray. I assure you it wasn't any bosh about honour or virtue that made me refuse to bribe the Wilvertonians; it was only laziness, on my word; I hated the bore of St. Stephen's, and didn't know how else to get rid of the affair. Indolence is hereditary and chronic in me. I can't help it."

"Well, well, you lost the election, so there's an end of it," said the Marquis, impatiently, in happy ignorance of the sneer on his son's lips, "but with regard to your marrying. Well, don't you think you could do it?"

"Decidedly I *could* do it," replied St. Albans, with a glance at himself in an opposite mirror.

"Then *do* do it. You have only to choose; any woman would have you. I don't mean a *nouvelle riche;* you shouldn't ally us with a parvenue to save yourself from starving; but such as Lady Elma Fer——"

"Not for an El Dorado! She is eight-and-twenty, is freckled, and has red hair——"

"Pray what does beauty matter in a wife? You will have plenty of beauties left elsewhere, won't you?"

"I hope so; but I shouldn't be able to enjoy them, for one tête-à-tête with a freckled woman would have killed me."

"Talk sense," interrupted old Glen, angrily. "One would think you had no brains, Cyril. Look at it rationally. Is there anything for you but to make a rich marriage?"

St. Albans took a few silent puffs from his hookah with a profound sigh, and answered not.

"I can give you no money, and you have a terrible taste for expensive pleasures; you have lived at double the rate your brothers have for the last fifteen years. Go on as you are now, you must go to the dogs your own way; *I* can't help you; I'm en route there myself. Marry an heiress, your difficulties are cleared, and you can have your pleasures *a votre gré*. As for wanting beauty in your wife—one would think you were twenty! Your mother was plain; she had good blood and money, but she was remarkably plain; you take all your beauty from me. Now there is Avarina Sansreproche, most unobjectionable in every way, will be Baroness Turquoise and Malachite in her own right; not exactly pretty, perhaps, but very good style: a woman who would never do a silly thing, or make a dubious acquaintance. Her mother, I know, would not object to the alliance; in fact, you need only be a little rational and passive, and I could arrange it for you; the mere whisper of an engagement with her would quiet those Jews in a moment. Are you listening, Cyril?"

St. Albans yawned and stretched himself a little more comfortably:

"Most attentively, sir; but you must really excuse my answering; it's too warm to talk."

"Well, say yes or no, if that's not too much exertion.

You are in a perfect Gordian knot of difficulties. Do you see any way of cutting it but the one I propose?"

His son yawned again, sighed, and took a long whiff of his perfumed hubble-bubble:

"My dear governor, if you *will* make me speak, no, I don't see any other way; I wish I did, because really the trouble of thinking is odious; the day's so much too close to do anything but drink Seltzer."

"You admit you don't see any other way of getting out of your labyrinth of debts, and going on smoothly in the future?"

St. Albans shut his eyes and shifted his cushions:

"I said I didn't—pray don't worry. I dare say I could get a very good living as model to the artist fellows; they want handsome men, and I've no doubt my hand alone would bring in a very fair sum. But you'd think that rather derogatory to the family, you see; so that career isn't open to me."

Lord Glen laughed, and rose from his chair:

"Don't be a fool, Cyril, but go and call in Wilton-crescent. Think over what I have said, and act like a practical man for once, if you can. You *must* marry Avarina, for I can tell you for your comfort that book-makers are beginning to back Coronation very confidently, and that I know on good authority Caradoc hasn't himself the confidence in Grey Royal that you fancy; that mare will no more win the Cup than your Park hack."

With which consolatory last hit the Marquis shut the door, and went down-stairs to his brougham, while St. Albans, letting fall the mouthpiece of his hookah, dropped his head on his hands with a bitter sigh:

"If she doesn't win I shall be ruined. What a fool I have been to mesh myself in such a net of debts and entanglements! How I shall get out of them, God knows.

And now he wants me to patch up my fortunes by marriage. Avarina Sansreproche! Faugh!—the Queen's Bench were better than that. He is right—I am going to the dogs, and dragging others with me too. By Jove! if he knew all, poor old fellow, it would bring on a fit, or he would console himself by cutting me in Pall Mall. I can't go on long like this; yet Heaven knows what I had better do. Marry Avarina Sansreproche! Faugh!"

His rooms were the most luxurious in any bachelor house in town; his breakfast was served in a silver and Dresden service fit for a young Princess; piles of rose, green, and cream-hued little notes, and a swarm of invitation-cards to all the best houses, lay on his writing-table; he belonged to the best set, drove the best horses, and was a member of the best clubs in London; but for all that St. Albans, as he leaned his head on his hands, with a very real and unmistakable sigh, and dropped the languid, bored tone he had used about his difficulties to his father, had about as much worry just then on his shoulders as any man going in London.

"Marry!" he said to himself, picking up his hookah again. "What on earth put that into his head? What's the time—two? I'll order the tilbury, and go and see her again."

"I want Cyril to marry," said Lord Glen, that same morning, in one of the windows of the Conservative, to me and Charlie de Vesci, another Coldstreamer, and St. Albans' special friend—"I want him to marry: you're a good deal with him; do your best to persuade him, there's a good fellow."

"You want him to marry, sir? What for, in the name of Heaven? St. Albans is the last man in the world to suit that sort of harness, and I thought you——"

"Were the last man to advocate it? Of course I am.

At the same time, if you're going to the deuce, you must put on any drag that'll keep the wheels from going down hill, must you not? You know Cyril's extravagance as well as I do. The best thing in the world would be for him to marry well, and the alliance I desire for him is Avarina Sansreproche. I have reason to believe, too, that Lady Turquoise is as inclined to the arrangement as myself. Nothing can be more suitable. She is three-and-twenty, eminently good style——"

"As cold as a statue, sir!"

The Marquis took a pinch out of his enamelled tabatière with a picture of Clara d'Ische by Mignard.

"The most desirable thing a wife can be. Secures you from all scandal!"

"But not at all fit for Cyril!"

"I hardly apprehend you. Fit for him? I am not asking them to *raffole* of each other—he is a man of the world, she is a woman of good sense—I merely want them to marry. I think she is admirably fitted for Cyril. She has good blood, great fortune; he would be exacting, indeed, to ask more."

"Perhaps; for all that, sir, I doubt if you will ever bring St. Albans round to think with you. Miss Sansreproche isn't pretty enough to please him, and I am sure he will hate being tied, however light you may make his fetters."

"What will you bet me that I, being allowed to manage it as I find best, shall see Cyril married within—let me see—I will say by the end of the season?"

I laughed:

"Very well, sir. I don't know anything about it, but I would bet you twenty guineas that by the end of the season you'll see no such thing. My dear Lord!—St. Albans will no more let himself be married than I shall."

Lord Glen entered the wager duly in his mem.-book.

"You will lose, my good fellow. He will marry when I wish him. He must. He lives very gaily and expensively. I don't expect him to do otherwise. But you know he has nothing—*we* never have; the *racaille* get all the money in these democratic days. So you and Bellaysse tied at Hornsey Wood yesterday? You shot off the ties early; Delamere told me the sun was so in your eyes you could hardly mark the birds."

"What were you doing with yourself yesterday at noon? I thought you never went out before two, and I positively called at twelve, because I particularly wanted to see you, and your man said you weren't at home," said Lord Glenallerton, in a considerably injured tone two days after in the smoking-room of the Guards' Club.

St. Albans dropped his eye-glass, and laid down the paper.

"My dear governor, if you will call on men at barbarian hours, you must expect valets, who have a decent idea of the blessings of slumber and peace, to tell a mild fib in their masters' service. You don't *really* mean you would have had the heart to get me up at noon, do you?"

"Certainly I should. You can get up early at Glen-Albans to go after deer, surely you can get up early in town to talk to me. It is seldom enough I want the trouble of seeing you. But your man said positively you were out. I asked him if he meant 'Not visible,' and he said no, you were not at home."

"Stupid fool!" said Cyril, sotto voce, as he took his cigarette out of his mouth. "*Bon père!* is it possible I should remember so far back as yesterday what I did with myself. Be reasonable! I have lived—let me see—

thirty-one, thirty-two—positively thirty-four hours since then!"

The Marquis looked at him, took out his snuff-box, and shrugged his shoulders.

"You can leave your memory behind you sometimes, my good fellow, as completely and conveniently as a bribed witness! *I* don't want to know what you did with yourself, Heaven forbid! I came to advise you to hedge as much as possible. From all I hear, I am certain Grey Royal is very unsafe. None of that breed ever had any pace in them yet. Listen a minute, Cyril, and take counsel, if you can."

With which he dropped his voice, and detailed some chronique scandaleuse of the unsoundness of Grey Royal, second favourite for the Ascot Cup, which was going the round of some Turf circles, and altering the odds at the Rooms.

"I have warned you. I have said my last word about that cursed mare," said the Marquis, as he rose. "You will come to my house to-night, Cyril?"

"Do you want me dreadfully? Can't you let me off?"

"No; it is very odd if you cannot spare an hour to show yourself in my rooms. I do not choose that every one in town should be seen at my parties but you, and that my sons should shun my house alone of anybody in London. Fainéant is abroad, I don't speak of him; and Julian I have done with long ago. He has taken up the patriotic and philanthropic clap-trap, let him keep to it. It is so excessively low! I don't know what we should have thought in the Regency of men who ought to be gentlemen, lecturing as if they were the drunken cobblers of a Methodist gathering, and pottering about Ragged Schools to get a little vulgar toadying, and heading Social Movements as if they were Chartists or Sensationalists—

it is so horridly low all that! But you, *you* are a man of good taste and good breeding, Cyril; it hurts me that you should never be seen at my house."

That speech was quite true. If Lord Glen likes anybody it is his second son, who has his wit, his beauty, and is, as the Marquis will complacently tell us, "exactly what I was forty years ago." But it was a craftily timed speech for all that, and St. Albans fell into the trap; he looked kindly at his father, and drank some hock and Seltzer.

"I'll come, governor!"

"The deuce, I never remembered that woman!" said St. Albans, under his breath, on the top of the staircase of his father's house in Berkeley-square. "That's what he bothered me to come here for, and I never thought of her!"

I, remembering the Marquis's wager, followed his glance, which was through the doorway, into the Marquis's salons, where all the *crême de la crême* were gathering and commingling; and there, among other young Belgraviennes, saw Avarina Sansreproche, the subject of the Marquis's diplomacy, the future Lady Cyril St. Albans, and sole heiress prospective to her mother's barony of Turquoise and Malachite. She was what we call by complaisance a fine girl: she was not handsome, or interesting, or brilliant, but she was clever, dressed well of course, and was eminently good style, as Lord Glen averred; she was very cold in manner, and rumour said of not the sweetest temper; but she had a distinguished air, and from her height and figure told well in a ball-room.

Altogether, considering how good an alliance she would be, she was not a woman to merit the disdainful and disgusted tone with which St. Albans murmured his uncomplimentary words on the staircase as he caught sight of her at his father's ball, which made me smile as I heard them, to think how little likely the Marquis was to win his bet and shackle his son with matrimonial handcuffs, with all his skill at diplomacy, and his Rochefoucauldean knowledge of men and their weaknesses.

Avarina looked very well that night, and her mother smiled her most gracious smile when St. Albans drew near them, and stopped to say a few words to them before passing on. True, the future Baroness might have looked for an elder rather than a younger son, but the St. Albans were one of the oldest and noblest houses in the Peerage. A cadet of that family was preferable to the head of many others, and Lord Glenallerton was leader in the Upper House of that great political party to which Lady Turquoise, as vehement an intriguer as Madame de Longueville or the Duchess of Devonshire, belonged heart and soul. Cyril was his favourite son; he did not care about Fainéant, who was plain, like the late Lady Glen, and had never been in his good graces for that reason, the Marquis rating beauty as highly as any woman. His third son, Julian, he had, as he said, done with long ago, Julian being an M.P., and taking a utilitarian and educating-of-the-masses line, which was naturally the antipodes of all his predilections, and disgusted him too much for remonstrance; but Cyril always pleased him: his manner, his air, his tastes, his person, his way of life, were all in accordance with all his father's views of what a gentleman and a St. Albans ought to be. Cyril was his favourite son, and therefore did he and Lady Turquoise tacitly agree—perhaps, even, in a little boudoir conference, admit to each other their agreement—in the choice of an alliance for Avarina.

"Cyril, you entreated me to be your envoy, and I have had the happiness to succeed in my embassy. Miss

Sansreproche has done you the honour to reserve you a place on her tablets," said the clever old Lord, with that gallant grace of air which had gained him so many *bonnes fortunes*, and won him so brilliant a reputation in the old Regency days with Alvanley and Pierrepoint. Men of condition, as Walter Scott says, never show what they feel, let them be startled, bewildered, or dismayed as they may, or, for a certainty, St. Albans would have shown his amazement at his father's adroit invention. "For a lie gracefully told, commend me to the governor!" he thought, as, *bon gré mal gré*, he bowed his thanks to Avarina for an honour he had certainly been most innocent of soliciting.

Cootes and Tinney's band were playing the Dinorah Quadrilles, and he had to give her his arm and lead her to the ball-room, let in for it as neatly as any man could be, while the Marquis stroked a little moth off his Blue Riband with an inward smile of complacency. His first minor move in diplomacy had succeeded, and perhaps St. Albans, though it bored him just then, would thank him afterwards. When one is drowning, one is grateful to anybody that flings us a rope, however tarred and rough a one.

"Hallo, old fellow, you are leaving early. Avarina Sansreproche won't be flattered, will she?" said I, as, about an hour afterwards, having three or four other places to go to that night, I left Lord Glen's, and met St. Albans just going to his cab.

"Avarina Sansreproche be hanged!" said he, between his teeth, as he stopped to light a Manilla. "Marry merely for money—buy freedom from my difficulties with that girl's gold—how low my father must think that I have sunk! Live on your wife's money! Good God, what lower degradation could there be?"

"Lots of men do it, though, old fellow, and think it none, when there's no better way of clearing themselves out of their difficulties."

"Exactly," said St. Albans, in his ordinary languid tone, with his pet semi-yawn, semi-sigh; "but only think of the horror of having to hear settlements read, and the worry of going through the marriage ceremony! It's far better of the two to go to the dogs quietly and gently, in a pleasant way, than to put the matrimonial drag on the wheels, and avoid Cerberus only to fall into the hug of Hecate. I've no scruples about anything, except about worrying myself. I don't care how low I sink, but you must please line the pit with rose-leaves. I wouldn't mind selling myself to the devil at all if that gentleman were in that style of trade now, and paid handsomely, but I couldn't sell myself to a wife—indeed I couldn't; marriage is an awful price to pay for a little monetary security. Fancy a woman who'd think she had a right over you, and who'd persist in bothering you, and lecturing you, and ferreting out where you went! It's better to give Leoni Levi cent. per cent. than to go through the ennui of a honeymoon. Fancy doing rural felicity, and raptures, and all the rest of it, and having to make love to the same woman one whole month long! I'd rather go to a Neapolitan prison. Why, a week of it would kill me. Milner, drive as fast as you can," said St. Albans, flinging his fusee into the gutter, and getting into his Hansom.

"Are you going to La Bonbonnière's? If you are, we can go together."

"La Bonbonnière's! No. I rarely go there now."

"What for? Have you quarrelled?"

The Comtesse de la Bonbonnière was a very charming little woman, and St. Albans had found no boudoir so attractive, and no opera suppers so agreeable, as those in her Section of the French embassy.

"Quarrelled? Not at all! But we idolised each other last season; it's in the nature of things that we're tired of one another this! Good-night. Drive fast, Milner!"

"Where to, my Lord?"

"To Richmond!"

His Hansom dashed round the corner at a pace that might have won a trotting-match, and I got into my own cab, and drove off to a ball at Carlton House-terrace, thinking that, with Cyril's views of marriage, the old Lord, with all his diplomacy, was not very likely to win his bet, and persuade his son to enter the holy bond, St. Albans being about the last man in town to assume the matrimonial fetters, or endure them when they were on. He was in the Coldstream Guards; he was a man sworn to pleasure, and to pleasure alone; he led a gay, easy, agreeable, extravagant life; was a leader of fashion, and a referee at clubs; hated worry, loved luxury, was utterly unused to any restrictions, and was the very last sort of person to be coaxed, driven, coerced, propelled, or led in any way into the shackles Lord Glen proposed for him. But great is the might of money, and when you have Ruin on one side of you and Hanover-square on the other, there is no knowing *what* you may do, mon ami, or which of the evils you may fancy the lesser; so, with all the odds in my favour, I hardly felt sure of winning the bet I had made.

"You *must* marry, Cyril," said old Glen, imperatively, as meeting the Coldstreamer in St. James's-street the next morning between two and three, he walked down there with him.

"My dear governor, so we must all *die*, but the obligation isn't an agreeable one; why refer to it? Positively, you're as cruel as a priest laying the skull and cross-bones right on the top of one's rose chaplets. The idea of bringing up horrid topics on a cool pleasant May morning like this!"

The Marquis gave a little growl and a contemptuous sneer.

"I thought you were a man of the world."

"Did you? Far from it. I'm a most innocent and unsophisticated person; no man more so; but merit's always misjudged."

Lord Glen gave a short laugh of amusement, as well he might.

"I thought you were a man of the world, too much of one not to know that such a very unimportant step as marriage can matter nothing in our ranks. If your wife be in a bad temper, you have nothing to do but to leave her; if she begin a quarrel, go and dine at White's or the Guards'; if she bother you very much, have a separate establishment. You are not like a man of the middle class with a limited income, resting on a clientela who *viser* all his actions, and would desert him if he tried to get a little liberty, or openly infringed their pet clap-trap of the domesticities. Be sensible, Cyril; of all the married men we know, on which of them has his wife any influence? Which of them allows her to trouble him the least? Of course not; *he* is in the world, *she* is in the world: they go their own ways, and neither troubles the other. So will you and Avarina; she is far too sensible a woman to want a lover's devotion from you, or any of that nonsense, you may keep it for Madame de la Bonbonnière; she is a Frenchwoman, and likes sentiment. I perfectly understand your reluctance: you are a man of pleasure, naturally you dislike anything that may interfere with or limit your pleasure, but, believe me, in seventy-eight years I have seen a little of life, Cyril! marriage will not make the slightest difference to you; you will live in Belgrave-square instead of Albemarle-street, that is all."

St. Albans listened and walked on in silence.

"You *must* marry," reiterated the Marquis. "Grey Royal has no more pace in her than a cab-horse; what could possess you, my dear boy, to venture so much on that miserable chesnut?"

St. Albans drew his breath hard, and turned paler for a second.

"You recommend me to marry, governor?" he said after a pause.

"I do, most decidedly."

"Very well, I'll think about it; don't worry me any more," said St. Albans, languidly. "Faugh! how that fellow that passed us was scented with musk! Are you going into White's? I am."

I have always liked the Marquis myself; he has no deep feelings to trouble him, he is an egotistical and worldly old gentleman; he sometimes tilts with the most amiable unconsciousness against your tenderest wounds, and makes you writhe without ever noticing it; but I always liked him, always shall; he is very clever, very amusing, ever good natured, ever hospitable, and is as fond of his second son, in his own way, as he could be of any one. I should be very glad if anybody would tell me why novelists always fancy it necessary to make their characters *either* good or bad, quite one or quite the other; the majority of people about in the world are, it seems to me, *neither* the one nor the other exclusively, but a mixture of both, as the Mocha your valet brings you up in the morning is coffee and chicory equally mixed. Five people out of six have no marked characters at all, and the generality one meets could neither be taxed with any remarkable vice nor honoured for any remarkable virtue; they would ruin your peace with their malice, but would not touch you with a dagger for the world, and are capable neither of a positively noble action nor of a positively bad one. You must have force of character for the extreme of both good and evil. Half the people in society are like my friend Lord Glen, who would have been insulted, no person more so, had you asked him to do anything dishonourable; but could see nothing degrading in the advice he gave his son, honestly thinking it was the best St. Albans could receive and follow, to make a rich marriage, that he might quiet his creditors now, and live on his wife's money afterwards.

"I shall win, my dear fellow," said he to me at a morning party at Fulham, as he stood stirring the cream in a cup of Souchong under a great chesnut-tree on the lawn, where the band was playing Trovatore airs and new waltzes, and we were eating Neapolitan ices, flirting, and playing croquet or lawn billiards with some hundred or so of our kind in the grounds of Lady Rosediamonds' bijou of a dower-house. I followed his glance, which was to where Avarina sat, looking more animated than usual, and talking to St. Albans.

"Do you think so, sir? I hope not. Wealth is the best of all blessings, Heaven knows, but, my dear Lord, he's the last fellow in the world to be put into bondage, even for that. The idea of St. Albans married!"

"I was just such a man as Cyril at his age, and *I* married, but I can assure you I made the fetters so light I did not know I wore them. Any sensible man may, if he likes. Cyril will marry Avarina, and will thank me very much for having made him the alliance. I knew I should bring him round to my views; he is a sensible fellow, really, though he has a few strange Quixotic ideas, like those about his election. I cannot imagine where he has got them; the St. Albans were never romantic, nor the Dormers either, and romance is such a *very* queer thing to linger in a man who has lived as my son has done. He will marry Avarina, *bon garçon*, and I am very glad of it—very glad." And the Marquis finished his tea, and turned to Lady Rosediamonds in the best possible spirits at the coming success of his diplomacy.

"Dine with me to-night?" he asked, when Avarina and her mother were rolling back to Belgravia. "And you, Cyril?"

"I sir?" said St. Albans. "Thanks, no. I'm engaged for this evening."

"Ah! no doubt; where to, may I ask?"

I dare say Lord Glen had a fond hope that the answer would be Wilton-crescent, but it wasn't; it was brief enough: "Richmond."

"Richmond? A man dinner, or a boating party, or what? You are always dining at Richmond, it seems to me; you were there on Monday, and yesterday too; with all the best houses in town open to you, I wonder you take the trouble to go all the way down there with a few men, or a few little dancers. Yesterday you threw over the Duchess's dinner for some Richmond affair. I have no business with what you do with yourself, of course, but it is unlike you, and bad taste, you are generally so very exclusive. Won't you be back in time for Protocol's reception to-night?"

St. Albans shook his head.

"My dear governor, why should I go to Protocol's? The atmosphere will be at 70 deg. I should be crushed as usual, and should only reach the green drawing-room and the Countess after three hours' steady toil. I've done so many of these things, please don't ask me; my health's too delicate to stand the fatigues of an assembly just yet again."

"Very odd," said Lord Glen to himself, as the Coldstreamer drove off, nodding a good-bye to his father. "Last season Cyril was at every reception in town; he is surely never losing his taste for good society!"

I don't suppose the Marquis liked Avarina Sansreproche, as he had a special contempt for any but very lovely women, save for matrimonial alliances. The St. Albans women and men are a family of great beauty, and have been famed for it for many generations; and Lord Glen sets the greatest possible store on it, both in himself and others, therefore I don't suppose he had any particular admiration for his future daughter-in-law; but if he made love for himself in the Regency days half so gracefully and gallantly as he now made it for his son, the reputation he won when he was Viscount Fainéant was not to be wondered at. And if St. Albans was rather lax in his courtship, the Marquis did his best to cover and make up for his shortcomings. St. Albans, though I suppose reconciled, was hardly as enchanted as his father; I fancied, now and then, there came over his face a look of genuine worry; and he was less in society than usual, which, considering he was a man whom you met everywhere each season, and lived in the highest and gayest *mondes*, was only traceable to one cause not complimentary to Miss Sansreproche—that he did not care to have more of her society than he was forced, till he should be linked to her for life. But Avarina bore it heroically; she went on her ways, showing herself with her equable grace of manner at concerts, and dinners, balls, and déjeûners. She was evidently, as Lord Glen said, a sensible woman, who neither gave nor expected any romantic nonsense; and though she smiled pleasantly when she and the Guardsman met in the Ride, or at the Opera, or any of the numerous balls, dinners, and assemblies, she smiled just as pleasantly at me, or at the old Duchess of Lapislazuli, or at her terrier Azor. She did not seem to want St. Albans' attention, which was particularly lucky, for he did not seem inclined to pay it, but let that part of the affair devolve on his father. The rumour of their engagement got among the on dits of town, and one morning, in the club, I read, among other fashionable intelligence, "It is rumoured that a matrimonial alliance is projected between Lord Cyril St. Albans, of the Coldstreams, second son of the Most Hon. the Marquis of Glenallerton, and the Hon. Avarina Sansreproche, only daughter and sole heiress of the Baroness of Turquoise and Malachite and the late Hon. George Sansreproche."

The old Lord standing by me pointed to the paragraph, smiled, and took out his enamelled box.

"Never bet with an old diplomatist!"

"Is it settled then?"

"Of course!"

The Marquis gave me a glance that said: "Do you suppose anything *I* undertook could fail to be?"

"Has St. Albans positively proposed to her, sir?"

"Proposed? No, I believe not; but the affair is quite arranged, and perfectly understood by every one. Lady Turquoise and I——"

"Then there is no hope for him?"

"No *fear*, you mean! No, the marriage is as certain as if it had already taken place, and it will be the best step of his life."

"Well, my Lord, I hope it may: but, on my life, for

St. Albans to marry seems as bad as for him to shoot himself. He's the last man in the world——"

The Marquis shrugged his shoulders, and tapped his box-lid amusedly.

"You men of the present generation are strange fellows! You speak of a good alliance made from social and sensible motives as dolefully as if it were a miserable, infatuated love-match. Cyril will marry, and will thank me very much for my advice. I told you I should win; there was never any doubt about it."

St. Albans was sitting in the bay-window of the Guards' Club half an hour after, when I went there, reading the morning papers, and, as his eyes fell on the paragraph that concerned himself, something suspiciously like a sneer went over his face. I suppose he thought it was an announcement of his own sale, similar to the announcement of the sale of a noble and costly library by Christie, or of a chesnut two-year-old by Tattersall.

"So you are really going in for marriage, St. Albans?" said Brabazon of the Grenadiers.

St. Albans looked up for a moment, as if he were positively startled by the very innocent and natural query; then he yawned behind his paper, stroked his moustaches, and stretched himself:

"My good fellow, if I were going to be hanged to-morrow, would you think it good taste to remind me of my doom?"

"By George! I wish Avarina heard you. *Is* that paragraph true? *You* married! Jupiter! who will credit it? You're a fit fellow to take matrimonial vows, certainly. Your wife will little know what a Tartar she has caught! if she heard some stories *I* could tell her!"

St. Albans smiled a little:

"Even if you did, Charlie, I would bet you my wife

would like me better, with all my faults, than any creature (if there be one) without any at all. My dear fellow, you forget you talk to the most attractive man in town."

He spoke the first words half sadly, but the last in his own light, languid way, with a gay laugh. Brabazon laughed too, and began to talk of the latest odds for the Ascot Cup next week.

"Grey Royal hasn't a chance with Coronation and Beau Sire; she'll never win. I never knew one of Capel Caradoc's horses that did," said Wyndham, contemptuously.

"Grey Royal! I believe you. She's a clever-looking little mare, but she wouldn't win the Consolation Scramble," added Tom Vane. "She'll let you in heavily, St. Albans, take my word."

St. Albans laughed:

"Very likely. Most things feminine betray confidence, whether equine or human. But I'm resigned. Where's the good of worrying? It never makes anything better; there's nothing worth vexing oneself about under the sun; it only makes lines in your forehead, and spoils your good looks. The governor's an Epicurean, and so am I; we never bother ourselves; if things go smoothly, well and good; if they don't, we turn our backs on them."

"What a lucky dog that is," said Brabazon to me, as St. Albans went out of the club. "Nothing troubles him; his life's one long lounge of delicious far niente, except, I suppose, he's deep with the Jews; but if they know he's going to marry into such a lot of tin as the Sansreproche's, they'll let him alone fast enough."

St. Albans went home to the Albany, drank down some iced water, and threw himself into an écarté-chair, worry enough on him, now that he was alone and could give reins to it.

"By Heaven! if that mare only win I will never bet again, I swear," he mused, in his solitude. "If she lose, I must sell my horses and everything available, pay the debts of honour as best I may, and leave England. My father is right: I live at the rate of a man with thirty thousand a year, and if I lose on that race, God knows what I am to do! And I have drawn her into my fate as well! She loves me: she would endure anything on earth for me. But she knows nothing of the world; she little dreams what it is for a man of pleasure to have ruin stare him in the face, and threaten to rob him of all his luxuries, pleasures, appliances, all he values, even perhaps to his good name. Poverty, I verily believe, would be bearable to her with me; but, God help her! I am too spoiled by the world to reach her standard, or learn her unselfishness."

Ascot week came, and Grey Royal won! beating Coronation, who had been winner of the Two Thousand the year before, and Beau Sire, who had been second at the Derby, throwing everybody out of their calculations, and gaining the Red Riband of the Turf for Capel Caradoc; giving the lie to all her foes' predictions, and proving herself worthy of her few staunch friends' trust, like a well-bred, clever, unpretending little chesnut as she was. Grey Royal won, and so by her did St. Albans.

He drove me down on the Cup Day, and never had I seen him so agitated about the issue of a race. He always betted considerably, and always took his gains or his losses with that light philosophy arising from the mixture in his character of generosity and carelessness, sweet temper and indolence, which he had practised all his life; but that day it deserted him. He was very pale;

he looked anxious and agitated; and as for the last ten yards Coronation and Grey Royal held neck by neck together, I heard his quick, loud breathings, that told how much was at stake for him on the issue of the race. Grey Royal won, the Marquis was fain to confess he had been in the wrong, and his son looked like a man who had received a reprieve from the gallows or the guillotine, and drove us back to town in spirits too genuinely gay to be forced or assumed.

"So that chesnut of Caradoc's beat, after all!" said the Marquis to me on the Heath. "I am glad she did. I know Cyril has risked a great deal of money upon her, and if he have won considerably he can free himself of one or two of his more pressing debts before his marriage. But I dare say you know more of how his affairs stand than I do."

"St. Albans, you must dine with us at the Star and Garter to-morrow," said Brabazon, as we drove home. "You must. No, hang it! we won't let you off. You're beginning to grow unsociable. That's what comes of being an engaged man, or next door to it. There won't be any women, so Avarina can't be scandalised if she hears of it."

St. Albans laughed:

"My dear fellow, I shouldn't mind scandalising Miss Sansreproche in the least."

"As a preface to what she'll have to encounter afterwards, eh? Well, that's only fair. You'll come then, Cyril? I'll call for you at half-past seven, if you like?"

"Very well, do."

He didn't seem over-willing, I thought, despite the preference his father had accused him of giving to Richmond dinners over private ones. Whether he was or not, however, Brabazon took him and me up at White's the next day, and the Marquis nodded his son a good-humoured adieu from the bay-window.

"Cyril asked me what time he could see me alone to-morrow," he thought, complacently, as he returned to his papers. "To tell me he has proposed to Avarina, no doubt! Ah! adroit management always succeeds. It is only your bunglers who fail—your maladroits, who push the thing too far, or do not push it far enough."

Brabazon's dinner was a very pleasant one. He had about ten or a dozen men, and we were as comfortable as men ever are when alone. We could talk what we liked, we could smoke when we would, we had not to rake up current chit-chat for Lady Adeliza nor go through an examination in chamber-music for Miss Concerto; it was a pleasant dinner from the fish to the move, which did not inaugurate the exit of ladies, but the entrance of coffee, and a lounge at the windows to scent the honeysuckles and drink iced waters.

"I say," said Brabazon, suddenly, "do you remember that girl we saw as we came back from Telfer's boating party? You do? Well, I told you I'd find out something about her? I sent Evans down to inquire what he could, but he's such a fool, he only brought me word that the house was called Brooke Lodge, as if I cared a hang for the name of the *place!* I must ferret her out somehow. She was such a pretty creature! If I see her in that garden again, I'll speak to her, I vow, for all she flew away as if we were ogres."

"How do you know your acquaintance will be desired or accepted?" said St. Albans from another window.

I looked at him surprised. There was a flush of annoyance on his face, and he pulled down his left wristband impatiently. Brabazon laughed:

"What a shocking fellow you are, St. Albans! Can't

you let one talk of any one woman without wanting to appropriate her? Poor Avarina! But do you know my little beauty?"

"What may her name be?" said St. Albans, with his teeth set hard on his cigarette.

"Marchmont, I think; I mean to find out more about her. She's too good to be lost, if attainable; she's the loveliest thing, on my honour, and you know——"

St. Albans stroked his moustaches impatiently, an angry flush mounting over his forehead. I had never seen him look so irritated in his life.

"I know one thing, that if you want to be home in time for Lady Wentworth's theatricals, you must start. It is ten o'clock," he said, looking at his watch, and flinging his cigarette into the garden below.

We did want to be in time for Lady Wentworth's, so we broke up and drove homewards. St. Albans chose the back seat, and was unusually silent, smoking, and entering but little into mine and Brabazon's conversation, which was chiefly on the score of the beauty whom we had seen a few days before, when we were on the river. She had been throwing a stick into the water, towards which her garden sloped down, for her dog to fetch; her face had caught Brabazon's eye, and pleased him so well that he couldn't forget it, and being an inflammable fellow, had sworn to see it again, which appeared to him tolerably practicable, as, by all his servant could hear, she seemed to be living alone, and to be rather a mysterious young lady altogether, going by the name of Miss Marchmont. He was destined to keep his oath. Just as we drove out of Richmond we passed the palings of a garden, with laburnums and lilacs nodding their heads over them in the summer moonlight, and leaning on the top rail of the little iron gate stood this identical woman; the June evening was well-nigh as bright as day, and very fair and striking she certainly looked in it.

"By George!" cried Brabazon, who was a devil-may-care young fellow, and that night, thanks to his having won by Grey Royal, in the mood for any sort of mischief, "there's my little beauty, I vow, looking for somebody—for me, perhaps. By Jove, I will go and ask her!"

"Stop! Good God! are you mad?" began St. Albans, in a tone I'd never heard from him in his life; but before the words were off his lips, Brabazon pulled up, flung the reins to me, jumped down, and with a laugh, lifting his hat, went up to the gate. The girl stood as if uncertain in the dusky light whether he were the person, whoever he was, whom she expected or not; but before he could speak to her, St. Albans sprang down and caught hold of his arm.

"Take care what you say!"

The other looked up and laughed:

"Hallo! I beg your pardon, St. Albans. I didn't know I was poaching on your manor; couldn't tell, could I? The deuce! I fancied you'd some proprietorship in——"

"Be silent, for Heaven's sake! She is my *wife!*"

Brabazon stared aghast.

"Your wife! Good God! I thought Avarina——"

"Is nothing to me; never was, never will be. This is my wife. Our marriage has been secret, owing to many reasons, but it must be secret no longer now insult has once approached her," said St. Albans, as he turned and beckoned to me, in his old languid, indolent style. "It's a queer place for an introduction, twelve o'clock at night at a garden gate, I must say, but will you allow me to present you to Lady Cyril St. Albans?"

"I told Cyril twelve o'clock, and it is twenty to one; but he is never punctual. He might as well come at once; he knows I shall be delighted to hear his news, though I know what it will be. If you set to work adroitly you are safe to succeed; skilful diplomacy always——Ah! there you are at last. Good morning," said the Marquis, next morning, looking up from his breakfast in his house in Berkeley-square, awaiting the interview his son had requested.

St. Albans tossed himself into an easy-chair, laid his head back on the cushion, and stroked an infinitesimal terrier.

"Good morning, governor. I'm come to speak to you, please."

"Speak, my dear fellow," smiled the Marquis, graciously. "I can guess your errand, but go on."

"Did I understand you rightly, sir, that you wished me to marry?"

"Quite rightly. I do wish you—most earnestly."

"You think I couldn't do better?"

"Decidedly I do. You have my full concurrence."

"I'm glad to hear that, because it's troublesome to dispute, and you know I am always happy to please you. Will you come and be introduced to my wife, then?"

The Marquis laughed and stirred his chocolate.

"My dear Cyril, I congratulate you most warmly; you have acted most wisely; believe me, it will be the happiest step of your life."

"I think it will!"

"I know it will. I could not tell you how much I myself am pleased. Of course you have said nothing about time yet, but if I might advise, I should hurry it on as much as possible. Your Jews——"

"I have hurried it on. I went through the ceremony, and bore it nobly, I assure you, a month ago."

The Marquis stared. "Went through the ceremony? Pardon me, I don't quite understand your jest. What do you mean?"

"I mean, bon père, that I *am* married!"

"Good Heavens! Avarina would never——"

"Avarina has nothing to do with it. My dear governor, I'm very sorry, but I had anticipated your advice. Don't be vexed, governor, she will do the St. Albans credit; surely you can trust my taste. I was married the day you counselled me first. We have had to keep it private, because of those deuced Jews; but there is no longer any need. I won enough at Ascot to quiet the most troublesome, and I am able to proclaim it, and introduce her now. Don't go into a fit, my dear father, for God's sake! I know you meant all kindness, but had I never met Violet, neither you nor any man would have made me sell myself for money——"

"*Violet!*" gasped the Marquis, white and breathless.

"Poor Marchmont's daughter—his only child, indeed. Do you remember him—a man in the Bays, who ran through every sou and cut to France? I met her in Paris this spring, under very singular circumstances—romantic ones if you like. No matter to relate them now; her father was dead, she was only seventeen, alone and unhappy with some wretched French people, and, in a word," said St. Albans, nestling into his chair and resuming his old tone, "she pleased me, and I was so dreadfully afraid of your fettering me one day to some red-haired woman with money, that I married her in Paris, and gave her a right to protect me."

Lord Glenallerton gasped for breath, then rose, his indignation too great to be uttered. He looked at his son with deep, mournful, contemptuous pity.

"Seventeen—alone—unprotected—and you *married* her."

St. Albans rose too:

"Yes, my Lord, I married her! Good for very little I may be, but I did not utterly abuse trust innocently and entirely placed in me."

The Marquis waved his hand to the door.

"I decline to express my opinion of your conduct, or I should be obliged to use words I should regret to use to a man who bears my name. You will see your own folly in time without any enlightenment from me. I need not say I wish our acquaintance to cease from to-day. May I trouble you to leave me?—Married a woman without a farthing! Good God! And he calls himself a man of the world!" murmured the Marquis, as the door closed on his son; and he sank back in his arm-chair, crushed, paralysed, and speechless, at the ruin of all his diplomacy.

And so our wager was drawn! The MARQUIS'S TACTICS were the best joke of that season; but Rochefoucauldean philosopher though he might be, I believe their failure rankled more cruelly in Lord Glen's breast than any lack of success at a European congress or a meeting of the Powers. He had never been foiled before—and he had made a fool of himself to so many! As for cutting St. Albans, he was too good natured to do that, and in his heart liked his son too well to be able to sit in the same club window many days without speaking to him. He considers him an *enfant perdu*, a wasted alliance—in a word, a very great fool—but told him so one day with much unction, regretted that romantic element in his character, to which his downfall was to be attributed, with deep pathos, and was reconciled to him for ever afterwards. He had some slight consolation when Fainéant returned from Athens, in wedding *him* to Avarina Sansreproche; and if you asked him which he preferred of his two daughters-in-law, he would tell you —and possibly persuade himself that he told the truth— that he admires and respects the future Baroness of Turquoise and Malachite *de tout son cœur*, and has never pardoned "Cyril's Folly," as he terms the other; but as Lady Fainéant grows decidedly plainer as years roll on, and it is Violet St. Albans with whom he laughs, jokes, and tells his Regency stories, and at whom he looked most complacently at the Drawing-room, when they were both presented "on their marriage," the next season, I have my doubts as to his veracity.

SIR GALAHAD'S RAID:

AN ADVENTURE ON THE SWEET WATERS.

For the punishment of my sins may the gods never again send me to Pera! That I might have plenty on my shoulders I am frankly willing to concede; all I protest is, that when one submissively acknowledges the justice of one's future terminating in Tophet, it comes a little hard to get purgatory in this world into the bargain. Purgatory lies *perdu* for one all over the earth. I have had fifty times more than my share already, and the gout still remains an untried experience, a Gehenna grimly waiting to avenge every morsel of white truffle and every glass of comet claret with which I innocently solace my frail mortality. Purgatory!—I have been chained in it fifty times; *et vous?*

When you rush to a Chancellerie, with the English Arms gorgeous above its doorway, on the spur of a frightfully mysterious and autocratic telegram, that makes it life or death to catch the train for England in ten minutes, and have time enough to smoke about two dozen very big cheroots, cooling your heels in the bureau, and then hear (when properly tortured into the due amount of frantic agony for the intelligence to be fully appreciated) that his Excellency is gone snipe shooting to ———, and that the First Secretary is in his bath, and has given orders not to be disturbed; your informant languidly pricking his cigar with his toothpick, and politely intimating, by his eye-brows, that you and your necessities may go to the deuce;—what's *that?* When you are doing the sanitary at Weedon, by some hideous conjunction of evil destinies, in the very Ducal week itself, and thinking of the rush with which Tom Alcroft will land the filly, or the close finish with which Fordham will get the cup, while you are not there to see, are sorely tempted to realise the Parisian vision of Anglo suicide, and load the apple-trees with suspended human fruit; what's *that?* When, having got leave, and established yourself in cozy hunting quarters, with some cattle not to be beat in stay, blood, and pace, close to a killing pack that never score a blank day, there falls a bitter black frost, locking the country up in iron bonds, and making every bit of ridge and furrow like a sheet of glass;—what's *that?*

Bah! I could go on ad infinitum, and cite "circles of purgatory" in which mortal man is doomed to pass his time, beside which Dante's Caïna, Antenora, and Ptolomea sink into insignificance. But of all Purgatories, chiefest in my memory, is——Pera. Pera in the old Crimean time—Pera the "beautiful suburb" of fond "fiction"—Pera, with the dirt, the fleas, the murders, the mosquitoes, the crooked streets, the lying Greeks, the stench, the hubbub, the dulness, and the everlasting "Bono Johnny."

"Call a dog Hervey, and I shall love him," said Johnson, so dear was his friend to him:—"call a dog Johnny, and I shall kick him," so abominable grew that word in the eternal Turkish jabber! Tell me, O prettiest, softest-voiced, most beguiling, feminine Æothen, in as romantic periods as you will, of bird-like feluccas darting over the Bosphorus, of curled caïques gliding through fragrant water-weeds; of Arabian Nights reproduced, when up through the darkness peal the roll of the drums calling the Faithful to prayers; of the nights of Ramadan, with the starry clusters of light gleaming all down Stamboul, and flashing, firefly-like, through the dark citron groves; —tell me of it as you will, I don't care; you may think me a Goth, *ce m'est bien égal*, and *you* were not in cavalry quarters at Pera. I wasn't exacting; I did not mind having ants in my jam, nor centipedes in my boots, nor a shirt in six months, nor bacon for a luxury that strongly resembled an old file rusted by sea-water, nor any little trifle of that sort up in the front; all that is in the fortune of war: but I confess that Pera put me fairly out of patience, specially when a certain trusty friend of mine, who has no earthly fault, that I wot of, except that of perpetually looking at life through a Claude glass (which is the most aggravating opticism to a dispassionate and unblinded mind that the world holds), *would* poetise upon it, or at least on the East in general, which came pretty much to the same thing.

The sun poured down on me till (conscience, probably) I remembered the scriptural threat to the wicked, "their brains shall boil in their skulls like pots;"—Sir Galahad, as I will call him, would murmur to himself, with his cheroot in his teeth, Manfred's *salut* to the sun, looking as lovingly at it as any eagle. Mosquitoes reduced me to the very borders of madness—Sir Galahad would placidly remark, how Buckland would revel here in all those gorgeous beetles. A Greek told crackers till I had to double-thong him like a puppy—Sir Galahad would shout to me to let the fellow alone, he looked so deuced picturesque, he must have him for a study. I made myself wretched in a ticklish caïque, the size of a cockle-shell, where, when one was going full harness to the Great Effendi's, it was a moral impossibility to be doubled without one's sash swinging into the water, one's sword sticking over the side, and the liveliest sensation of cramp pervading one's body—Sir Galahad, blandly indifferent, would discourse, with superb Ruskin obscurity, of "tone," and "colouring," and "harmonised light," while he looked down the Golden Horn, for he was a little Art-mad, and painted so well that if he had been a professional the hanging committee would have shut him out to a certainty.

Now he was a good fellow, a *beau sabreur*, who had fetched some superb back strokes in the battery at Balaclava, who could send a line spinning, and land his horse in a gentleman riders' race, and pot the big game, and lead the first flight over Northamptonshire doubles at home, as well as a man wants to do; but I put it to any dispassionate person, whether this persistent poetism of his, flying in the face of facts and of fleas, was not enough to make anybody swear in that mosquito-purgatorio of Pera?

Sir Galahad was a capital fellow, and the men would have gone after him to the death; the fair, frank, handsome face, a little womanish perhaps, was very pleasant to look at, and he got the Victoria not long ago for a deed that would suit Arthur's Table; but in Pera, I avow, he made me swear hard, and if he would just have set his heel on his Claude glass, cursed the Turks, and growled refreshingly, I should have loved him better. He was philosophic and he was poetic; and the combination of temperaments lifted him in a mortifying altitude above ordinary humanity, that was baked, broiled, grumbling, savage, bitten, fleeced, and holding its own against miserable rats, Greeks, and Bono Johnnies, with an Aristides thieving its last shirt, and a Pisistratus getting drunk at its case-bottle! That sublime serenity of his in Pera ended in making me unholy and ungenerous; if he would but have sworn once at the confounded country I should have borne it, but he never did, and I longed to see him out of temper, I pined and thirsted to get him disenchanted. "*Tout vient a point, à qui sait attendre,*" they say; a motto, by the way, that might be written over the Horse Guards for the comfort of gloomy souls, when, in the words of the Psalmist, "Promotion cometh neither from the south, nor from the east, nor from the west"—by which lament one might conclude David of Israel to have been a sufferer by the Purchase-system!

"Delicious!" said Sir Galahad, sending a whiff of Turkish tobacco into the air one morning after exercise, when he and I, having ridden out a good many miles along the Sweet Waters, turned the horses loose, bought some grapes and figs of an old Turk, dispossessed him of his bit of cocoa-matting, and flung ourselves under a plane-tree. And the fellow looked round him through his race-glass at the cypress woods, the mosques and minarets, the almond thickets, the "soft creamy distance," as he called it in his *argot d'atelier*, and the Greek fishermen near, drawing up a net full of silvery prismatic fishes, with a relish absolutely exasperating. Exasperating—when the sun was broiling one's brain through the linen, and there wasn't a drop of Bass or Soda-and-B to be got for love or money, and one thought thirstily of days at home in England, with the birds whirring up from the stubble in the cool morning, and the cold punch uncorked for luncheon, under the home woods fringing the open.

"One wants Hunt to catch that bit of colour," murmured Sir Galahad, luxuriously eyeing a mutilated Janissary's tomb covered with scarlet creepers.

"Hunt be hanged!" said I (meaning no disrespect to that eminent Pre-Raphaelite, whose "Light of the

World" I took at first sight to be a policeman going his night rounds, and come out in his shirt by mistake; by the way, it *is* a droll idea to symbolise the "light of the world" by a watchman with a dark lantern, *lux in tenebras* with a vengeance!") "Give me the sweet shady side of Pall Mall, and the devil may take the Sweet Waters. What's the Feast of Bairam beside the Derby Day, or your confounded colouring beside a well-done cutlet? What's lemonade by Brighton Tipper, and a veiled bundle by a pretty blonde, and an eternity of Stamboul by an hour of Piccadilly?"

Sir Galahad smiled superior, and shied a date at me.

"Goth! can't you be content to feed like the Patriarchs, and live like an idyl?"

"No! I'd rather feed like a Parisian, and live an idler! Eat grapes if you choose; I agree with Brillat-Savarin, and don't like my wine in pills."

"My good fellow, you're all prose."

"And you're all poetry. You're as bad as that pretty little commissariat girl who lisped me to death last night at the Embassy with platitudes of bosh about the 'poetry of marriage.'"

"The deuce!" said Sir Galahad, with a whistle, "that must be like most other poetry now-a-days—uncommon dull prose, sliced up in uneven lengths! Didn't you tell her so?"

"Couldn't; I should have pulled the string for a shower-bath of sentiment! When a woman's bolted on romance you only make the pace worse if you gall her with the curb of common sense. When romance is in, reason's out—excuse the personality!"

He didn't hear me; he was up like a retriever who scents a wild duck or a water-rat among the sedges, for sweeping near us with soft gliding motion, as pretty as a toy and as graceful as a swan, came a caïque, with the wife of a Pacha of at least a hundred tails in it, to judge by the costliness of her exquisite attire. Now, women were not rare, but then they were always veiled, which is like giving a man a nugget he mustn't take out of the quartz, a case of champagne he musn't undo, a coverside he is never to beat, a trout stream in which he must never fling a fly; and Sir Galahad, whose loves were not, I admit, quite so saintly as Arthur's code exacted, lost his head in a second as the caïque drifted past us, and, raising herself on her cushions, the Leilah Duda or Salya within it, glanced towards the myrtle screen that half hid us, with the divinest antelope eyes in the world, and letting the silver gauze folds of her veil float half aside, showed us the beautiful warm bloom, the proud lips, and the chesnut tresses braided with pearls and threaded with gold, of your genuine Circassian beauty. Shade of Don Juan! what a face it was!

A yataghan might have been at his throat, a bowstring at his neck, eunuchs might have slaughtered, and Pachas have impaled him, Galahad would have seen more of that loveliness: headlong he plunged down the slope, crushing through the almond thickets and scattering the green tree frogs right and left; the caïque was just rounding past as he reached the water's edge, and the beauty's veil was drawn in terror of her guard. But as the little cockleshell, pretty and ticklish as a nautilus, was moored to a broad flight of marble stairs, the Circassian turned her head towards the place where the Unbeliever stood in the sunlight—her eyes were left her, and with them women speak in an universal tongue. Then the green lattice gate shut, the white impenetrable walls hid her from sight, and Sir Galahad stood looking down the Sweet Waters in a sort of beatific vision, in love for the 1360th time in his life. And certainly he had never been in love with better reason; for is there anything on earth so divine as your antelope-eyed and gold-haired Circassian?

"I shall be inside those walls or know the reason why," said he, whom two gazelle eyes had fired and captured, there by the side of the sunny Sweet Waters, where the lazy air was full of syringa and rose odours, and there was no sound but the indolent beating of the tired oars on the ripples.

"Which reason you will rapidly find," I suggested, "in a knock on the head from the Faithful!"

"Well! a very picturesque way of coming to grief; to go off the scene in the sick-wards, from raki and fruit, would be common-place and humiliating, but to die in a serail, stabbed through and through by green-eyed jealousy, would be piquant and refreshing to the last degree; do you really think there's a chance of it?" said Galahad, rather anxiously—the eager wistful anxiety of a man who, athirst for the forest, hears of the rumoured slot of an outlying deer—while he shouted the Greek fishermen to him, and learned, after sore travail through a slough of mixed Italian, Turkish, and Albanian, that the white palace, with its green lattice and its hanging gardens, belonged to a rich merchant of Constantinople, and that this veiled angel was the favourite of his harem, Leilah Derran, a recent purchase in Circassia, and the queen of the Anderûn.

"The old rascal!" swore Galahad, in his wrath, which was not, however, I think, caused by any particular Christian disgust at polygamy. "A fat old sinner, I'll be bound, who sits on his divan puffing his chibouque and stuffing his sweetmeats, as yellow as Beppo, and as round as a ball. Bah! what pearls before swine! It's enough to make a saint swear. Those heavenly eyes! . . . ." And

Galahad went into a somewhat earthly reverie, coloured with a thirsty jealousy of the purchaser and the possessor of this Circassian gazelle, as he rode reluctantly back towards Pera. The Circassian was in his head, and did not get out again. He let himself be bewitched by that lovely face which had flashed on him for a second, and began to feel himself as aggrieved by that innocent and unoffending Turkish lord of hers, as if the unlucky gentleman had stolen his own property! The antelope eyes had looked softly and hauntingly sad, moreover: I demonstrated to him that it was nothing more than the way that the eyelashes drooped, but nobody in love (very few people out of it) have any taste for logic; he was simply disgusted with my realism, and saw an instant vision for himself of this loveliest of slaves, captive in a bazaar and sold into the splendid bondage of the harem as into an inevitable fate, mournful in her royalty as a nightingale in a cage, stifled with roses, and as little able to escape as the bird. A vision which intoxicated and enraptured Sir Galahad, who, in the teeth of every abomination of Pera, had been content to see only what he wished to see, and had maintained that the execrable East, to make it the East of Hafiz and all the poets, only wanted—available Haidees! "Hang it! I think it's nothing *but* Hades;" said an Aide, overhearing that statement one night, as we stumbled out of a half-café, half-gambling-booth pandemonium into the crooked, narrow, pitch-dark street, where dogs were snarling over offal, jackals screaming, Turkish bands shrieking, cannon booming out the hour of prayer, women yelling alarms of fire, a Zouave was spitting a Greek by way of practice, and an Irishman had just potted a Dalmatian, in as brawling, rowing, pestiferous, unodorous an earthly Gehenna as men ever succeeded in making.

Sir Galahad was the least vain of mortals; nevertheless, being as well-beloved by the "maidens and young widows" for his fair handsome face as Harold the Gold-haired, he would have been more than mortal if he had not been tolerably confident of "killing," and luxuriously practised in that pleasant pastime. That if he could once get the antelope eyes to look at him, they would look lovingly before long, he was in comfortable security; but how to get into a presence, which it was death for an Unbeliever and a male creature to approach, was a knottier question, and the difficulty absorbed him. There were several rather telling Englishwomen out there, with whom he had flirted *faute de mieux*, at the cavalry balls we managed to get up in Pera, at the Embassy costume-ball, on board the yacht decks in the harbour, and in picnics to Therapia or the Monastery. But they became as flavourless as twice-told tales and twice-warmed entremets beside the new piquance, the delicious loveliness, the divine difficulty of this captive Circassian. That he had no more earthly business to covet her than he had to covet the unlucky Turkish trader's lumps of lapis-lazuli and agate, never occurred to him; the stones didn't tempt him, you see, but the beauty did. That those rich, soft, unrivalled Eastern charms, "merely born to bloom and drop," should be caged from the world and only rejoice the eyes of a fat old opium-soddened Stamboul merchant, seemed a downright reversal of all the laws of nature, a tampering with the balance of just apportion that clamoured for redress; but like most other crying injustice, the remedy was hard to compass.

Day after day he rode down to the same place on the Sweet waters on the chance of the caïque's passing; and, sure enough, the caïque did pass nine times out of ten, and, when opportunity served for such a hideous

Oriental crime not to be too perilous, the silver gauze floated aside unveiling a face as fair as the morning, or, when that was impossible, the eyes turned on him shyly and sadly in their lustrous appeal, as though mutely bewailing such cruel captivity. Those eyes said as plainly as language could speak that the lovely Favourite plaintively resisted her bondage, and thought the Frank with his long fair beard, and his six feet of height, little short of an angel of light, though he might be an infidel.

Given—hot languid days, nothing to do, sultry air heavy with orange and rose odours, and those "silent passages," repeating themselves every time that Leilah Derran's caïque glided past the myrtle screen, where her Giaour lay *perdu*, the result is conjectural; though they had never spoken a word they had both fallen in love. Voiceless *amourettes* have their advantages:—when a woman speaks, how often she snaps her spell! For instance, when the lips are divine but the utterance is slangy, when the mouth is adorably rosebud but what it says is most horribly horsy!

A tender pity, too, gave its spur to his passion; he saw that, all Queen of the Serail though she might be, this fettered gazelle was not happy in her rose-chains, and to Galahad, who had a wonderful twist of the knight-errant, and lived decidedly some eight centuries too late, no wiliest temptation would have been so fatal as this.

He swore to get inside those white inexorable walls, and he kept his oath: one morning the latticed door stood ajar, with the pomegranates and the citrons nodding through the opening; he flung prudence to the winds and peril to the devil, and entered the forbidden ground where it was death for any man, save the fat Omar himself, to be found. The fountains were falling into marble basins, the sun was tempered by the screen of leaves the lories and humming-birds were flying among the trumpet-flowers, altogether a most poetic and pleasant place for an erratic adventure; more so still when, as he went farther, he saw reclining alone by the mosaic edge of a fountain his lovely Circassian unveiled. With a cry of terror she sprang to her feet, graceful as a startled antelope, and casting the silver shroud about her head, would have fled; but the scream was not loud enough to give the alarm—perhaps she attuned it so—and flight he prevented. Such Turkish as he had he poured out in passionate eloquence, his love declaration only made the more piquant by the knowledge that in a trice the gardens might swarm with the Mussulman's guards and a scimitar smite his head into the fountain. But the danger he disdained, *la belle* Leilah remembered; rebuke him she did not, nor yet call her eunuchs to rid her of this terrible Giaour, but the antelope eyes filled with piteous tears, and she prayed him begone—if he were seen here, in the gardens of the women, it were his death, it were hers! Her terror at the infidel was outweighed by her fear for his peril; how handsome he was with his blue eyes and fair locks, after the bald, black-browed, yellow, obese little Omar!

"Let me see again the face that is the light of my soul and I will obey thee; thou shalt do with thy slave as thou wilt!" whispered Galahad in the most impassioned and poetical Turkish he could muster, thinking the style of Hafiz understood better here than the style of Belgravia, while the almond-eyed Leilah trembled like a netted bird under his look and his touch, conscious, pretty creature, that were it once known that a Giaour had looked on her, poison in her coffee or a sullen plunge by night into the Bosphorus, would expiate the insult to the honour of Omar, a master whom she piteously hated. She let her veil float aside, nevertheless, blushing like a sea-shell under the shame of an unbeliever's gaze—a genuine blush that is banished from Europe—his eyes rested on the lovely youth of her face, his cheek brushed the

Loose train of her amber dropping hair,

his lips met her own; then, with a startled stifled cry, his coy gazelle sprang away, lost in the aisles of the roses, and Galahad quitted the dangerous precincts, in safety so far, not quite clear whether he had been drinking or dreaming, and of conviction that Pera had changed into Paradise. For he was in love with two things at once: a romance and a woman; and an anchorite would fairly have lost his head after the divine dawn of beauty in Leilah Derran.

The morrow, of course, found him at the same place, at the same hour, hoping for a similar fortune, but the lattice door was shut, and defied all force; he was just about to try scaling the high slippery walls by the fibres of a clinging fig-tree, when a negress, the sole living thing in sight, beckoned him, a hideous Abyssinian enough for a messenger of Eros; a grinning good-natured black, who had been bought in the same bazaar and of the same owner as the lovely Circassian, to whose service she was sworn. She told him by scraps of Turkish, and signs, that Leilah had bidden her watch for and warn him, that it were as much as both their lives were worth for him to be seen again in the women's gardens, or anywhere near her presence; that the merchant Omar was a monster of jealousy, and that the rest of the harem, jealous of her supremacy and of the unusual liberty her ascendancy procured her, would love nothing so well as to compass her destruction. Further meeting with her infidel lover she pronounced impossible, unless he would see her consigned to the Bosphorus; an ice avalanche of intelligence, which, falling on the tropical Eden of his passion, had the effect, as it was probably meant that it should have, of drowning the lingering remnant of prudence and sanity that had remained to him after his lips had once touched the exquisite Eastern's.

Under the circumstances the negress was his sole hope and chance; he pressed her into his service and made her Mercury and mediatrix in one. She took his messages, sent in the only alphabet the pretty gazelle could read, *i. e.*, flowers, plotted against her owner with true Eastern finesse, wrought on the Circassian's tenderness for the Giaour, and her terrified hatred of her grim lord Omar, and threw herself into the intrigue with the avidity of all womanhood, be it black or be it white, for anything on the face of the earth that has the charm of being forbidden. The affair was admirably *en train*, and Galahad was profoundly happy; he was deliciously in love—a pleasant spice as difficult to find in its full flavour as it is to bag a sand grouse;—and had an adventure to amuse him that might very likely cost him his head, and might fairly claim to rise into the poetic. The only reward he received (or ever got, for that matter) for the Balaclava brush, where he cut down three gunners, and had a ball put in his hip, had been a cavil raised by a critic, not there, of doubt whether he had ever ridden inside the lines at all; but his Circassian would have recompensed him at once for a score years of Chersonnesus campaigning, and unprofessional chroniclers: he was perfectly happy, and his soft, careless, couleur de rose enjoyment of the paradise was aggravating to behold—when one was in Pera, and the heat broiled alive every mortal thing that wasn't a negro, and Bass was limited, and there were no Dailies, and one thought even lovingly and regretfully of the old "beastly shells," that had at least this merit, that they scattered bores when they burst!

"Old fellow!—want something to do?" he asked me one day. I nodded, being silent and savage from having had to dance attendance on the Sultan at an Embassy reception. Peace to his *manes* now! but I know I wished him heartily in Eblis at that time.

"Come with me to-night then, if you don't mind a probability of being potted by a True Believer," went on Leilah Derran's lover, going into some golden water Soyer had sent me.

"For the big game? Like it of all things; but you know I'm tied by the leg here."

Galahad laughed. "Oh, I only want you an hour or two. I've got six days' leave for the pigs and the deer; but the hills won't see much of me, I'm going to make a raid in the rose-gardens. It may be hot work, so I thought you would like it."

Of course I did, and asked the programme, which Sir Galahad, as lucidly as a man utterly in love can tell anything, unfolded me. Fortune favoured him: it was the night of the Feast of Bairam, when all the world of Turkey lights its lamps and turns out; he had got leave under pretext of a shooting trip into Roumelia, but the game he was intent on was the captive Circassian, who in the confusion and *tintamarrie* attendant on Bairam, was to escape to him by the rose-gardens, and being carried off as swiftly as Syrian stallions could take them, would be borne away by her infidel lover on board a yacht belonging to a man whom he knew who was cruising in the Bosphorus, which would steam them away down the Dardanelles before the Turk had a chance of getting in chase. Nothing could be better planned for everybody but the luckless Mussulman who was to be robbed—and the whole thing had a fine flavour about it of dash and difficulty, of piquance and poetry, of Mediæval errantry and Oriental colouring, that put Leilah's Giaour most deliciously in his element, setting apart the treasure that he would carry off in that rich, soft, antelope-eyed, bright-haired Circassian loveliness which made all the dreams in Lalla Rookh and Don Juan look pale.

So his raid was planned, and I agreed to go with him to cover the rear in case of pursuit, which was likely enough to be hot and sharp, for the Moslems, for all their apathy, lack the philosophic gratitude which your British husband usually exhibits towards his despoiler—but then, to be sure, an Englishman can't make a fresh purchase unless he's first robbed of the old! Night came; and the nights, I am forced to admit, have a witching charm of their own in the East that the West never knows. The Commander of the Faithful went to prayer, with the roar of cannon and the roll of drums pealing down the Golden Horn, and along the cypress-clad valleys. The mosques and minarets, starred and circled with a myriad of lamps, gleamed through the dark foliage, and were mirrored in the silvery sheet of the waves. The caïques, as they swept along, left tracks of light in the phosphor-lit waves, and while the chant of the Muezzin rang through the air, the children of Allah, from one end of the Bosphorus to the other, held festival on the most holy eve of Bairam. A splendid night for a lyric of Swinburne's!—a superb scene for an amorous adventure! And as we mingled amongst the crowds of the Faithful, swarming with their painted lanterns, their wild music, their gorgeous colours, their booming guns, in street and caïque, on land and sea, Sir Galahad, though an infidel, had certainly entered the Seventh Heaven. He had never been more intensely in love in his life; and, if the fates should decree that the dogs of Islam should slay him at her feet in the sanctuary of her rose-paradise, was ready to say, in his pet poet's words, with the last breath of his lips,

> It was ordained to be so, sweet, and best
> Comes now beneath thine eyes and on thy breast,
> Still kiss me! Care not for the cowards! Care
> Only to put aside thy beauteous hair
> My blood will hurt!

In the night of the feast all the world was astir, Franks and Moslems, believers and unbelievers, and we made our way through the press unwatched to where Omar's house was illumined, the cressets, and wreaths, and stars of light sparkling through the black foliage. Under the walls, hidden by a group of planes, we fastened the stallions in readiness, and Galahad, at the latticed door, gave the signal word, "Kef," low whispered. The door unclosed, and, true to her tryst, in the silvery Bosphorus moonlight, crouching in terror and shame, was the veiled and trembling Circassian.

But not in peace was her capture decreed to be made; scarce had the door flown open, when the shrill yell of "Allah hu! Allah hu!" sung through the air; and from the dark aisles of the gardens poured Mussulmans, slaves, and eunuchs, the Turk with a shoal at his back, giving the alarm with hideous bellowings, while their drawn scimitars flashed in the white starlight, and their cries filled the air with their din. "Make off while I hold the gate!" I shouted to Galahad, who, catching Leilah Derran, in his arms before the Moslems could be nigh us, held her close with one hand, while with his right he levelled his revolver, as I did, and backed—

facing the Turks. At sight of the lean shining barrels, the Moslems paused in their rush for a second—only a second; the next, shouting to Allah, till the minarets gave back the echo, they sprang at us, their curled naked yataghans whirling above their heads, their jetty eyeballs flaming like tigers' on the spring. Our days looked numbered ;—I gave them the contents of one barrel, and in the moment's check we gained the outside of the gardens; the swarm rushed after us, their shots flying wide, and whistling with a shrill hiss harmlessly past; we reserved further fire, not wishing to kill, if we could manage to cut our way through without bloodshed, and backed to the plane-trees, where the horses were waiting. There was a moment's blind but breathless struggle, swift and indistinct to remembrance as a flash of lightning; the Turks swarmed around us, while we beat them off, and hurled them asunder somehow. Omar sprang like a rattlesnake on to his spoiler, his yataghan circling viciously in the air, to crash down upon Galahad's skull, who was encumbered by the clinging embrace of his stolen Circassian. I straightened my left arm with a remnant of "science" that savoured more of old Cambridge than of Crimean custom; the Moslem went down like an ox, and keeping the yelling pack at bay with the levelled death-dealer, I threw myself into saddle just as Galahad flung himself on his stallion, and the Syrians, fleet as Arab breeding could make them, tore down the beach in the rich Eastern night, while the balls shrieked through the air past our ears, and the shouts of our laughter, with the salute of a ringing English cheer in victorious farewell, answered the howls of our distanced and baffled pursuers.

Sir Galahad's Raid was a triumph !

On we went through the hot fragrant air, through

the silvery moonlight, through the deep shade of cypress and pine woods; on we went through gorge, and ravine, and defile, through stretches of sweet wild lavender, of shining sands, of trampled rose-fields, with the phosphor-lit sea gleaming beside us, and the Islam Feast of Bairam left far distant behind. On and on—while the glorious night itself was elixir, and one shouted to the starry silence Robert Browning's grand challenge—

> How good is man's life, the mere living! how fit to employ
> All the heart, and the soul, and the senses, for ever in joy!

That ride was superb!

We never drew rein till some ten miles farther on, where we saw against the clear skies the dark outline of the yacht with a blue light burning at her mast-head, the signal selected; then Galahad checked the good Syrian, who had proved pace as fleet as the "wild pigeon blue" is ever vouched in the desert, and bent over his prize, who, through that long ride, had been held close to his breast, with her arms wound about him, and the beautiful veiled face bowed on his heart. The moon was bright as day, and he stooped his head to uplift the envious veil, and see the radiant beauty that never again would be shrouded, and to meet once more the lips which his own had touched before but in one single caress; he bowed his head, and I thought that my disinterested ungrudging friendship made the friendships of antiquity look small; when——an oath that chilled my blood rang through the night and over the seas, startling the echoes from rock and hill; the veiled captive reeled from the saddle with a wailing scream, hurled to earth by the impetus with which his arms loosed her from him and away into the night, without word or sign, plunging headlong down the dark defile, riding as men may ride from a field that reeks with death, far out of sight into the heart of the black dank woods his Syrian bore Sir Galahad. And lo! in the white moonlight, against the luminous sea, slowly there rose before me, unveiled and confessed—THE NEGRESS!

* * * * *

The history of that night we never learnt. Whether Leilah Derran herself played the cruel trick on her Giaour lover (but this *he* always scouted), whether Omar himself was a man of grim humour, whether the Abyssinian, having betrayed her mistress, was used as a decoy-bird, dressed like the Circassian, to lure the infidels into the rose-gardens where the Faithful intended to despatch them hastily to Eblis—no one knows. We could never find out. The negress escaped me before my surprise let me stay her, and the fray made the place too hot for close investigation. Nor do I know where Galahad tore in that wild night-ride, whose spur was the first maddened pain and rage of shame that his life had tasted. I never heard where he spent the six days of his absence; but when he joined us again, six weeks in the sick-wards would not have altered him more; all he said to me was one piteous phrase—"For God's sake don't tell the fellows!"—and I never did; I liked him well enough not to make chaff of him. Unholily had I thirsted to see him disenchanted, ungenerously had I pined to see him goaded out of temper; I had my wish, and I don't think I enjoyed it. I saw him at last in passion that I had much to do to tame down from a deadly vengeance that would have rung through the Allied Armies; and I saw him loathe the East, curse romance, burn all the poets with Hafiz at their head, and shun a woman's beauty like the pestilence. To this day I believe that the image of Leilah Derran haunts his memory, and that a certain remorse consumes him for his lost gazelle, whom *he* always thought paid penalty for their love under the silent waves of the Bosphorus, with those lost ones whose souls, according to the faith of Stamboul, flit ceaselessly above its waters, in the guise of its white-winged unrestful sea-gulls. He is far enough away just now —in which of the death-pots where we are simmering and frittering away in little wretched driblets men and money that would have sufficed Cæsar or Scipio to conquer an Empire, matters not to his story. When he reads this, he will remember the bitterest night of his life, and the fiasco that ended SIR GALAHAD'S RAID!

THE END.

www.ingramcontent.com/pod-product-compliance
Lightning Source LLC
Chambersburg PA
CBHW022100230426
43672CB00008B/1235